"This book presents a simple, practic

create exactly what the title offers: effective, mindful employees. It's a must-have in the armamentarium of any psychologist or HR professional who wants to help people increase their satisfaction, improve their performance, create better relationships, or enhance well-being in the workplace."

—**Russ Harris**, author of *The Happiness Trap*

"This book is a remarkable step forward in accelerating productivity in the workplace while caring for the well-being and vitality of employees. When companies blend the proven ideas of mindfulness and value-directed actions into the work culture, the employees will blossom, the work teams will strengthen, and the organization will prosper. Research clearly suggests that applying the principles in this book will yield a solid return on investment. It is easy to envision leading-edge companies capitalizing on this training manual. These forward-thinking companies will not only advance their bottom line, but will also benefit the people of the organization. *The Mindful and Effective Employee* training manual presents a solid how-to handbook for achieving the elusive win-win scenario of creating productive and healthy work environments."

—**D.J. Moran, PhD, BCBA-D**, senior vice president of Quality Safety Edge and founder of Pickslyde Consulting

"After reading *The Mindful and Effective Employee* I felt inspired, wiser, and very well equipped to deal with both individual career coaching and brief but effective group exercises. This is a glistening gem of a book, and it provides the reader with a smart 'how-to' rationale for delivering cutting-edge, evidence-based workplace training. I want to start practicing what I learned right now!"

—**Walter Osika, MD, PhD**, specialist in internal medicine and author of *The Stressed Heart*

"This book is a must for those wishing to make a significant contribution to workplace health and well-being. It is built out of workplace experience and research and written by authors who are experts in their field, offering techniques that are carefully crafted, known to work, and readily transferable into the workplace. More than just a valuable resource, this book gives support and confidence to those wanting to improve the quality of working lives."

—**Philip Dewe**, professor of organizational behavior, department of organizational psychology, Birkbeck, University of London

"Even though work is often defined as a necessary evil, having a job tops the list of what makes people happy in life. Work is a great source of both stress and joy. We spend more time working than doing any other single activity in our lives. It stands to reason that psychotherapists help us to learn to react to the challenges of work in ways that are healthy in the long run. The aim of this book is to demonstrate how ACT can be implemented in the workplace. The authors are internationally acclaimed experts in the field. The book is helpful for both the newcomer to ACT and the seasoned expert. It covers the theoretical aspects as well as practical session-by-session protocols and handouts. This book is the first of its kind; don't miss it!"

—**JoAnne Dahl, PhD**, professor in the department of psychology, Uppsala University, Sweden

The Mindful and Effective Employee

An Acceptance & Commitment Therapy Training Manual for Improving Well-Being and Performance

Paul E. Flaxman, PhD
Frank W. Bond, PhD
Fredrik Livheim, MS

New Harbinger Publications, Inc.

Distributed in Canada by Raincoast Books

New Harbinger Publications, Inc.
5674 Shattuck Avenue
Oakland, CA 94609
www.newharbinger.com

Cover design by Amy Shoup
Acquired by Catharine Meyers
Edited by Rosalie Wieder

Library of Congress Cataloging-in-Publication Data

Flaxman, Paul Edward.
The mindful and effective employee : an acceptance and commitment therapy training manual for improving well-being and performance / Paul E. Flaxman, PhD, Frank W. Bond, PhD, and Fredrik Livheim, MS.
pages cm
Includes bibliographical references and index.
ISBN 978-1-60882-021-4 (pbk. : alk. paper) -- ISBN 978-1-60882-022-1 (pdf e-book) -- ISBN 978-1-60882-632-2 (epub) 1. Psychology, Industrial. 2. Acceptance and commitment therapy. 3. Job stress. 4. Personnel management--Psychological aspects. I. Bond, Frank W. II. Livheim, Fredrik. III. Title.
HF5548.8.F554 2013
158.7'2--dc23

2013003021

Printed in the United States of America

15 14 13

10 9 8 7 6 5 4 3 2 1 First printing

In memory of my great friend, "Uncle" Brendan,
and to Sherylin, my fellow traveller
— P.E.F.

To Aidan Conway, my source of love and psychological flexibility
— F.W.B.

In memory of my beloved big brother and friend, Jan, and to my
sources of inspiration: my husband, Tobias Livheim, and my
colleagues, friends, and teachers, JoAnne Dahl and Steven C. Hayes
— F.L.

Contents

Foreword

Many people spend more time on work than on any other single thing they do. Work can be a source of satisfaction, stress, support, conflict, meaning, emotion, connection, anger, community, and hopelessness. For many, it is a hugely important part of life.

Surprisingly, however, the world of work is not often a central focus of practitioners in the mental health professions, and industrial and organizational consultants do not often consult the work of psychotherapists for inspiration. Historically, the worlds of clinical work and organizational work are separated by a vast chasm of professional differences and disinterest.

That is not true in the ACT world. The very first randomized trial done on ACT following the publication of *Acceptance and Commitment Therapy* by Hayes, Strosahl, & Wilson in 1999 was a worksite intervention (Bond & Bunce, 2000), and ACT practitioners have continued to research the world of work since that initial study. What the ACT community has learned in the clinic finds its way into the workplace and vice versa.

There is a reason. ACT is based on a reticulated (i.e., network-like) functional contextual intervention development model—a model that is at the core of the contextual behavioral science (CBS) tradition that gave birth to ACT. And that development model facilitates the interconnection between practitioners in clinic and work settings.

Functional contextualists are focused on changeable contextual causes because they want analysis that both predicts and influences psychological events. They are focused on basic principles and have also actively sought the new principles needed to address human cognition. They want to explain human complexity and behavioral problems by addressing both the external environment and the internal world, but they try to model problem areas based on an understanding of normal psychological processes. Finally, they have learned how to use multiple language systems—high-precision systems in the lab and looser ones in practical settings—without becoming incoherent.

That combination has allowed what has been learned in the clinic to be brought into the workplace and vice versa. ACT is not just applicable to, say, worksite stress—it is also applicable to leadership development. It is not just applicable to mental health but also to worker effectiveness. The flexible employee prospers in the flexible workplace, and ACT consultants have important things to say to employers, managers, and employees alike.

So it is by design that ACT is able to make the link between the clinic and the workplace. There is, however, a big "but." Modifications need to be made when adapting ACT for nonclinical settings. You cannot simply understand ACT and waltz into business and industry making a difference that lasts. There are some tricks of the trade and helpful hints that need to be assimilated by workplace practitioners in order for them to deliver ACT-based interventions effectively. The transfer is substantial, but so too are the unique features of the world of work.

While there have been theoretical accounts that address the application of ACT and RFT principles to the world of work (for example, Hayes, Bond, Barnes-Holmes, & Austin, 2006), the present volume is the first "how to" book on applying ACT to the work setting. It describes the need, the model, and the research, but most of all it walks practitioners through a step-by-step approach to creating mindful and values-guided employees. This volume should enable practitioners who are reasonably skilled in dealing with groups and applying ACT or related approaches to take a huge leap forward in their ability to effectively deliver ACT interventions in the workplace. The book offers numerous examples of interventions that have been used (and evaluated) in workplace settings, and you can turn to it as you would turn to a trusted adviser. The authors are the best in the field. They know how to do this work because they've done it. And now they are ready to share their expertise.

You can help create the mindful and effective employee using ACT principles—for the good of employees and employers alike. You are about to learn a carefully researched method for doing just that.

Steven C. Hayes
University of Nevada

Acknowledgments

Paul Flaxman: I begin by sending warm and sincere thanks to my coauthors, Frank Bond and Fredrik Livheim. It was Frank who first introduced me to ACT and I am forever in his debt. Frank continues to be a source of inspiration, a mentor, and a friend. Warm thanks also to you, Fredrik, for being so willing to share details of your ACT Train the Trainer program, and for always offering the kindest words of encouragement as this book gradually took shape.

Thanks as always to the ACT community in the UK and worldwide for pursuing principles of open dialogue and for sharing information and resources. Many thanks to DJ Moran, Rachel Collis, and Rob Archer for your contributions to this book. Here in the UK, special thanks to Joe Oliver, Eric Morris, and Vasiliki Christodoulou, who helped me to reflect on aspects of our ACT sessions. Thanks also to Mia Söderberg, who sat through many ACT sessions and provided some very insightful feedback that helped to shape subsequent interventions.

I take this opportunity to thank Michael Chaskalson and Bhante Bodhidhamma, who helped me to strengthen my mindfulness practice, and who each in his own unique way helped me to contact some profound personal insights. Many thanks to the New Harbinger team, especially Melissa Valentine, Catharine Meyers, and Rosalie Wieder. I am most grateful for your patience and editorial support at various points along the way.

Thank you to the funding bodies that saw value in supporting ACT workplace programs, including Economic and Social Research Council and Guy's and St Thomas' Charity.

I extend my gratitude to some key contacts in various organizations who have helped to advertise and implement our training and associated research: Catharine Anderson and Susan Folwell, who supported me in those early days, as well as Barbara Wren, Teresa Jennings, Clare Allen, Leslie Morrison, Jan Hill-Tout, and Anthony Schwartz. A wonderful group of individuals, you have supported me, my career, and the work described in this book. I am constantly grateful to be part of your network.

I save my final thanks for all those individuals who took time out from their busy schedules to attend our ACT workshops. For all those laughs, moments of sadness, dodgy pictures of passengers on the bus, flashes of wonder and insight, and shared stories of pursuing a value-guided life, this work is as much yours as it is ours.

Frank Bond: The material in this book very nicely summarizes the first twelve years of my academic career. As a result, it is impossible for me to publicly thank everyone who has guided me on the journey that has led to this publication. I will, however, thank a few. The generosity that Steve Hayes showed me as a young clinician and researcher led me onto this wonderful academic path down which I travel and for that I will always be grateful to him. David Bunce and Michael Bruch were mentors of mine who helped me to rigorously test the initial "ACT at Work" intervention that Steve and I developed, and I am thankful for their support. The worldwide ACT community has not only been a source of intellectual and scientific inspiration for the work in this book, but also has given me some of my best friends, including Fredrik Livheim. Finally, I wish to acknowledge Paul Flaxman, whose idea it was to write this book. It is difficult to believe that I could ever have a finer PhD student or colleague. (Paul is also the best person with whom to spend a year traveling around the UK conducting research; it was one of my favorite years of work.)

Fredrik Livheim: I am grateful to my coauthors for the invitation to participate in creating this book. It is so inspiring working with both of you. And thanks, Frank, for showing up in that car on a warm summer's day in Sweden in 2003 and introducing me to ACT work for groups in the workplace. It was exactly what I was looking for. I also want to thank the hundreds of group leaders I have trained. You have taught me so much. To me, you are my teachers.

There are three persons I am eternally grateful to and want to thank especially. Tobias Livheim, thank you for your unconditional love and for sharing this cool journey called life with me! And thanks for your wise input and your patience. JoAnne Dahl, thank you for your valuable friendship, for teaching me ACT, and for gently pushing me out in the world. Steven Hayes, thank you for your incredible generosity, support, and helpfulness, and for being my favorite "Research and Psychology Super-Star."

Introduction

Although the beneficial effects of gainful employment on psychological well-being and quality of life are widely recognized, high rates of mental ill health are nevertheless found among working populations. For example, in the United Kingdom, workforce surveys of various industry sectors suggest that around one in four workers is experiencing a common mental health problem (typically anxiety and/or depression). In some occupational groups this figure can be as high as 40 percent (Hardy, Shapiro, Haynes, & Rick, 1999; Stride et al., 2007). A range of similar prevalence statistics (see chapter 1) shows that this problem is faced by most industrialized nations.

Picture the faces of your own coworkers and managers. A significant number of those you bring to mind could, right now, be lost in worries about the future, have their behavior unhelpfully influenced by feelings of inadequacy, or find themselves somewhat out of touch with their sense of purpose in life.

Of course, some of the distress and dysfunction we find in the workplace stems directly from aspects of the work environment itself, including excessive work demands, low levels of autonomy or control over work tasks, a lack of adequate support or respect from managers, and a chronic imbalance between workplace rewards or recognition and efforts a person expends on the job. Interventions that address such stressors in the work environment play an important role in protecting and promoting employees' health and job satisfaction, and the quality of their work life.

However, this is only half the picture. The promotion of mental health at work also requires occupational health professionals to focus on enhancing the psychological and behavioral resources of individual workers. In this domain the principles and practices of *acceptance and commitment therapy* (ACT) can make a significant contribution to employees' psychological health, resilience, and behavioral effectiveness. ACT employs a distinctive set of mindfulness and acceptance strategies, alongside a range of interventions, that are ultimately designed to increase people's ability to identify and pursue patterns of personally valued behavior. It is important to recognize from the outset that ACT differs from more traditional approaches to promoting employees' mental health, which have traditionally fallen under the broad banner of stress management interventions. Most notably, ACT does not set out to change the form, frequency, or intensity of undesirable thoughts and feelings—or what we might refer to as *internal* events. Instead, ACT cultivates mindfulness and acceptance skills that are then used in the active and deliberate pursuit of value-guided goals and actions. ACT is, at its core, a behavioral approach, and in this book you will find various interventions that encourage employees to identify and engage in patterns of action that manifest their most valued personal strengths and qualities.

This book is the product of some fifteen years of workplace training and research. The approach to using ACT at work that is described here has emerged and evolved from an initial protocol developed in 1996 by Frank Bond and Steven Hayes for the use of ACT in the workplace. Paul Flaxman has extended Frank's work, adapting his original three-session ACT-based training protocol for delivery to employees of some of London's large public-sector organizations. Fredrik Livheim and his colleagues in Sweden have developed an innovative and evidence-based ACT train-the-trainer program that is leading to ACT being delivered to ever-increasing numbers of the working population (his train-the-trainer program is outlined in chapter 8 of this book).

We have designed the book to demonstrate how ACT can be translated into training programs suitable for delivery to groups of workers in a range of different organizations, with the goal of achieving a much greater dissemination of ACT-based interventions to working populations. This work is not without its challenges: ACT interventions routinely invite people to open up to what might be difficult inner experiences in the service of actively pursuing a value-guided life. Participants in this training are asked to reflect on profound questions such as "What do I most want my life to *be about*?" and then assess the degree to which their recent behavior has been consistent with the answers. As people take steps to bring their personal values to life, they may become more aware of unhelpful or difficult thoughts, feelings, and sensations than ever before. Thus, we need an army of suitably trained practitioners who are willing, first of all, to spend a sufficient amount of time applying ACT's core processes to their own personal and professional lives. Once armed with an intimate and *experiential* understanding of the ACT approach, these practitioners will be prepared for the task of training others to do the same. And if we are going to reach as many people as possible, the workplace seems the ideal place to do it.

This book is intended to be of interest and use to those relatively new to this intervention approach and also to those who have more experience with ACT's principles and procedures. In the opening chapters, we set out a rationale for increasing the availability of ACT interventions in workplace settings. This rationale is informed by the high rates of common mental health problems found among working-age adults, the breadth and utility of ACT's underlying intervention model, and an interesting alignment between ACT's philosophy and current trends within the field of occupational health. In the chapters that follow, we describe a three-session ACT-based training program that has been successfully delivered in various public- and private-sector organizations. In this part of the book, we outline key ACT interventions and include extracts of participant–trainer interactions that reflect a few of the more common participant experiences we have observed when delivering this type of training. We have altered some of the specific content in these extracts to protect the anonymity of participants and organizations while still retaining what we see as the essence of each contribution. In the final chapters of the book, we consider the skills and experiential knowledge required to deliver this type of workplace intervention in a way that is consistent with the ACT approach; we also review the evidence base for delivering ACT-based training in the workplace and, finally, describe how ACT principles are increasingly being used to support a variety of organizational initiatives, such as team and leadership development and career coaching.

Our overriding hope is that the book will prove to be a valuable resource for those interested in using ACT to improve the psychological well-being and behavioral effectiveness of working individuals.

CHAPTER 1

The Prevalence and Impact of Psychological Distress in the Workplace

Prior to presenting our three-session ACT-based training protocol, we aim to reveal our rationale for using ACT to promote mental health and enhance behavioral functioning in the workplace. We begin that task in this first chapter by providing some estimates of the pervasiveness and costs of mental ill health found among working populations. To show that this is a global phenomenon, we deliberately extracted the reported prevalence estimates from workforce (and general population) surveys conducted in various countries, including the United States, the United Kingdom, various countries of the European Union, and Australia.

It is of course possible that we are "preaching to the converted"; readers of this book might already be cognizant of the considerable costs that psychological distress exacts from individual workers, their organizations, and the wider society. Nonetheless, we believe it is vital that the prevalence and cost statistics outlined in this chapter be widely disseminated, as organizational stakeholders are not always fully aware of the nature and extent of the problems associated with workplace distress. For example, while senior managers in an organization may express an interest in ACT for its potential to reduce absence due to sickness, they can be surprised to learn that even greater costs may arise from employees with common mental health problems showing up for work but being unable to perform effectively (Kessler & Frank, 1997). In addition, employers have been known to grossly underestimate the rates of mental ill health in their own workforce (Shaw Trust, 2006), and this will in turn influence the extent to which they are willing to invest resources and staff time in interventions such as ACT. Hence, an important role for mental health professionals interested in delivering ACT in workplace settings is to ensure that organizational decision makers are familiar with the ethical and business arguments for improving employees' psychological health. We provide the following information to facilitate this task.

Prevalence of Psychological Distress in the Workplace

Numerous epidemiological studies have established that mental health problems are highly prevalent among human societies. Evidence collated from across the globe suggests that clinically relevant psychological distress was probably experienced by somewhere between 19 and 30 percent of your nation's general population in the past twelve months (Hilton et al., 2008). We are particularly familiar with the prevalence statistics for the United Kingdom, where it is estimated that nearly a quarter (23.4 percent) of the general adult population is suffering from a mental health difficulty at any one time (Sainsbury Centre for Mental Health, 2007). By far the most prevalent conditions in the general population are anxiety and depression. These common mental health problems are placing a formidable financial burden on many of the world's national economies, and a significant proportion of that burden is being attributed to lost work productivity (see, for example, Kessler, Merikangas, & Wang, 2008; Sobocki, Jönsson, Angst, & Rehnberg, 2006; Thomas & Morris, 2003).

Despite the broad consensus surrounding the societal prevalence of mental ill health, there remains a common misconception that prevalence rates would be considerably lower among working populations (Sainsbury Centre for Mental Health, 2007). After all, employees must drag themselves out of bed each morning, commute to their workplaces, and then perform at a level that ensures both remuneration and continued employment. Given the demands of working life, it might be assumed that a significant proportion of people with mental health problems would simply drop out of the workforce. However, there is plenty of evidence to suggest that the most common mental health problems are almost as pervasive in the workplace as they are in the wider population.

In U.S. workforce surveys, around one in three workers report high levels of stress or stress-related disability, with an average of one in ten workers experiencing poor mental health for fourteen or more days in the past month (National Institute for Occupational Safety and Health, 2002). Similarly, Kessler and Frank (1997) found an average thirty-day prevalence of 18 percent for any DSM psychiatric disorder among U.S. workers, with some variation across occupational groups (ranging from 11 to 30 percent). The fourth European Survey of Working Conditions (Parent-Thirion, Macias, Hurley, & Vermeylen, 2007) concluded that stress is the second most reported workplace health problem in Europe, affecting on average 22 percent of workers across twenty-seven countries. Finally, data from the United Kingdom indicate that around one worker in six will be experiencing a common mental health problem, such as depression, anxiety, or problems related to stress, at any one time. This figure rises to one in five if problems related to drug and alcohol misuse are also included. In contrast, severe mental health problems, such as psychotic and bipolar disorders, are estimated to affect around 1 to 3 percent of the working population (Seymour & Grove, 2005).

Although these estimates show some variation (due in part to differing data collection methods and classification criteria), it is not difficult to find the commonalities. Taken together, the results of these (and many other) large-scale surveys lead to the conclusion that mental health problems are highly prevalent in the workplaces of the industrialized world. For us, the implication is obvious: the workplace offers an ideal context for improving people's psychological health. This view receives further endorsement from the findings discussed next, which imply that the majority of distressed employees are unlikely to receive psychological intervention unless it is delivered in the workplace.

Treatment Rates among Psychologically Distressed Workers

In their survey of the Australian labor force, Hilton et al. (2008) assessed treatment prevalence rates among the most highly distressed workers. They found that only 22 percent of workers exhibiting clinically relevant distress were currently receiving treatment. This low treatment prevalence rate was influenced by the following factors:

- 31 percent of workers with high psychological distress were unaware that they might have a mental health problem;
- 29 percent of distressed employees were aware of having a mental health problem but had not sought treatment;
- 19 percent of distressed workers had previously sought treatment but were not currently receiving treatment, even though their current level of distress warranted intervention.

The low treatment rate found among distressed Australian workers is mirrored in other working populations. For example, it has been estimated that around three-quarters of British working adults with a common mental health problem (anxiety and/or depression) do not receive intervention (Seymour & Grove, 2005). In addition to the influencing factors identified by Hilton et al. (2008), a number of other reasons have been proposed to account for the fact that so few distressed workers seek or access recognized psychological intervention. First, employees may be unwilling to reveal a psychological difficulty to their coworkers and may be reluctant to request time off work to visit a mental health professional (Black, 2008). In addition, some workers may believe that mental health care is directed primarily at those with severe mental illness and therefore remain unaware that professional help is also appropriate for more common mental health problems (Sainsbury Centre for Mental Health, 2007). Finally, there may be subgroups of workers, such as young males, who show low levels of help-seeking behavior for any type of health problem (and particularly a mental health problem; see, for example, Oliver, Pearson, Coe, & Gunnell, 2005).

Taken together, these observations indicate that psychological interventions often fail to reach the vast ranks of workers experiencing the most common forms of mental ill health. Of course, we are not suggesting that delivering ACT to groups of employees in the workplace is the only solution to the combined problem of workplace distress and low rates of treatment. Toward the end of this chapter we discuss some other important worksite intervention approaches that should also be considered in light of the prevalence and cost statistics outlined here. Nonetheless, given that so many employees are failing to seek or access recognized psychological interventions elsewhere, we propose that group-based ACT worksite programs can serve an important role in improving the well-being, behavioral functioning, and quality of life of significant numbers of people. This proposal is supported by the ACT and psychological flexibility research reviewed later in this book (see chapter 9).

When delivering and evaluating ACT in UK organizations, we have become particularly interested in those workers who are perhaps aware of having difficulties with a common mental health problem and (for whatever reason) have not sought intervention elsewhere. The volume of moderately or highly distressed employees who have volunteered for our ACT programs suggests that such workers are attracted to psychological interventions if those interventions are made highly accessible (for example, offered as a worksite training program rather than as therapy, and delivered during working hours). We return to this issue when considering how ACT training programs might be marketed to employees in work settings, as well as the types of employees who typically volunteer (see chapter 4).

Business Costs of Psychological Distress in the Workplace

The business costs associated with employee distress are substantial. Such costs stem from staff turnover, elevated sickness absence rates, and reduced output found among distressed workers. Let's take a look at some of the estimates.

Data from the Annual Survey of Occupational Injuries and Illnesses, which collects information from private industry in the United States on reported reasons for and duration of absences from work, indicate that anxiety, stress, and neurotic disorders account for a much higher percentage of long-term sickness absences than do other types of injuries or health problems. Specifically, in data collected in 2001, 42.1 percent of absence cases attributed to mental ill health involved thirty-one or more days away from work. As a result, the number of workdays lost among workers in the United States with these common mental health problems was on average four times greater than the number of workdays lost for all other nonfatal injuries and illnesses (National Institute for Occupational Safety and Health, 2004). It has been argued that, compared to injuries and physical illnesses, psychological distress is more likely to remain undiagnosed and untreated until it becomes so problematic that the worker needs a significant period away from work in order to recover (Black, 2008).

In the United Kingdom, researchers at the Sainsbury Centre for Mental Health have set out a convincing business case for tackling mental health problems in the workplace. They estimate that mental ill health costs UK businesses in the region of £26 billion per annum (or approximately $40.6 billion). This overall cost breaks down as follows:

- £8.4 billion ($13 billion) per year in sickness absence (with approximately 40 percent of all sickness absences attributed to mental ill health)
- £15.1 billion ($23.5 billion) per year in reduced productivity in the workplace
- £2.4 billion ($3.7 billion) per year in replacing staff who leave their jobs because of mental ill health

What is interesting about the above estimates is that reduced on-the-job productivity due to mental health problems far exceeds the costs associated with sickness absence. This reflects the phenomenon of "presenteeism," which is attracting considerable interest from occupational health researchers and policy makers (for example, see Johns, 2010). Presenteeism occurs when employees appear at work but are unable to function at their full or usual capacity due to symptoms of ill health. Presenteesim is particularly likely in cases of mental ill health, as employees may fear being stigmatized if they are absent from work due to emotional or psychological difficulties. Depending on the country of origin, estimates of the costs to industry range from 1.5 to several times larger than the costs associated with sickness absence. Moreover, there is some evidence to suggest that presenteeism is more common among white collar and professional (hence more highly paid) occupational groups (Sainsbury Centre for Mental Health, 2007).

While progress is undoubtedly being made, it is important that the business costs associated with mental ill health continue to be communicated to organizational decision makers and employers. In this way, workplace programs that can be shown to enhance employees' psychological well-being and behavioral functioning will come to be viewed less as an indulgence and more as an investment with considerable cost-saving potential. Data from Australia suggest that employers who do invest in mental health initiatives, such as screening and facilitating help-seeking behavior, can expect a fivefold return on that investment (Hilton, 2005). To paraphrase the author of a major workplace well-being review conducted in the United Kingdom: Good *mental* health is good business (Black, 2008).

Societal Costs of Psychological Distress in the Workplace

The costs associated with psychological distress among working populations inevitably impact the wider society and economy. At this more macro level, costs stem from increased health care and welfare spending required to support large numbers of working-age adults with mental health problems, and also the aggregated output losses resulting from reduced productivity of distressed workers.

A large-scale study of U.S. workers indicated that health care expenditures for employees with high levels of stress were 46 percent higher than those for employees with low stress levels (Goetzel et al., 1998). Among the member states of the European Union, mental health problems are estimated to cost an average of 3 to 4 percent of gross national product (GNP), including treatment costs and output losses associated with employee absence and low productivity (Seymour & Grove, 2005). Every year in the United Kingdom, an average of 200,000 working-age adults become dependent on welfare (incapacity benefit) payments because of a mental health problem (Black, 2008). Finally, the Centre for Mental Health (2010) recently estimated the increase in the economic and social costs of mental health problems for England between

2002/2003 and 2009/2010. The overall societal cost in 2009/10 was estimated at £105.2 billion ($164 billion), representing a 36 percent increase since 2002/3 (the largest increase was in the costs of health and social care, which rose by 70 percent). Moreover, the output losses included in their report should be considered an underestimate, as they do not include reduced productivity resulting from presenteeism. The authors of this particular report offer a rather startling perspective on their estimates of the societal costs: mental health problems carry a larger cost to English society than crime.

Intervention Approaches

Various types of workplace intervention have been applied to improve employees' psychological health and work/life functioning. Traditionally, many of these interventions have been labeled as stress management interventions (SMIs). *Organization*-focused SMIs seek to modify aspects of the design and management of work to prevent or reduce psychological ill health among working populations. Such initiatives are often considered to operate at a primary level of prevention because of their potential to reduce work-related stressors at their source (Cox et al., 2000; Giga, Cooper, & Faragher, 2003). The most common organization-focused programs adopt a highly participative approach, in which employees are closely involved in the identification of problems and solutions, and in the implementation of any problem-solving initiatives. Although the research evidence for these programs has been somewhat mixed, a number of studies have found that such initiatives are able to improve important work characteristics (such as the amount of control or autonomy people have over their jobs) and improve workers' well-being (Bond, Flaxman, & Bunce, 2008; Holman, Axtell, Sprigg, Totterdell, & Wall, 2010). These interventions do need to be implemented with some care, as there is evidence to suggest that some employees lack the personal coping resources to benefit from work redesign programs (see, for example, Bond et al., 2008; Jex, Bliese, Buzzell, & Primeau, 2001; Meier, Semmer, Elfering, & Jacobshagen, 2008; Schaubroeck, Jones, & Xie, 2001).

In contrast to these organizationally oriented initiatives, *individual*-focused worksite SMIs generally seek to modify the way that individuals appraise stressful events and aim to improve workers' coping resources.

By far the most common (and empirically evaluated) approach takes the form of stress management training (SMT) programs. These programs are delivered to small groups of employees in the workplace and usually comprise a combination of traditional CBT techniques (such as cognitive restructuring, muscular relaxation training, and time management training). Many of these programs are based on variants of Donald Meichenbaum's (1985) well-validated stress inoculation training protocol. Recent reviews of the SMT research literature have found that these multifaceted CBT-based programs are an effective way of improving mental health in the workplace (Murphy, 1996; Richardson & Rothstein, 2008; van der Klink, Blonk, Schene, & van Dijk, 2001). Interestingly, the research also suggests that adding too many different components to these programs may reduce their effectiveness (perhaps by overwhelming already busy employees; Richardson & Rothstein, 2008).

Consistent with the recent expansion of the CBT movement, we are already seeing the influence of mindfulness-based approaches on worksite mental health promotion. MBSR programs are increasingly being delivered to employees in the workplace (see, for example, Chaskalson, 2011; Williams, Kolar, Reger, & Pearson, 2001), and researchers have shown that abbreviated (or "low-dose") versions of traditional mindfulness programs can elicit impressive improvements in employees' psychological health (Klatt, Buckworth, & Malarkey, 2009). We fully support these efforts to make mindfulness interventions more accessible and available to working populations.

Based on the intervention classification system described above, ACT would primarily be considered an individual-focused approach as it seeks to improve employees' personal levels of psychological flexibility. In this respect, the present book aims to build on the historical link between CBT and worksite SMT programs by describing a workplace adaptation of the ACT intervention approach. In subsequent chapters we also consider the use of ACT to meet objectives beyond improvements to employees' psychological health, including applications of the ACT model and intervention technology for leadership, career, or organizational development (see chapter 10).

Readers of this book won't be surprised to learn that we believe ACT has the potential to advance the theory and practice of worksite mental health promotion. Unlike more traditional SMT programs, ACT is underpinned by a unified theoretical model that offers clear guidance to researchers interested in identifying, measuring, and testing intervention processes of change (see, for example, Bunce, 1997). Moreover, ACT's focus on promoting psychological flexibility rather than "symptom reduction" is congruent with current trends in occupational health policy and practice. We shall return to these issues in chapter 3, where we set out a rationale for increasing the availability of ACT programs to promote mental health in the workplace.

Summary

In view of the various prevalence statistics documented in this chapter, it is perhaps not surprising that mental health problems are considered by many to be the predominant health issue facing working-age populations. Indeed, a number of influential commentators have suggested that such problems could be exacerbated in the future by the trends toward greater work intensity (requirements to work faster and meet increasingly stringent deadlines with fewer resources) and the increased job insecurity and economic uncertainty gripping many parts of the industrialized world (see Milczarek, Schneider, & Gonzalez, 2009; Seymour, 2010). Given that employees can spend around 60 percent of their waking hours at work, it follows that the workplace provides an important context for improving people's psychological health and quality of life. Most of the reports cited in this chapter recommend that organizations move beyond the traditionally more reactive approach to mental ill health and toward prevention and mental health promotion. The research that has emerged over the last decade or so suggests that ACT can play an important role in such efforts.

CHAPTER 2

What Is ACT?

ACT has emerged at the forefront of a new generation of cognitive behavioral therapies (CBTs). What has been referred to as the "third wave" of CBT is perhaps most obviously characterized by a modern scientific and clinical interest in the ancient practice of mindfulness as an important route to mental health and behavioral functioning (Hayes, 2004). Whereas the CBT movement has more traditionally focused on changing the content (that is, the form or frequency) of people's undesirable or dysfunctional thoughts, feelings, and physical sensations, mindfulness-based approaches focus on changing the fundamental way that people *relate to* their inner experiences.

ACT is perhaps best described as a *contextual CBT* (Hayes, Villatte, Levin, & Hildebrandt, 2011) in that the ACT intervention model and technology focus on altering the problematic psychological contexts in which people experience cognitive and emotional content. ACT differs from other prominent mindfulness-based programs, such as mindfulness-based stress reduction (MBSR) and mindfulness-based cognitive therapy (MBCT), because of its strong emphasis on personally valued behavioral activation. ACT is, at its heart, a behavior therapy, and it is firmly rooted in a well-established behavior analytic theory of the fundamental nature of human language and cognition (known as *relational frame theory*, or RFT—see below). Thus, while ACT is quite rightly recognized as a mindfulness-based approach, ACT interventions do not seek to cultivate mindfulness as an end in itself. Instead, ACT utilizes various mindfulness and acceptance processes in the service of enhancing people's ability to pursue personally valued life goals and actions.

In this chapter, we highlight ACT's links to RFT before defining each of the six interrelated processes that combine to create ACT's widely applicable model of psychological flexibility. Toward the end of the chapter we explain how we have translated this intervention model into a group-based training program that cultivates the functional combination of psychological and behavioral skills, namely mindfulness and values-based action.

ACT and RFT

As noted above, ACT is based on RFT (Hayes, Barnes-Holmes, & Roche, 2001), which maintains that at the core of human language and cognition is people's ability to relate events or objects in complex ways. In particular, we can relate events not just by their physical (e.g., bigger than) or temporal (e.g., before and after) characteristics but also by their arbitrary (e.g., culturally defined, conventional, or agreed) features. For example, one of the many ways in which we can relate objects is by comparing them physically. People can see that a nickel is physically bigger than a dime; however, they learn that the smaller coin is worth more than the bigger one, despite their physical sizes. Importantly, we make these relations, such as more than/less than, only in certain contexts (for example, when deciding how much to tip a waiter). This is advantageous, as it makes us less likely to make relations at unhelpful times (noticing that a dime is worth more than a nickel, which is physically bigger than the dime, is not helpful when trying to count your change); in addition, it allows us to learn and make very fine discriminations, and to see intricate and complex patterns in events.

RFT emphasizes that when we learn to relate events and objects in a certain way, such as comparing them, the function (or meaning/properties) of one event or object transfers to (or rubs off on) the other. This *transformation of stimulus functions* helps to explain why we can feel happy, for example, when we hear a piece of music that we listened to during a fun holiday: the functions of a beach, friends, and food are not only related to the song (that is, we think about the holiday when we hear the song), but the song has also taken on the enjoyable stimulus functions of the holiday.

A large number of objects and events can be related in many ways; that is, people learn to compare stimuli, contrast them, see them as equivalent, see them as opposite, put them in a hierarchy or an arbitrary temporal order. Put more technically, there are many *relational frames*, or relational webs, in which people can learn to relate events and objects. This means that a large number of stimuli can alter the function of other stimuli. In essence, people are "relating machines": we often do it without awareness, which means that transformations of stimulus functions (including our feelings and concerns) are constantly occurring and changing.

We have given this extremely brief and nontechnical account of RFT to emphasize that ACT is based on a theory of language and cognition that has received considerable empirical support (Hayes, Bunting, Herbst, Bond, & Barnes-Holmes, 2006). We next use this account to highlight why contextual CBTs do not try to get people to change, or challenge the veracity of, their cognitions. (For a readable, yet detailed, account of RFT see Törneke, 2010; Hayes et al., 2001, present a more technical account of RFT.)

ACT as a Contextual CBT

One of the most important implications of RFT for improving people's mental health and behavioral effectiveness is that relations among objects and events are learned. In the early twentieth century, Pavlov's experiments with his salivating dogs showed that learned reflexes do not entirely disappear, or extinguish. They can become inhibited but are liable to spontaneous recovery and can easily be reestablished.

It appears that the same is true with relations among language, cognitions, and emotions. This implies that psychological interventions that attempt to change these relations (that is, to extinguish them) are unlikely to prove effective at doing so. Indeed, this hypothesis is consistent with the findings of researchers such as Longmore and Worrell (2007), who noted that attempting to challenge and change the content of people's cognitions does not particularly enhance the efficacy of content-focused CBTs. One of the distinctive features of ACT and the other contextual CBTs (such as MBCT) is that they do not attempt to question the validity, or change the frequency or form, of people's internal events; rather, they attempt to change how people respond or relate to their internal events so that they can live more "open, aware, and active" lives (Hayes et al., 2011, p. 141). More specifically, contextual CBTs are conceptualized in the following way:

> Grounded in an empirical, principle-focused approach, the third wave of behavioral and cognitive therapy is particularly sensitive to the context and functions of psychological phenomena, not just their form, and thus tends to emphasize contextual and experiential change strategies in addition to more direct and didactic ones. These treatments tend to seek the construction of broad, flexible and effective repertoires over an eliminative approach to narrowly defined problems, and to emphasize the relevance of the issues they examine for clinicians as well as clients. (Hayes, 2004, pp. 5–6)

The contextual CBTs maintain that mental health and behavioral effectiveness are influenced more by how people relate to their thoughts and feelings than by their form (that is, how negative they are), and there is growing empirical evidence to support this proposition. Indeed, this hypothesis has been supported in many areas of human functioning. For example, in chronic pain, psychosocial disability is predicted more by the experiential *avoidance* of pain than it is by the degree of pain (McCracken, 1998). A number of concepts central to modern empirical clinical methods have emerged with this same basic theme, including distress tolerance (e.g., Brown, Lejuez, Kahler, & Strong, 2002; Schmidt, Richey, Cromer, & Buckner, 2007), thought suppression (e.g., Wenzlaff & Wegner, 2000), and mindfulness (Baer, 2003).

The ACT Model of Mental Health and Behavioral Effectiveness

From the perspective of ACT and RFT, psychological health is largely determined by how our cognition interacts with our current situation or environment (or contingencies of reinforcement) to help or hinder our ability to pursue our long-term values and goals (Hayes, Luoma, Bond, Masuda, & Lillis, 2006). ACT and RFT hypothesize that, depending upon the values-related opportunities afforded in a given situation, people need to be flexible in the degree to which they base their actions on private experiences (current thoughts, feelings, and physiological sensations) on the one hand, or opportunities that exist in that given situation on the other. Entanglement with the literal content of thought (cognitive *fusion*) and attempts to avoid undesirable private experiences (experiential avoidance) are argued to increase the impact and influence of emotional and cognitive content on people's actions, even when these sources of behavioral regulation are unhelpful (Hayes et al., 2001). As a result, suppressive and avoidant approaches to thoughts and feelings not only enhance distress (e.g., Wenzlaff & Wegner, 2000), they also interfere with effective behavior by minimizing the influence of useful opportunities in a given situation on people's actions (Hayes, Luoma, et al. 2006).

When ACT was originally developed, the overarching term used for its model of psychological ill health was *experiential avoidance*—the attempt to alter the form, frequency, or situational sensitivity of negative private events, even when doing so leads to behavioral difficulties (Hayes, Wilson, Gifford, Follette, & Strosahl, 1996). *Acceptance* was the term used to describe the adaptive form of this model, acceptance in this context being defined as the willingness to experience (i.e., not alter the form, frequency, or sensitivity of) unwanted private events in the pursuit of one's values and goals (Hayes et al., 1996).

The terms "acceptance" and "experiential avoidance" are still useful in highlighting how the avoidance of undesirable internal events can decrease people's sensitivity to values-related contingencies that exist in a given situation. However, when taken to represent the entire ACT model, these terms have their limitations. For one, the focus of these terms is on how people respond to unwanted thoughts, feelings, and physiological sensations, so they fail to highlight the breadth of ACT's more general claim that it is important how people respond to *all* of their internal events, whether they are unwanted, wanted, or neutral. Behavioral effectiveness (for example, performing well at work) and the ability to live a vital life can be just as inhibited when pleasant or simply mundane thoughts or feelings decrease people's sensitivity to values-related contingencies. For example, believing that one is wonderful can reduce behavioral flexibility when mistakes are made and "wonderful" no longer fits as a description; similarly, daydreaming about an upcoming holiday can decrease people's ability to respond to goal-related contingencies that are perhaps more important or pressing. Under such circumstances, people are not necessarily avoiding their internal events (indeed, they may be actively engaging in them); however, as with people who are avoiding their private events, their actions are disproportionally under the control of their internal events at the expense of values-related contingencies. You will see these principles being played out in the training described in this book as participants are shown how it is possible to make one's personally chosen values a more prominent guide to daily action (reducing the unhelpful influence of momentary thoughts and feelings over behavior).

According to the ACT model and its underlying basic account, depending upon the values-related opportunities afforded in a given situation, people need to be flexible in the degree to which they base their actions on opportunities in their current situation or on their internal events—no matter whether those internal events are unwanted, wanted, or neutral. In order to highlight ACT's emphasis on flexibility, its core psychological process has, over the past few years, been increasingly referred to as *psychological flexibility*. Psychological flexibility is defined as the ability to fully contact the present moment and the thoughts and feelings it contains without needless defense and, depending upon the situation, persist in or change behavior in the pursuit of values and values-based goals (Hayes, Luoma, et al., 2006).

Acceptance and experiential avoidance are examples of psychological flexibility and inflexibility, respectively, and it is still appropriate to use those terms. They refer to psychological stances that people take when the present moment contains unwanted thoughts and feelings they would prefer to avoid; as a result, these terms are often used when psychopathology and psychotherapy are discussed. However, ACT principles and techniques are increasingly being used in nontherapeutic situations to maximize behavioral effectiveness, for example, to facilitate employees' work and life functioning (e.g., Bond & Bunce, 2000; Bond et al., 2008). When ACT is delivered outside the clinical context, people's propensity to avoid unwanted thoughts and feelings may not be the central focus. Instead, greater emphasis may be placed on how excessive "entanglement" with cognitive and emotional content can interfere with the effective pursuit of personally valued actions and goals.

Producing Psychological Flexibility: The Hexagon

It is fairly straightforward to maintain that, in its essence, psychological flexibility is about people being able to base their actions on opportunities that exist in their current situation or their internal events, depending on the degree to which each will help them to pursue their values (being an effective worker, available parent, or loving spouse) in any given situation. It is quite another matter to specify what actions people can take to do this—that is, how people might become more psychologically flexible. A less technical definition of psychological flexibility is useful to this end: contacting the present moment as a conscious human being and, based on what that situation affords, acting in accordance with one's chosen values (Hayes, Strosahl, Bunting, Twohig, & Wilson, 2004). This more descriptive definition is represented by six interactive processes (see figure 2.1) that, together, help people to create a context of psychological flexibility. It is important to note that psychological flexibility is not literally made up of these six processes like a jigsaw puzzle is mad up of separate pieces that come together to form a whole. Rather, the processes are more like guidelines that help people to contact psychological flexibility (represented in the figure as the center of the hexagon). We now discuss these core processes.

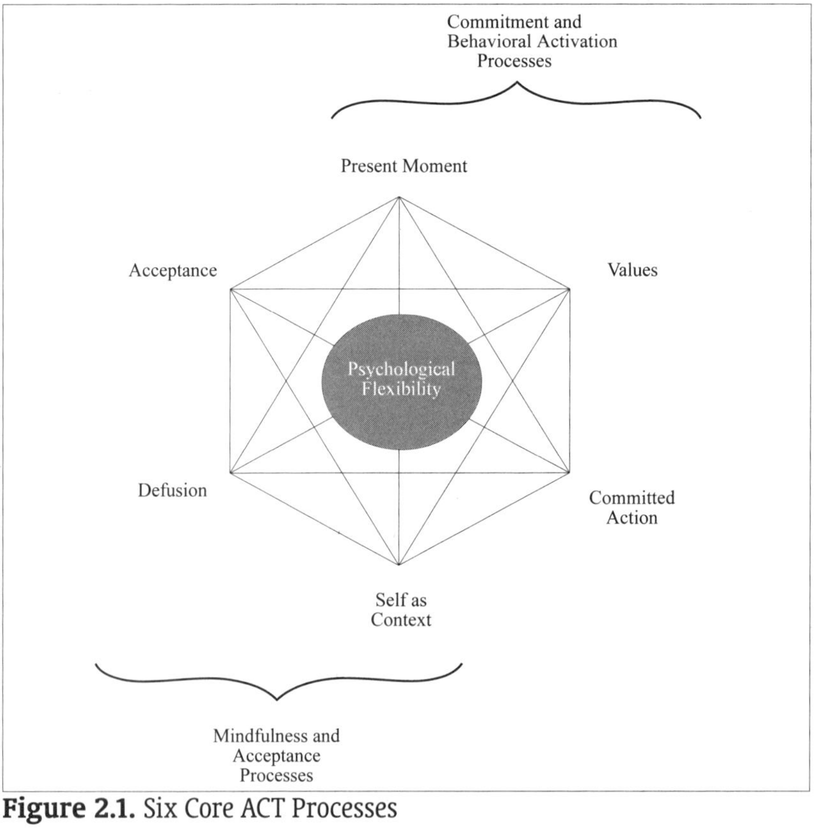

Figure 2.1. Six Core ACT Processes

Cognitive Defusion

Cognitive fusion occurs when our thoughts and feelings have too much control over our actions in comparison with the values-related opportunities in a given situation. Such unhelpful dominance of our thoughts and feelings results from people failing to notice that our internal events—our thoughts, feelings, memories, physiological sensations—are linked and that one (for example, a thought) can activate another one (for example, a feeling). Also, if we are cognitively fused, we fail to notice that there can be rigid patterns to how we typically think and feel in specific situations. We fail to see that whenever we get an e-mail from a particular person, we think, feel, and act in a specific way. That is, we may normally think, "What have I screwed up?" We feel a bit of anxiety and catch our breath, and we avoid opening the e-mail for a few minutes. In a state of cognitive fusion, we allow this automatic, or relational, process to disproportionately control our behavior, and our actions (whether or not we open the e-mail) are more likely to be controlled by the automatic process than by our goals and values, such as performing to our best ability at work.

The inverse of fusion is *cognitive defusion*, whereby people create a context in which their momentary thoughts and feelings are not excessively regulating their actions. In such a context, people notice, for example, that their fearful thoughts are related to fearful feelings; however, this relational process no longer has disproportionate control over their actions. Their goals and values can now exert more control over their behavior. Cognitive defusion is a key component of an ACT/RFT interpretation of what is usually termed "mindfulness" (Fletcher & Hayes, 2005). In essence, defusion involves techniques that increase our observations of thoughts and feelings as they occur in the moment. In a defused state, a person may notice that he or she is currently experiencing particular thoughts, while remaining flexible enough to choose whether or not to allow those thoughts to influence behavior.

When we are cognitively fused, we fail to notice the relational network that links unwanted thoughts with difficult feelings, and such failure tends to evoke predictable, habitual, or stereotypical actions, such as avoidance, inaction, and compulsions. We fail to properly notice this network because we are entangled in it, and our actions are excessively controlled by it. To escape its unwanted effects, we may try not to activate this unwanted network, so we avoid situations that might evoke the unwanted thoughts and feelings connected to it. This strategy, however, leads to psychological inflexibility, as our actions are based not on our values but, rather, on the desire not to experience certain unwanted internal events. This experiential avoidance leads to a very constrained and narrow existence, and even more unwanted thoughts and feelings tend to emerge (Bond, Hayes, Baer, Carpenter, Guenole, Orcutt & Zettle, 2011).

Acceptance

For most of us, the internal events that most profoundly constrain our psychological flexibility are ones that we do not want to experience: unhappy memories, unpleasant or self-critical thoughts, or scary feelings. Often these unwanted internal events rapidly, comprehensively, and automatically divert our responses away from the present moment, toward getting rid of, changing, or minimizing them. Such an inflexible response to these types of inner experiences is unlikely to promote our values, because we are guided by our desire to avoid or change them, rather than by seeing how we can best work toward our values and goals in the present situation. To act more flexibly with regard to these unwanted psychological events, people can respond to them with *acceptance*, which interacts with defusion to help undermine the domination of our internal events in determining behavior.

Acceptance involves a particular approach to experiencing one's thoughts, feelings, and physiological sensations. In particular, ACT argues that no matter how toxic one's thoughts and feelings might be ("I can't cope with this"; "I'm useless at my job"; "I feel terribly anxious"), they will not directly lead to mental illness and poor performance. Rather, it is only when people hold these unwanted internal events in a specific context that they will lead to harmful effects. This harmful context is one in which (1) people are cognitively fused with, or completely buy into, the literal meaning of their cognitive content ("if I have the thought 'I am a fool,' then I am really a fool") and cannot see this content as an automatic, idiosyncratic reaction to certain types of events; and (2) they avoid further internal events (such as anxiety) that are triggered by the content with which they are fused (Bond & Hayes, 2002).

As noted above, a key aim of ACT is to break down this context of cognitive fusion and experiential avoidance so that people's actions are not overwhelmingly regulated by the content of their thoughts and feelings; instead, their actions are also based on how they can work toward their goals and values in their present situation (Hayes, Strosahl & Wilson, 1999). To this end, ACT shows people how to contact their psychological content from a context of defusion and acceptance so that they merely notice, rather than engage, their thoughts and feelings as a continuous flow of psychological material and are willing to observe even their painful cognitive and emotional content without necessarily seeking to avoid it. In this context of defusion and acceptance, people treat their thoughts, feelings, memories, and physiological sensations as automatic chatter, or more technically, as the classically and operantly conditioned responses that they are.

The two processes of psychological flexibility discussed so far involve undermining the domination that human language and cognition have over our actions. The next two processes involve changes in how events are understood, known, and experienced.

Contact with the Present Moment

We do not want to give the impression that cognitive fusion is always bad. Its ability to envelop us in our relational frames, or internal events, also allows us to problem solve. We have evolved as a species (and have come to dominate the earth) precisely because we can evaluate a scenario we have never experienced ("being eaten by a lion would be bad") and then make ordered plans to prevent that from occurring ("first I'll find a cave, then I'll build a fire at the entrance of it"). Thus, anticipating, evaluating, and planning have been, and still are, essential skills for our survival and enrichment.

We tend, though, to overuse these skills, and so we get caught up in, or fused with, these temporal and evaluative relational frames. In doing so, we lose contact with the present moment: both in terms of contact with the immediate physical and social environment, as well as contact with our own psychological reactions. Defusion and acceptance help to foster such contact, and they are aided in doing so by actions that make the range, sensitivity, and depth of our experiences more flexible so that people can better "attend" to broad or narrow ranges of the current moment, as the situation demands. At times, it will be beneficial for people to attend to a broad range in the present moment, such as when crossing a busy intersection; at other times (when listening to a lecture), it is more useful for people to focus on a narrow range in a particular situation. Being in the present moment will help us determine and utilize the degree of focus that is most advantageous to us in a given situation.

Self-as-Context

The fourth process that helps to produce psychological flexibility involves viewing one's self as an observer, as the context in which we experience life. As a child, we learn to take various perspectives: I versus you, here versus there, and now versus then. These relational frames emerge through learning to talk about our perspective in relation to the perspective of other people, "What did you see at the park today, and did Johnny see it too?" (Hayes, 1984). As a result of children answering these countless questions, they can learn that what they see and experience constantly changes, but the *perspective* from which they notice that their experience constantly changes remains the same. In this sense, they experience a stable context of knowing: a *self-as-context.*

From this perspective, people can be aware of the changing flow of their thoughts, memories, feelings, and experiences without needing to avoid or be defensive about them; they do not have to maintain that they are correct about their viewpoints, memories, or reasons why something happened because from the perspective of self-as-context, *they* are not that memory, that feeling of humiliation or fear; they are the stage on which those experiences play out, but they are not those transient players and uncomfortable scenes—they are more stable and enduring than those internal events.

Importantly, this perspective of self can promote acceptance and defusion, especially with difficult internal events such as fear, because it is a perspective that is stable, and such stability and security can help people willingly experience difficult internal events. Thus, this sense of self makes moments of psychological flexibility—of persisting in valued actions even when doing so creates discomfort—less aversive and threatening, and thus more likely.

Conversely, inflexibility is fostered by attachment to a conceptualized self: the rigid network of verbal relations that are *about* ourselves, particularly those self-conceptualizations that are evaluative, dispositional, or predictive in nature. From this sense of self, *I* am a hard worker, a mother, a caring person, a loving husband. A conceptualized self is something to defend, to be right about, even when doing so gets in the way of pursuing our goals and values. For example, when we argue with our partner about "who's right" on an issue, we cease to pursue our value of being intimate with him or her; instead, we are defending the conceptualization of our self as a clever, strong, capable, or accurate person. In that moment, we are not viewing ourselves from the context of the observer (self-as-context), and we are also probably not defusing ourselves from our thoughts of needing to be right, nor accepting (making room for) our feelings of irritation; in short, we are acting in a manner that is psychologically inflexible.

Hewing to a conceptualized self is also problematic, as many of the events in a network of self-conceptualizations are not changeable. For example, the thought "I was intimidated by my demanding father, and I'll be damned if I will let my exacting boss do so as well" suggests that a resolution requires either a new boss or a new childhood, neither of which is likely.

The purpose of psychological flexibility is to allow individuals to contact, take in, and evaluate their current circumstance so as to act *effectively* in that situation. We must now define "effective" from an ACT perspective, and, in doing so, we specify the two remaining key processes that constitute psychological flexibility: *values* and *committed action.*

Values

Values are defined in ACT and RFT as chosen qualities of action patterns (e.g., being a good manager) that people can work toward, but that they cannot arrive at once and for all (people have to work constantly at being a good manager or they cease to be one) (Hayes, Strosahl, Bunting, et al., 2004). As such, values involve verbally constructed rules that motivate us to act in ways that are meaningful to us (Hayes et al., 1999). To the extent that people act according to their chosen values, they are living an effective life, *for them.* Thus, in accord with the philosophy of science that underlies both ACT and RFT (functional contextualism), judgments regarding what is effective, "right," or workable for individuals need to be made against a priori statements of their own personally chosen values.

As suggested by the interrelations among the six processes (as shown in figure 2.1 and discussed below), defusion and acceptance are not ends in themselves. Rather, these processes help people to see situations more clearly and to be more flexible in acting in accordance with their values. Thus, in ACT, living a valued life provides the raison d'être for defusing from unhelpful cognitive content, accepting discomforting emotions, and contacting the present moment as a conscious person (from the perspective of self-as-context). All of these processes are mutually facilitative: they are aspects of the same behavioral pattern, namely, psychological flexibility.

In the absence of values, people tend to be motivated by being right, looking good in the eyes of others, avoiding difficult internal events, or doing what feels good at the time, even if doing so is not in one's long-term interests (that is, consistent with one's values). In short, from an ACT/ RFT perspective, acting in the absence of values (or with vague or poorly articulated values) tends to promote psychological rigidity and inflexibility (Bond, 2004).

An important goal of ACT, therefore, is not only to promote acceptance and defusion and, hence, contact with the present moment as a conscious person, but it is also to have individuals, and indeed organizations, clarify and specify their values. When people do not behave according to their values, they risk denying themselves contact with positive reinforcers that foster good mental health and effective action in a given context, such as work (Bond, Hayes, & Barnes-Holmes, 2006). Reinforcement deprivation often results when people avoid difficult psychological experiences and the values-consistent actions that may occasion them (Wilson & Blackledge, 1999). Thus, once again, all aspects of this model interrelate.

Committed Action

Finally, ACT promotes the development of larger and larger patterns of values-based action. Once ACT participants have defined personally chosen values for different areas of their lives, they are encouraged to identify (and pursue) specific patterns of action that will help to bring those values to life. The aim is for participants to begin noticing the vitality and sense of purpose that can come through value-consistent behavior and to learn to relate skillfully (mindfully and with acceptance) to any unhelpful thoughts and feelings that arise during this process.

Combining the Six Core Processes

Each of these six processes relates to, and interacts with, all of the other processes, as represented by the lines connecting all points in figure 2.1. Some of these relations have similar functions: the three vertical lines are all of that kind. Acceptance and defusion both undermine destructive language processes; self-as-context and contact with the present moment both involve increasing effective contact with the *here and now*—the present moment; values and committed action both involve harnessing the positive aspects of language (e.g., stating and specifying values) in order to create patterns of values-driven actions.

Notice in figure 2.1 how these six processes can be chunked into two larger groups: mindfulness and acceptance processes (the four processes to the left of the figure) and commitment and behavioral activation processes (the four to the right). The two middle processes, contact with the present moment and self-as-context, are relevant to both groups. We draw readers' attention to these larger groups of processes because the two related skills at the heart of our workplace training program have been designed to reflect and target them.

How the ACT Model Has Informed Our Workplace Training Program

We have translated the model of psychological flexibility shown in figure 2.1 into the three-session psychological and behavioral skills training program that is described in this book. This type of brief ACT-based workplace training has been successfully delivered in a wide range of organizations, and its effectiveness has been demonstrated in a series of randomized controlled trials (e.g., Bond & Bunce, 2000; Flaxman & Bond, 2010a, b; Flaxman, Söderberg, Bond, & Lloyd, 2011; also see chapter 9). The ultimate aim of the program is the same as for all ACT interventions: to increase psychological flexibility. We have found this can be achieved in the workplace by communicating ACT principles to groups of employees in an accessible format and repeatedly seeking to provide employees with an *experiential* understanding of ACT's core processes, by encouraging participants to engage in value-based actions and to notice what happens when they do so. Most of the techniques we use in the program have been adopted (and in some cases adapted slightly) from the wider ACT literature. In addition, some strategies have been borrowed from other mindfulness training programs and from the field of behavioral activation.

Our two-skills diagram (figure 2.2) shows how we have explicitly designed the training to target two related skills: *mindfulness* and *values-based action*. It is not difficult to see from this overview how the training has been directly influenced by the ACT model.

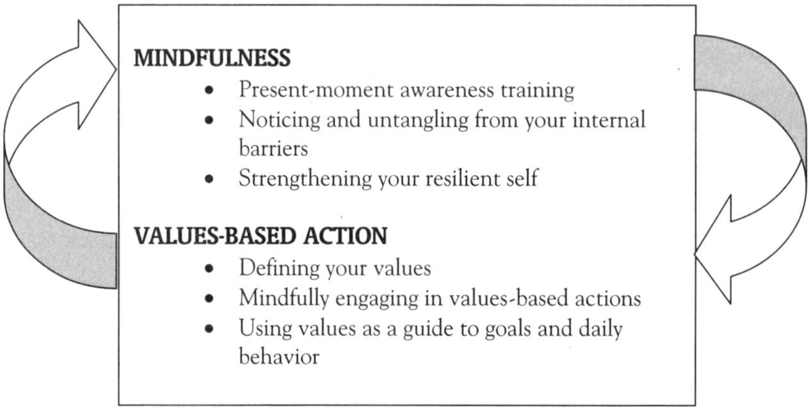

Figure 2.2. The Two-Skills Diagram

Specifically, the mindfulness skill component reflects ACT's aforementioned higher-order cluster of mindfulness and acceptance processes, while the values-based action component reflects commitment and behavioral activation processes. The subcomponents of the two skills reflect the terminology we use to communicate ACT's six core processes. For example, "noticing and untangling from internal barriers" captures both defusion and acceptance, while the subskills found within the values-based action component capture both values and committed action.

Finally, note the arrows linking mindfulness and values-based action in the diagram. These arrows reflect the fact that mindfulness and valued action are being presented to employees as intimately related psychological and behavioral skills. For example, in session 2 of our training protocol, you will learn how the trainer explicitly introduces defusion and acceptance practices as strategies that help us "untangle" from internal barriers to personally valued action. Similarly, the trainer repeatedly employs certain techniques and metaphors that are specifically designed to highlight the functional links between mindfulness and value-directed behavior.

Summary

As we have discussed in this chapter, ACT is a contextual CBT. As such, it emphasizes a particular way of dealing with difficult or unhelpful internal experiences: instead of trying to change and control them, participants are encouraged to approach their thoughts, feelings, and sensations from a more mindful and open perspective. Unlike most other third-generation CBTs, ACT maintains that mindfulness is not an end in itself. Rather, ACT helps facilitate people's ability to identify their values and then actively and deliberately to pursue them, even when experiencing unwanted or unhelpful thoughts, feelings, memories, and physiological sensations. Research shows that promoting such psychological flexibility helps to reduce psychological distress (Hayes, Luoma, et al., 2006). In addition, it can help people become more productive at work, not only by reducing their distress and related occasions of absence from work, but also by helping them become much more sensitive to the performance- and productivity-related opportunities that exist in their work and home environments (Bond, Hayes, & Barnes-Holmes, 2006). In short, psychological flexibility allows people to learn how to do their jobs more effectively, to pursue values in their personal lives, and to have better mental health. Having described the distinctive features of ACT, in the next chapter we further unpack our rationale for implementing this approach in the workplace.

CHAPTER 3

The Rationale for Applying ACT in the Workplace

As described in the previous chapter, ACT is at the forefront of recent developments within the wider field of CBT. As we have seen, unlike more traditional forms of CBT, ACT does not seek to change the content, frequency, or intensity of people's unwanted thoughts, feelings, and sensations. Instead, ACT aims to change the way that people fundamentally relate to all internal events in order to increase psychological flexibility and value-guided behavioral effectiveness. Accordingly, when evaluating the impact of ACT interventions, researchers often prioritize indicators of improved quality of life or life satisfaction over more traditional measures of symptom reduction. Research suggests that ACT can produce significant improvements in life functioning that are independent of any changes in the content or frequency of people's undesirable thoughts or feelings (Hayes, Luoma, et al., 2006). In the present chapter, we consider why the emergence of ACT has important implications for those interested in improving mental health and effectiveness among working populations.

The following rationale for implementing ACT in the workplace is organized into three main sections. First, we discuss the practical benefits that stem from ACT's unified model of psychological flexibility (shown in figure 2.1), which is presumed to apply across most (if not all) areas of human functioning. Second, we consider how features of ACT's intervention technology, such as mindfulness skills training and values-based goal setting, are well suited for delivery to groups of employees in the workplace. We also describe how ACT's broad scope and technical flexibility allow ACT interventions to be adapted according to context and desired outcome. In the third section, we highlight an interesting alignment between ACT's philosophy and recent trends in occupational health policy, which has seen a shift away from the traditional focus on reducing symptoms of mental ill health and toward fostering engagement in work and improving people's quality of life. We hope that by the end of this chapter, readers will begin to share our view that the emergence of ACT represents an exciting development for those of us interested in enhancing employees' well-being and behavioral effectiveness.

ACT's Unified Model of Human Functioning

One of the strongest arguments for applying ACT in the workplace stems from its generic underlying model of psychological flexibility. As discussed in the previous chapter, ACT's model is itself based on an established theory and research program (RFT), which holds that most forms of psychological distress and behavioral ineffectiveness are consequences of certain features of human language and cognition. As a result of this link to basic principles and processes, the model is presumed to apply across a wide range of human experience.

In particular, experiential avoidance (an important feature of psychological inflexibility) is now widely viewed as an important risk factor (or diathesis) that has implications for human functioning in general (Biglan, Hayes, & Pistorello, 2008; Hayes et al., 1996; Kashdan, Barrios, Forsyth, & Steger, 2006). To reiterate, experiential avoidance refers to the tendency to try to change, avoid, or remove unwanted thoughts and feelings. Unfortunately, many forms of experiential avoidance are futile and counterproductive, resulting in more difficulties rather than less. For example, there is a large body of research evidence showing that attempts to suppress unwanted thoughts actually lead to a greater frequency of those thoughts and associated undesirable emotions (Wenzlaff & Wenger, 2000). We humans try hard not to think about something, and our minds can think about little else. Similarly, experientially avoidant individuals, who are unwilling to experience certain thoughts and feelings, will tend to avoid situations, events, and interpersonal interactions that are likely to elicit those thoughts and feelings. In this way, people's lives can become restricted as they avoid pursuing valued life goals and actions in order to avoid experiencing particular internal states. There is certainly strong evidence in favor of viewing experiential avoidance as an important factor in many manifestations of psychological distress and behavioral dysfunction. Higher levels of experiential avoidance are associated with a wide range of mental health problems including anxiety, depression, phobias, posttraumatic stress, eating disorders, and various forms of self-harm (Hayes et al., 1996; see Hayes, Luoma, et al., 2006, for a more recent review).

So what relevance does all this have for implementing ACT in the workplace? Well, given that we already have a good understanding of the core processes (such as experiential avoidance) implicated in the development and maintenance of psychological distress, behavioral ineffectiveness, and reduced quality of life, it seems somewhat unethical to wait for these processes to create serious dysfunction before offering intervention. While tertiary, or therapeutic, interventions are undoubtedly important, we believe it is equally appropriate to adopt a more preventive approach—that is, offering interventions such as ACT to much greater numbers of people in the general population to prevent such processes from leading to unnecessary problems. As we saw in chapter 1, even among working populations we can expect to find a high proportion of individuals experiencing common mental health problems, the vast majority of whom will not seek treatment from mainstream mental health services. Moreover, the benefits of ACT can go beyond helping those workers who are already experiencing chronic psychological distress. ACT interventions potentially have something important to offer individuals who are already functioning well enough but looking to function even better (for example, by increasing present-moment awareness and value- and goal-consistent behavior).

Consistent with these arguments, Biglan et al. (2008) recently proposed that our growing knowledge of experiential avoidance as a common risk factor should now be harnessed in the service of prevention. It is notable that their recommendations include delivering ACT in the workplace as a promising, yet underutilized, preventive intervention strategy.

Suitability of ACT's Technical Features for Workplace Delivery

The second strand in our rationale relates to the nature of the techniques and exercises that are employed in ACT interventions. To start at a general level, the six facets of psychological flexibility (contact with the present moment, acceptance, cognitive defusion, self-as-context, values, and committed action) can be conceptualized as psychological skills that can be developed through experiential practice (such as mindfulness) and engagement in values-consistent action (Hayes, 2004). Similar to more traditional forms of CBT, a skills-based approach to therapeutic change and behavioral functioning is well suited to group delivery, across a range of different contexts.

More specifically, we have found mindfulness work in ACT to be very useful for worksite interventions. ACT has a higher purpose that goes beyond simply showing people how to "cope" with undesirable thoughts, emotions, and physiological sensations. Instead, ACT seeks to change the relationship that people have with *all* of their internal experiences. The emphasis in ACT is not on whether the content of particular thoughts and feelings is deemed "negative" or "positive," but rather on how our thoughts and feelings *function* (for example, whether being entangled in particular thoughts influences our behavior in unhelpful ways).

From a practical perspective, this means that mindfulness skills can be cultivated regardless of whether the participant is currently experiencing a high volume or intensity of negatively evaluated thoughts and emotions. To take one example, when using mindfulness strategies to help participants cultivate defusion (learning to notice the process of thinking in the moment), the tone of the thoughts being experienced during the exercise is unimportant. Rather this skill can be cultivated by learning to "watch" whatever thoughts happen to show up, whether they are positive or negative. This feature of mindfulness practice is particularly useful in work settings, where ACT is often delivered to heterogeneous groups of individuals, not all of whom are currently experiencing high levels of negative psychological content.

Similarly, the values- and goal-oriented skills central to ACT seem highly suited to worksite delivery. In our experience, employees often are already reasonably familiar with the process of short-term, medium-term, and long-term behavioral goal setting and the assessment of potential barriers to goal achievement. Indeed, theories of work motivation and job performance have long emphasized the importance of having employees participate in setting their own work and career goals (e.g., Locke & Latham, 1990, 2002). We tend to harness people's previous experiences with goal setting both in work and in their nonwork lives. During ACT training sessions, we sometimes promote ACT's values work as "goal setting with a difference," the difference being that goals are explicitly linked to chosen values and are used to initiate and maintain behavioral movement in valued life directions. We have received plenty of anecdotal feedback reporting that participants derive benefit by aligning specific goals with more general values. Values tend to provide coherence to a set of goals within a particular area of life and help to keep us "on track" even when individual goals are not achieved on schedule (Hayes et al., 1999). When ACT is being employed to enhance work performance, we suggest that a combination of values and mindfulness (e.g., defusion) interventions adds a powerful dimension to more traditional goal-setting procedures—not only by providing a deeper sense of meaning and purpose but also by helping participants recognize and overcome their "psychological barriers" to performance enhancement.

Another practical benefit of ACT's model is that the six processes and related interventions are all part of a unified rationale that is always focused on the cultivation and promotion of psychological flexibility. This more coherent approach stands in contrast to more traditional multifaceted CBT-based programs that have been delivered in the workplace. These more traditional programs typically provide a mix of different intervention approaches (such as cognitive modification, progressive muscular relaxation, problem-solving training, and time management). While the idea is to offer employees a broad and flexible repertoire of stress management skills, it is not necessarily easy to show how such different approaches are to be integrated or oriented toward to a common purpose. Indeed, a recent review of workplace SMT research found that the more additional components are added to a traditional SMT program, the less effective the intervention generally becomes (Richardson & Rothstein, 2008). It may be that employees become overwhelmed if they are asked to learn an array of apparently different procedures in a relatively short space of time.

In view of these arguments, readers might not be surprised to learn that we have taken advantage of ACT's unified model when designing and developing the training protocol described in this book. As noted in the previous chapter, we organize the various metaphors, writing tasks, group discussions, and experiential exercises contained within our ACT protocol into two interrelated sets of skills, centering on mindfulness and values-based action. We have found that this approach 1) helps the trainer demonstrate how ACT's processes are not only intimately interrelated but also directed toward a common purpose; and 2) provides participants with a simple framework for organizing the numerous intervention strategies that will be introduced and practiced during (and between) the training sessions.

Finally, ACT can be delivered effectively in groups, which is the usual format for worksite training programs. Walser and Pistorello (2004) highlight a number of advantages associated with delivering ACT in groups, including the potential to normalize people's internal experiences, the opportunity to share insights into ACT's principles and procedures, the creation and sharing of new exercises and metaphors, and the creation of a context within which clients can publicly commit to chosen values. Also, we find that a fair amount of humor is typically shared among group members, and (when appropriate) this humor can be used in the service of one or more of ACT's processes.

Aligning ACT with Occupational Health Policy and Practice

The final strand in our rationale for implementing ACT in the workplace concerns general trends in the occupational health literature. The first trend reflects an attempt to expand occupational health policy and practice beyond mere compliance with health and safety regulations to place greater emphasis on prevention initiatives and on the promotion of psychological health in the workplace (Black, 2008). For example, a recent large-scale review of staff well-being in the British National Health Service (the largest employer in Europe) highlighted the importance of viewing staff health and well-being as more than the absence of disease and called for increased investment in interventions that show potential for improving employees' quality of life (Boorman, 2009).

Similarly, a recent review of workplace interventions for the most common mental health problems (such as anxiety and depression) suggests that it is time to let go of the view that employees with common mental health problems need to be "symptom free" to remain at work or return to work after a period of absence (Seymour, 2010). A related trend is the increased focus on "presenteeism" that was mentioned in chapter 1. Specifically, there is now growing recognition of the considerable costs associated with psychologically distressed employees who are present at work but are experiencing performance impairments and reduced productivity. This issue may be exacerbated during difficult economic periods as distressed employees may be more reluctant to take time off for reasons of mental ill health out of fear of losing their jobs.

There appears to be an interesting alignment between the philosophy of ACT and these trends in occupational health research, policy, and practice. ACT seeks to help people function more effectively, *even while* experiencing what would traditionally be referred to as symptoms of mental ill health (undesirable thoughts, feelings, and physiological sensations). Hence, ACT has the potential to help people perform in their jobs and stay productive even when they don't particularly feel like it. Also, if employees become less concerned or distressed about undesirable thoughts and emotions, then it is less likely they will feel the need to drop out of the workforce (or alter their behavior in other ways) when such difficult thoughts and feelings show up. Similarly, for those employees who value working life and the benefits it can bring, ACT can ensure that such values are operating as a prominent guide to work-related behavior.

Summary

Over the past dozen years or more, we have become increasingly convinced of the arguments in favor of implementing ACT in the workplace. The rationale outlined in this chapter starts with ACT's generic model of human functioning, which suggests that significant benefits will be gained by offering ACT interventions to nonclinical populations, including working people. In addition, we have found that ACT has a number of technical features that facilitate its delivery to groups of employees in work settings. Finally, we propose that ACT's focus on improving psychological flexibility (rather than on the reduction, modification, or removal of unwanted psychological content) sits well with current thinking among occupational health policy makers.

Having outlined our basic rationale for extending ACT interventions to working populations, we can now turn to the program itself. In the next chapter we outline some of the more practical issues associated with delivering this type of intervention in workplace settings and provide an overview of the technical content of our own ACT-based training program. Then, in chapters 5 through 7, we provide a more detailed account of the types of strategies we have used in the workplace to target ACT's core processes, along with examples of how the training tends to unfold across three sessions.

CHAPTER 4

Practical Considerations and Program Overview

Before providing a session-by-session account of our ACT-based protocol, we consider some of the more practical issues associated with the delivery of this type of psychological and behavioral skills training in the workplace. We begin by discussing whether the training is being delivered to meet broad or more specific objectives and reflect on how it might be marketed to employees, managers, and organizational decision makers. We also outline different training design and delivery options, issues related to the size and composition of training groups, and the skills and experience of the trainer.

In the second part of the chapter, we present an overview of the program, providing more detail on how we have built our training around mindfulness and values-based action skills. We also outline the basic structure and technical content of each of the three sessions that make up the protocol described in the subsequent chapters.

The theme that runs through this chapter is *flexibility*. Our aim is to show that this type of training can easily be adapted for delivery over a different number of sessions, to groups of various sizes, and tailored to fit the particular organizational context, desired outcomes, and employee groups likely to be involved. As noted in the introduction to this book, we present our training protocol not as a prescriptive manual for other trainers to follow verbatim, but rather as one worksite training approach that suits our own style of delivery and has been found to be effective in enhancing employees' psychological flexibility, mental health, and behavioral effectiveness.

Training Focus

One of the first things to consider is whether this type of training is to be implemented to meet specific or broad objectives. Over the years, we have tended to adopt a broad focus for the program, with our desired outcome being the enhancement of employees' levels of psychological flexibility as the key mechanism for enhancing both psychological health and values-oriented behavioral effectiveness. In less technical language, we often pitch the program as a way of strengthening employees' personal resilience by providing a set of skills for overcoming psychological obstacles to the effective pursuit of personally valued actions and goals. One practical implication of this approach is that we do not offer this program solely to improve work-related well-being and effectiveness. Instead, we offer a combination of mindfulness and values-based action skills and invite employees to apply these skills in each and every area of their lives (work/career, leisure time, relationships, personal growth, and health).

There are some notable advantages to offering ACT as a program of generalizable skills training. When the trainers are explicit about this approach from the outset, employees quickly get the sense that this training is designed "for them" and is not something being implemented by management to help them work harder, meet their performance targets, or prepare them for dealing with greater work demands. This is important for the way that employees view the training; if employees get the impression that the training is part of some unpopular management drive, the intervention is likely (at least initially) to be met with a degree of suspicion and cynicism. Moreover, the generic skills training approach supports one of our main ACT-inspired goals of helping employees make experiential contact with diverse sources of values-based behavioral reinforcement (see Dahl, Plumb, Stewart, & Lundgren, 2009).

Despite our preference for this general skills approach, ACT is also increasingly being delivered to support more specific organizational outcomes and to enhance the effects of other worksite training programs. One approach that has generated recent interest involves the use of the ACT model and intervention technology to improve leaders' effectiveness (e.g., Bond, 2012; Moran, 2011). Other applications include ACT-based career coaching, workplace safety training, team development, and interpersonal skills training (see chapter 10 for some examples of these more specific applications of the ACT model). It is perhaps not surprising that ACT is now being used to achieve such a wide range of objectives, given that it is underpinned by a broadly applicable model of human functioning. In addition, research from various sources indicates that ACT principles have an enhancing effect on other workplace training initiatives, on employees' experiences of organizational change, on how employees manage the emotional demands of work, and on job-related innovation and learning (see, for example, Biron & van Veldhoven, 2012; Bond & Bunce, 2000; Bond & Flaxman, 2006; Bond et al., 2008; Hayes, Bissett, et al., 2004; Varra, Hayes, Roget, & Fisher, 2008).

The protocol presented over the next three chapters has been designed as a generic employee skills training program. However, with simple modifications to the initial introduction and to the terms and examples used throughout, the program can be more specifically oriented toward specific objectives. For example, if other trainers wish to utilize this approach to support leadership development, then the values work that is conducted across all three sessions can be adapted to encourage reflection on the leadership strengths and qualities that participants personally value and the internal barriers or obstacles that hold them back from engaging more fully and frequently in daily patterns of behavior that would bring those valued leadership qualities to life. The ultimate goal is still to increase employees' psychological flexibility—it's just that this goal may be achieved within the context of pursuing other specific organizational and employee training outcomes. The ACT approach naturally encourages this sort of creativity and flexibility, and we hope that our protocol serves as a foundation for an array of innovative adaptations.

Recruitment and Marketing Strategy

The desired outcome of the training will obviously have an influence on the way the training is marketed to organizations and employees. There are usually two levels of marketing required—the initial approach to attract interest (and support/investment) from organizational decision makers, and then the recruitment strategy to attract employees to the training.

As researchers, we have often been able to secure research funding before approaching potential host organizations. This makes the training an attractive option as we are able to offer the program at minimal *direct* cost to the organization. Nonetheless, it is unlikely that even "free" training will automatically be taken up by an organization. While direct costs can be minimized during funded research projects, organizations will still need to consider the costs of staff coverage if people are to be released for training during working hours. Thus, whether or not an organization is being asked to make a direct financial investment, we usually find that senior managers and those responsible for organizational expenditure will need to be convinced of the merits of the training.

As a central part of our marketing strategy, we make full use of the evidence base that has demonstrated the role of psychological flexibility in employees' psychological health and work-related functioning, and the intervention studies that have repeatedly demonstrated the efficiency and effectiveness of ACT programs delivered to working populations (see chapter 9 for a review of this research). In a competitive training market, we view the underlying evidence base as an important selling point for ACT practitioners. Indeed, most organizations will have made considerable and long-term investments in other staff training programs that have not been subjected to such rigorous evaluation in terms of being shown to elicit significant and long-term improvements in employees' psychological health in a series of randomized controlled trials.

The key message we convey to potential host organizations is that this training has been shown in a number of different studies across the globe to improve an individual resilience factor (psychological flexibility) that is associated with people's mental health, levels of sickness absence, work task performance, and general life functioning. In fairness, we find that many senior managers do not need much convincing about the need to improve their staff members' psychological well-being. However, this is not always the case, and some will require a degree of persuasion that this type of training offers a sufficient return on investment. In such cases, ACT's empirical evidence base can be bolstered with estimates of the costs of mental ill health and associated dysfunction to individual employees and their employers (as discussed in chapter 1).

As noted above, if an organization shows little interest in ACT as a general personal resilience program, the marketing can be adapted so that ACT principles are used as the vehicle for other recognized initiatives such as leadership development, enhancing work-related functioning, or improving customer service (Archer, 2012; Bond, 2012). For example, following recent consultations with different health care organizations in the United Kingdom, we are in the process of tailoring ACT to fit the particular concerns of each organization, including helping employees stay psychologically healthy during a period of organizational change; improving shift workers' leisure time experiences; and helping health care managers untangle from work-related worry and rumination during evenings and weekends. In this way, we offer ACT as a general intervention approach or philosophy, which is then tailored to meet particular needs identified by organizational stakeholders. We generally find this to be an effective approach when consulting with organizations, as key stakeholders (including some of the employees who may attend the training) are given the opportunity to participate in decisions about the design and focus of the program.

The second level of marketing is aimed at attracting the target employee groups to the training. Here the key considerations become the title given to the training and the initial recruitment information provided. We also consult with organizational contacts regarding the title for our ACT-based training. We might suggest various titles and ask members of the organization (such as occupational health or human resource representatives) which of those options is most likely to attract people. The titles we have employed more than once over the years include "Work and Life Effectiveness Training," "Psychological Skills Training," "Personal Resilience Training," and "Psychological Resilience Training." Other ACT practitioners have used titles such as "ACT for Life" (Oliver, Morris, Johns, & Byrne, 2011) and "Living to the Full" (Fledderus, Bohlmeijer, Smit, & Westerhof, 2010). Such titles have been used when ACT is being delivered as a general resilience-enhancing intervention. If the training is being offered to achieve more specified outcomes, such as improving employees' leisure time experiences, then the title should be phrased to reflect that aim.

In addition to the title, it is important to provide a brief description of the training in the recruitment material. Our usual practice is to produce a one-page flyer that describes the training as an opportunity to reduce the impact of unhelpful thoughts and feelings (such as worry, low mood, self-doubt, irritation) on one's psychological well-being and life effectiveness, and clarify and more effectively pursue personally valued life goals. We also routinely mention potential performance-related benefits, such as improved concentration and task focus, that can stem from

ACT/mindfulness-based programs. We try to make the training as attractive as possible, with taglines such as "An opportunity to learn some of the latest skills and techniques that have been shown to improve people's well-being and effectiveness." It is often worth offering target groups a brief introductory taster session (perhaps during the lunch hour or at the end of the workday) to let potential participants meet the trainer(s) to further explain the nature of the program and address any concerns, such as self-disclosing personal issues in front of coworkers.

Aside from the need to be ACT-consistent, we do not wish to be prescriptive in making these suggestions, as the marketing materials and recruitment strategy should always be appropriately tailored to the organizational context and client group. For example, when one is offering this training in some working environments, recruitment materials that suggest a focus on "feelings" might deter the target audience. In such contexts, strengths-based terms such as "resilience," "hardiness," "performance development," and "pursuit of goals" are likely to be more effective (see White, 2000). In short, it usually pays for the training provider to gain some insight into the organizational culture in which this type of training is being offered.

Our basic position is that ACT should be made available to as many employees as possible regardless of their current levels of psychological distress. We therefore design our recruitment materials to attract a wide range of employees, from those struggling with a common mental health problem through to employees who are functioning well but who are interested in learning how to reach greater levels of effectiveness and how to obtain greater clarity about their life purpose and goals. We take a certain amount of pride in the fact that we are able to offer an ACT-based program that performs well even when delivered to highly heterogenous training groups.

Delivery Format

There are many different ways of delivering ACT in the workplace. We have mostly employed a "2 + 1" method of delivery, which involves participants attending three sessions of training during working hours—two of which occur in consecutive weeks, with a third "booster" session occurring somewhere between one and three months after session 2 (Bond & Bunce, 2000; Flaxman & Bond, 2006, 2010b). The three-session protocol described in the following chapters reflects this approach.

When the training is delivered in this way, each session is scheduled to last for a maximum of three hours, which includes plenty of time for a midsession break and the completion of any evaluation measures. With breaks and other pauses in the training, this method of delivery provides participants with approximately 7 to 7½ hours of in-session material, skill practice, and discussion.

We have found this delivery format has some advantages in the workplace. First, the organizations we have worked with have often viewed this training approach as less disruptive to people's working schedules, when compared to the option of having briefer sessions spread over a greater number of weeks. Second, the need to attend training on just three occasions makes it somewhat less likely that participants will have to miss a session due to work demands, illness, or for other personal reasons. Moreover, the gap between sessions 2 and 3 provides participants with the opportunity to practice combining mindfulness and values-based action in their daily lives and begin generalizing ACT principles and procedures across various life domains. Finally, scheduling a "booster" session some weeks after the initial training sessions allows the trainer to check on progress and may help to maintain benefits over a longer period of time.

So far, we have found that varying the timing of the final session has little impact on the overall improvements in mental health, behavioral functioning, and psychological flexibility that employees obtain from this type of training. The longest gap we have left between sessions 2 and 3 is three months. We have also successfully delivered ACT training with shorter gaps of one month, six weeks, and two months, and have to date observed no significant impact on participants' experiences of the program. The decision about the timing of the final session has often been influenced by practical considerations, such as the need to complete the training within a time period requested by host organizations or to reflect the time frame of a funded research project. The most important factor for us is that participants are given a period of a few weeks to apply and practice ACT-based skills in their daily lives and to notice what happens when they do so. Our current preference is to leave a gap of somewhere between one and two months between the initial training phase and the final session.

There are various other ways to deliver this type of training. Perhaps the most obvious is to deliver the same training in shorter sessions (e.g., 1½- to 2-hour sessions) over four or more weeks. This approach has the advantage of allowing participants and trainer to reflect on progress on a weekly basis. This training format is particularly helpful for completing and reviewing between-session assignments, with a new skill introduced each week, practiced between sessions, and discussed and reinforced in the following session. Mindfulness training programs (such as MBSR) and group CBT interventions are typically delivered in this way to facilitate the home practice requirement. Our ACT protocol can also be delivered in this format, with a useful option being weekly sessions of up to two hours for four consecutive weeks and a final booster session delivered one or two months later. At the time of writing, Paul Flaxman is in the process of helping to deliver and evaluate ACT in this format for employees working in health care organizations in the United Kingdom.

Particularly in the current economic climate, it is not always possible for organizations to commit to programs of this duration (at least not when the training is being offered during working hours). Some studies have demonstrated that one full day of ACT-based training can lead to improvements in general and work-related well-being and effectiveness (for example, see Hayes, Bissett, et al., 2004; Varra et al., 2008). Offering training over a single day does have some practical advantages over multisession programs, and many organizations may already deliver other types of training in this way. One important disadvantage is that one-day workshops do not provide participants with the opportunity to return and share their experiences of home practice and skill application. In addition, participants can easily become overwhelmed if required to absorb an ACT-based intervention in a single day. Nonetheless, if this is the only option on the table, there is some empirical evidence that single-day workshops are able to convey key ACT principles and skills. Where possible, we would strongly encourage some kind of participant follow-up (perhaps by e-mail) to check on skill development and utilization and to ensure the intervention strategies are functioning as intended.

There is also a place for even briefer ACT-based workplace training, ranging from a couple of hours' duration up to a single half-day workshop. Although we haven't conducted a rigorous empirical evaluation of such brief ACT interventions, we have delivered ACT taster workshops in this format (again in health care organizations) and have observed beneficial effects and received favorable feedback (particularly when the brief workshop is supported by handouts, recommended reading and supported by handouts and recommended reading). A colleague of ours (Vasiliki Christodoulou) has developed some excellent DVDs in which she covers the same basic messages and content as an in-person ACT-based program. Such films can be utilized as a useful adjunct to briefer training programs. Another colleague working in the United Kingdom (Rob Archer; http.lppconsulting.org) has developed series of two- and four-hour ACT-inspired training modules that are designed to achieve specific outcomes, such as supporting cultural change or leadership development. At a workshop at the recent ACT world conference, Rob described how he has generated most interest in ACT among senior managers and organizational decision makers by using ACT principles as the foundation for other recognized training initiatives, including leadership development, team performance, and time management (Archer, 2012). We provide an overview of some of Rob's ACT-based career development work in chapter 9.

Of course, many of the logistical difficulties and staff release costs mentioned in this section can be overcome by offering the training outside of normal working hours, for example, at the end of the workday or even on weekends. However, this does somewhat change the ethos of the program and can make it more difficult for some sections of the workforce to attend, including those with young children or other dependents. In some organizations, we have offered sessions both during and immediately after normal working hours to account for the fact that some staff members were unable to leave the workplace for this length of time and also to facilitate the attendance of people working nontraditional shift patterns. It is not unusual for employees to attend our training on their days off (as part of their annual leave entitlement). Where possible, we prefer it when organizations are able to commit to releasing staff to attend during the workday.

Group Size and Composition

We would suggest that ACT-based training can be delivered effectively to groups with as few as two or three employees up to groups of perhaps sixty or more. The size of the group will have an influence on the style of delivery (see below). With smaller groups (ten employees or fewer) there is likely to be more in-depth discussion of people's individual experiences with mindfulness and values-based action exercises, and it is easier for the trainer to harness natural group processes in the service of promoting psychological flexibility. In much larger groups, two or more trainers may be required, with the larger group frequently broken into subgroups to facilitate reflection on the various exercises.

When considering a larger group format, we would particularly recommend that readers inspect the delivery rationale and implementation process developed by Jim White in Scotland (White, 2000; see also Brown, Cochrane, Mack, Leung, & Hancox, 1998). Although the technical content of Jim White's training is based on more traditional CBT (for anxiety management and stress control), his general implementation approach seems ideal for the wide and efficient dissemination of ACT. It is notable that ACT practitioners are already adopting a similar approach by offering ACT workshops in community settings (e.g., Fledderus et al., 2010) and for the general public. In addition, other mindfulness training programs (such as MBSR) can be delivered effectively to groups of around twenty-five people (e.g., Chaskalson, 2011), and there is evidence that ACT workshops can be delivered effectively in the workplace to groups of this size (Brinkborg, Michanek, Hesser, & Berglund, 2011).

When delivering ACT training in the workplace, we usually work with groups of ten people or fewer (with one trainer). Across several ACT projects conducted over the past decade or so the average group size has probably been around five or six. Working with groups of this size facilitates our preferred style of delivery (discussed in more detail below), which makes use of a general structure to guide each session while remaining flexible enough to respond to and utilize group processes.

The composition of each training group will be influenced by a number of factors, including the marketing and recruitment strategy, the size of the host organization, and whether the training is being provided to intact work teams or open to volunteers from different parts of an organization. Much of our own ACT training has been implemented in large public-sector institutions (such as health care organizations). As a result, we most often find ourselves delivering this training to heterogenous groups of employees (who may not all know one another). In any one group, we might have very senior people in the organization completing the training alongside much more junior members of staff. There are both advantages and disadvantages to this approach. One key advantage is the process of *normalization*—participants learn that regardless of age or level of organizational seniority, humans are still prone to experience a range of thoughts and feelings that can have an unhelpful influence over behavior.

One potential challenge with heterogenous training groups is that some participants may feel intimidated if they attend the training alongside an immediate line manager or much more senior members of the organization. When implementing this training, we find it useful to offer a number of training sessions so that participants can choose a different group if they find themselves being trained alongside someone who inhibits their participation. However, we do not make a deliberate attempt to create homogenous groups, and we do not usually select people on the basis of seniority or current level of psychological health.

Training intact teams is also often an interesting experience. Sometimes the manager of a team will have "encouraged" the whole team to attend the training together. If there are well-established and warm relationships within the team, this can be highly beneficial. For example, when most or all members of a particular unit have attended the training, we often hear reports of ACT-consistent language being transferred back to the workplace. This supports our goal of helping people become more psychologically flexible in their work tasks and interactions, and also ensures that ACT stays on the agenda long after the training has been completed.

If relationships within a team seem more strained, some members of the group may be reluctant to share personal issues alongside their coworkers. Junior members of the team may find it difficult to speak in front of managers, and managers may not want to show any sign of "weakness" in front of the team. It is not always a bad sign if some members of a group remain quiet and subdued during the training. We have often observed individuals hardly saying a word during training sessions only to approach us at the end to thank us for an inspiring training program!

When faced with the possibility of training an existing team, we recommend having informal discussions with leaders and members of that team before the training. The trainer can convey what the training involves, learn more about what the team hopes to get out of the sessions, and gain a degree of initial insight into how willing team members might be to discuss psychological and behavioral skills with one another. This information can be used by the trainer to adapt the style of delivery to suit that particular work group.

One final issue to consider in this section is the range in psychological distress that is typically found within workplace training groups. When we employ the broad marketing and recruitment strategy described earlier, and the training is pitched as a personal resilience-enhancing program, we find that around 50 percent of the volunteers for this training would likely be diagnosed with a minor psychiatric disorder, such as anxiety and/or depression (Flaxman & Bond, 2010b). The fact that we attract a large number of these initially more distressed employees to the training is encouraging—it means we are getting ACT out to people in need of psychological intervention. Moreover, recent research indicates that many of these more distressed workers will experience clinically meaningful improvements in mental health as a direct result of their participation in this type of workplace training (Brinkborg et al., 2011; Flaxman & Bond, 2010b).

Thus, employees who may have moderate to high levels of distress or life dysfunction are being trained alongside coworkers with lower levels of distress and dysfunction. In our experience, this does not pose a significant problem, as the ACT model of human functioning is ideally suited to training such heterogenous groups. As we noted in chapter 3, a great advantage of the ACT approach is that people do not currently have to be experiencing a high frequency of negative psychological content to develop ACT-congruent psychological and behavioral skills. Indeed, we have designed the training protocol so that it has the potential to offer something to everyone in the room. Occasionally, participants will share their experiences of mental health difficulties in the group, and it can be unusual for people to hear such reports from coworkers. The skilled trainer can harness such contributions in the service of promoting psychological flexibility, perhaps by reflecting on how common such experiences are even though they are rarely revealed or discussed.

Trainer Background and Experience

To deliver this program we would suggest trainers have some educational background and experience in psychology or a related behavioral science profession, such as mental health promotion, psychiatric nursing, social work, vocational rehabilitation, counseling, or psychotherapy. Learning to deliver ACT in a manner consistent with its underlying principles requires both a conceptual and experiential understanding of the processes that combine to produce psychological flexibility (Luoma, Hayes, & Walser, 2007). Perhaps the most important qualification is that trainers have spent a sufficient amount of time applying ACT principles and practices in their own personal and professional lives before seeking to train others in this approach. It is only through a personal exposure to ACT's core processes that trainers develop an appropriate ACT facilitation stance, which is described in more detail in chapter 8.

For those completely new to ACT, there are now a number of very accessible books that provide knowledge of ACT's core processes and its model of psychological flexibility. The original ACT book, first published in 1999, is now in its second edition (Hayes, Strosahl, & Wilson, 2012); there are also more condensed books that provide concise overviews of ACT's theory and examples of its intervention technology (Batten, 2011; Flaxman, Blackledge, & Bond, 2011); finally, less technical accounts of the ACT approach can be found in the excellent writings of Russ Harris and in ACT-based self-help texts (Forsyth & Eifert, 2008; Harris, 2007, 2009; Hayes & Smith, 2005; Strosahl & Robinson, 2008; Lejeune, 2007). We recommend reading as many different ACT protocols as possible to get a sense of the different ways ACT processes can be cultivated.

Just reading about ACT will, however, not turn you into an effective ACT practitioner! To develop some expertise with this approach it is essential to attend a number of more experiential ACT workshops, which allow for the behavioral rehearsal of ACT strategies and help trainers recognize and respond to signs of psychological flexibility and inflexibility as they unfold during human interactions. Finally, if using this workplace protocol for the first time, we would suggest it is important to access supervision from relevant peers and from more experienced ACT practitioners so that you can discuss the challenges that arise during the intervention. The Association for Contextual Behavioral Science (ACBS) website (http://contextualpsychology.org/) is the central hub for ACT workshops, conferences, and contacts and offers a wealth of other useful training resources.

The encouraging news is that it does not necessarily take years to learn how to deliver this approach in a way that is ACT-consistent and that increases psychological flexibility and improves people's mental health. For instance, in chapter 8 we describe a focused ACT train-the-trainer initiative developed in Sweden that offers mental health professionals four days of training, along with supervisory support, as new trainers facilitate their own ACT workshops. A number of studies have demonstrated that even relatively novice ACT practitioners are able to elicit significant and meaningful outcomes with this approach (e.g., Brinkborg et al., 2011).

As we describe in the program overview below, our training includes some mainstream mindfulness practices that are designed to help participants strengthen present-moment awareness and that lay the experiential foundations for the defusion and acceptance exercises found in sessions 2 and 3. It is therefore important that trainers have sufficient personal experience with these practices. The mindfulness training in ACT is much less extensive than that found in other mindfulness-based programs (such as MBSR), but as *a minimum* we would suggest that trainers delivering this approach attend a full eight-week mindfulness program to strengthen their own practice, learn how challenging it is to maintain a daily practice, and observe the stance adopted by mindfulness trainers when responding to people's experiences of mindfulness skills training. In addition, attending mindfulness retreats is a highly recommended way to develop the required personal experience with mindfulness practices. For those readers interested in strengthening mindfulness training skills we recommend perusing the recommended training standards and other resources provided by the United Kingdom network for mindfulness-based teacher trainers (http://mindfulnessteachersuk.org.uk/).

Perhaps the most useful way of learning how to deliver ACT in groups is to seek out opportunities to be a co-trainer with a more experienced ACT practitioner working with groups in clinical or nonclinical settings. One of the richest learning experiences is personally to observe ACT training in action, facilitate some sections of a group program yourself, and discuss key moments with a fellow trainer immediately afterward.

For those readers who have been trained to deliver ACT in individualized clinical settings, it is not (in our opinion) much of a leap to begin delivering ACT-based training to groups. The key difference is the need to develop greater awareness and understanding of group processes—particularly the way that group members will quickly become disengaged if the trainer focuses too much on any one individual and forgets to include the rest of the group. We have improved our own training expertise by adopting strategies for utilizing group processes developed for CBT groups (we highly recommend a book on conducting CBT in groups by Bieling, McCabe, & Antony, 2006). We provide a few simple examples of how the trainer can utilize group processes in the training protocol described in chapters 5–7.

PROGRAM OVERVIEW

Having covered some of the practical and implementation considerations, we can now turn our attention to the technical content of the training protocol itself. In this section, we provide an overview of the intervention strategies we tend to employ in the program to cultivate a combination of two core skills: mindfulness and values-based action.

As we turn to the content of the training, it is important to be aware that our primary focus over the years has been on empirically evaluating the ACT approach when it is delivered to groups in the workplace. Thus, we have tried not to veer away too much from the most widely recognized exercises, client handouts, and metaphors that can be found throughout the ACT literature. The program therefore incorporates some instantly recognizable ACT strategies (such as the "passengers on the bus" metaphor), versions of which can be found in most ACT texts. As discussed below, we also find it useful to incorporate some basic mindfulness skills training and some other techniques we have borrowed from behavioral activation approaches.

The Two-Skills Framework: Mindfulness and Values-Based Action

As noted toward the end of the previous chapter, the two related skills that lie at the heart of this program are designed to mirror the mindfulness and acceptance processes and values-based commitment and behavioral activation processes that combine to form ACT's hexagonal model of psychological flexibility (Hayes et al., 2012; Hayes, Strosahl, Bunting, et al., 2004; and see figures 2.1 and 2.2). From an ACT perspective it is how these two core skills are related and combined that is important. Thus, the large arrows linking the two skills are a critical feature of figure 2.2. As will hopefully become evident over the next three chapters, we target mindfulness and acceptance skills to help our participants reduce excessive entanglements with thoughts and feelings that have the potential to function as internal barriers to the increased pursuit of personally valued actions and goals. We also promote participants' willingness to experience difficult or undesirable internal states in the service of actively pursuing values. In the following sections, we outline the main technical components of the two skill sets and then consider some of the strategies we use throughout the training to illustrate to participants how the skills are functionally related.

Mindfulness Techniques

As ACT practitioners, we tend to use the term "mindfulness" broadly to refer to all four of ACT's mindfulness and acceptance processes (namely contact with the present moment, acceptance, defusion, and self-as-context; Fletcher & Hayes, 2005). The techniques used in the program to cultivate these processes range from classic mindfulness practices (such as the raisin exercise and mindfulness of breath and body) to experiential exercises that are more specifically designed to cultivate acceptance (e.g., the physicalizing exercise) and defusion (e.g., thoughts on a blank screen exercise).

We have deliberately incorporated a gradual progression of mindfulness-oriented practices into the program. The primary purpose of the mindfulness work in session 1 is to help participants strengthen present-moment awareness and to lay the foundations for the subsequent experiential exercises. We also practice a mindfulness exercise at the beginning of both sessions 2 and 3 to help center participants and trainer in preparation for the session. The other mindfulness practices we conduct in sessions 2 and 3 are more explicitly linked to the values work. Most notably, the defusion- and acceptance-oriented meditative exercises are offered as strategies designed to help participants notice and untangle from internal barriers to the effective pursuit of valued behavior. As is common in other mindfulness-based programs, we encourage our participants to engage in both formal and informal mindful practices between the training sessions. To facilitate this home practice, we provide participants with audio recordings of the all the key exercises on CDs and as MP3 files. Examples of these techniques and other resources are available from the authors' website www.mindfulemployee.com.

It is worth reiterating that mindfulness is employed in our ACT program as a means to an end rather than an end in itself (Dimidjian & Linehan, 2008). In other words, the various mindfulness strategies are ultimately used to increase value-guided behavioral activation and to increase the likelihood of participants coming into contact with values-based behavioral reinforcement. Thus, the mindfulness training component is much briefer than those found in "pure" mindfulness-based programs. Despite this, one of our recent research studies indicates that this program leads to significant increases in established self-report measures of mindfulness, and our data suggest that an improvement in mindfulness skills operates as one of the mechanisms through which this training improves people's psychological health.

Values-Based Action Techniques

The design of the values-oriented components in this program has been informed by some of the basic behavioral principles that underpin the ACT approach (see, for example, Dahl et al., 2009; Törneke, 2010). In particular, we invite participants to engage in some self-reflection on values for different areas of their lives and then to engage in value-guided actions outside of the sessions. The underlying purpose of these exercises is to create repeated opportunities for participants to contact values-based behavioral reinforcement (that is, the reinforcement that derives from deliberately and actively pursuing a personally chosen value). In this regard, we subscribe to the importance of behavioral rehearsal. It is tempting to provide participants with new exercises in each session, but it can also pay to encourage participants to practice the same key values steps as many times as possible over the course of the training. This strategy tends to ensure that all participants will engage in this behavioral process at least once and helps participants "get the gist" of using values as a more prominent guide to daily behavior.

The values work found across all three sessions is primarily supported by two basic handouts: Handout 1, "Define Your Values," and Handout 2, "Values, Goals, and Actions Worksheet." Handout 1 has been designed to help participants define personal values in five life areas: health; relationship; work and career; leisure time; and personal growth. Handout 2 enables participants to chart specific values across the values—goals—actions progression. We include two completed samples of Handout 2, one for the life area of work/career (Handout 2a), and one for the area of relationships (Handout 2b). We have adopted this approach to keep the values work similar to the values-based exercises participants will find if they pick up one of the ACT-based self-help books we recommend during or after the training (e.g., Harris, 2007; Hayes & Smith, 2005).

The key steps in the values exercises are as follows: defining values; summarizing values in a few key reminder words; translating values into more specific goals; identifying values-based actions for the next week; performing those valued actions mindfully and noticing what happens; and noticing any thoughts or feelings that show up and threaten to "hijack" behavior.

From the first session, we support participants in translating a value into three actions for the next week. This forms the basis of the first home practice assignment participants are invited to complete between the first two sessions. Although our instructions and handouts focus on identifying valued actions for the next week, this period can be extended if the training is designed with a longer gap between training sessions. When preparing participants for valued action assignments, we encourage them to set up "cues" on their person or in their daily environment to help elicit the chosen actions. We provide participants with a range of resources for this, including small colored stickers that can be strategically placed on mobile phones, kettles, or mirrors; silicone wristbands for participants to wear during the week as a reminder to engage in valued actions and mindfulness practice; and small colored key fobs that have space to record value reminder words or actions. We adopted this strategy from behavioral activation (see, for example, Kanter, Busch, & Rusch, 2009) and have found it to be surprisingly effective in workplace interventions. When sufficient time is left to discuss the benefits of using visual and auditory cues to develop new behavioral skills, it is not unusual for most members of a group to engage in some valued action outside of the sessions and notice the consequences of doing so. To date, behavioral activation programs have mostly been used in the treatment of depression. Nonetheless, we have been struck by how effective and appreciated some of the simplest behavioral activation techniques have been when we introduce them to employees in the workplace and find they enhance the values-oriented elements of our ACT training.

Techniques for Demonstrating the Link between Mindfulness and Values-Based Action

As noted earlier, psychological flexibility results from the combination of mindfulness and values-based behavioral activation processes. Hence, in each session, we seek to provide participants with a straightforward rationale for how and why the two core skills are related. We use three main strategies to demonstrate the link. First, we refer to the arrows in our two skills framework to communicate that an important part of the trainer's role is to show how the two skills are mutually related. Also, in each session, we adopt what we refer to as the "two sheets of paper technique," which conveys the message that the training is ultimately designed to increase the prominence of personally chosen values as a meaningful, effective, and motivating guide to goals and daily actions. We use this particular technique not only to show the link between mindfulness and values-based action skills but also to deliver progressive ACT-consistent messages across the three sessions. For example, in session 1, we tend to use the two sheets technique simply to suggest that a main aim of the training is to increase the prominence of personally chosen values as a behavioral guide. In session 2, we might place more emphasis on developing the ability to pursue personally valued action in the presence of unhelpful thoughts, moods, emotions, and sensations. Finally, in the third session we use the same technique to communicate that becoming more effective at pursuing values requires a willingness to experience the whole range of internal experiences that may arise as part of that process.

Finally, we make use of ACT's highly versatile "passengers on the bus" metaphor when communicating the program rationale (Hayes et al., 1999). This metaphor portrays thoughts, feelings, moods, and other internal states as passengers, some of whom may be exerting an unhelpful influence over the pursuit of valued life directions.

The following four points summarize the basic messages we seek to convey to participants during this work:

- Our most effective and meaningful behavior is guided by and consistent with our personal values.

- Our own thoughts and feelings can sometimes operate as subtle yet powerful internal barriers to effective value-guided action.
- Mindfulness training helps us become much more aware of this process.
- Some mindfulness strategies are particularly useful for helping us untangle from internal barriers, thereby reducing the extent to which even our most unhelpful thoughts and feelings will interfere with effective, values-based behavior.

Alternative Summarizing Frameworks

As noted above, we organize our training around two core skills—mindfulness and values-based action—to reflect the higher-order cluster of processes that combine to produce psychological flexibility. There are also various other useful frameworks or tools that can be used in the workplace and these deserve mention. One tool that is now widely recognized within the ACT community is "The Matrix" developed by Kevin Polk, Jerold Hambright, and Mark Webster. This is a neat ACT-based learning tool that encourages participants to notice the distinction between different types of experiencing (five senses experiencing versus mental experiencing; moving toward values and goals versus moving away from undesirable internal states). Moreover, the matrix cultivates the self-as-context by encouraging participants to recognize who is noticing these different ways of experiencing. There are numerous YouTube clips demonstrating the use of the matrix to deliver ACT training.

Another simple framework is the "ACT triflex" presented by Harris (2009). This model organizes ACT's processes into a triangle, with "be present," "open up," and "do what matters" at its corners (see Harris, 2009, p. 13). More recently, Hayes et al. (2011) have set out a convincing argument that ACT and other contextual CBTs essentially encourage people to become more "open, aware, and active," and these three interrelated processes offer a useful way of organizing and conveying ACT's principles.

In sum, we have been organizing our training around mindfulness and values-based action skills for the past few years, and our research indicates that this is one way to increase psychological flexibility and mental health in workplace settings. However, we stake no claim that ours is the best or only way to deliver ACT in nonclinical settings, and we encourage readers to peruse the full range of other learning tools that are now available.

Undermining Experiential Avoidance

When ACT is delivered in therapeutic settings, the therapist often begins by building up a picture of the client's repertoire of avoidance coping strategies (for example, Hayes et al., 2012; Luoma, Hayes, & Walser, 2007; Zettle, 2007). The therapist then works with the client to explore the apparent effectiveness and life costs of seeking to avoid or change unwanted inner experiences. When ACT is delivered to groups in a workplace training context, this process is more difficult to implement. In the past, we have implemented a group version of this process by inviting participants to discuss their coping strategies and consider how useful they are for removing difficult thoughts and feelings, such as worry (see Bond & Hayes, 2002; Flaxman & Bond, 2006). In our more recent workshops we have taken a more gradual and progressive approach to undermining experiential avoidance and find that this also has the desired effect.

Specifically, as a natural part of the various exercises and metaphors we introduce, we make a point of communicating that struggling with undesirable thoughts and feelings is often not the most effective approach for enhancing well-being and behavioral effectiveness. For example, in presenting the two sheets of paper technique, we clearly convey the message that we are not looking to remove, change, or replace the unhelpful internal states that function as barriers to valued action but will instead be cultivating a more mindful perspective on them. Similarly, our mindfulness-oriented exercises (such as the physicalizing exercise practiced in sessions 2 and 3) offer an experiential demonstration that we are looking to promote acceptance rather than avoidance of even our more difficult thoughts and emotions.

Session Structure and Style of Delivery

When delivering this training, we tend to follow a basic structure not dissimilar to the sequencing of activities found in CBT groups and other psychological skills training programs (see, for example, Drossel, 2008; Meichenbaum, 1985; White, 2000). Specifically, apart from session 1 (where we open with a general introduction to the training), we begin the sessions with a brief mindfulness practice and then conduct a review of participants' experiences with the recommended home practice assignments. We then introduce a couple of skill development practices, provide a simple and accessible rationale for the program (for example, by using our two sheets of paper technique), and spend some time preparing participants for the next home practice assignment. Throughout the sessions participants are given the opportunity to discuss the training material and exercises in pairs and as a group.

Over the years, we have developed a rather flexible approach to delivering this training that would best be described as process-driven. Using this approach, we are primarily guided by the degree to which we have touched upon ACT's core processes during a session, rather than by whether we have introduced specific techniques. This process-oriented approach allows for both the manualization of the program (for research purposes) and for flexibility as to which specific exercises to introduce (according to how the group is responding).

There is a particular style we have found effective when delivering our ACT-based program, which we sense has evolved in part from the types of organizations we have worked with over the years. We have often worked in organizations that do not have a lot of internal resources or equipment at their disposal, and this has encouraged us to become "low tech" in our approach. Ideally, we have a flip chart or whiteboard in the room (although even these are not essential). We come simply prepared with packs of handouts and with a poster-sized print of our two-skills diagram (to be attached to the wall of the training room). In most of our workshops, we do not use PowerPoint slides, and this makes things considerably easier from a practical point of view. We like the idea of being able to deliver our training "anytime, anywhere." We have delivered this training in tiny rooms barely large enough to hold the group; in large conference suites; on the top floor of high-rise offices with spectacular views of the surrounding area; in hospitality rooms of a sports arena; and in dilapidated prefabricated offices that have water pouring through the ceiling and an unusual aroma seeping through the walls!

One thing we have observed is that this low-tech style of delivery is well suited to ACT's philosophy. When training smaller groups, we tend to sit among our participants rather than assuming the more traditional trainer's position of standing at one end of the room. This supports the ACT stance of the trainer being "in the same boat" as his or her clients or participants and naturally allows the trainer to reveal his or her own experiences with the human condition, rather than hiding behind the role of the "all-knowing" trainer. Regardless of the context, we find it is a style that supports the development of a strong and equalizing alliance with the other people in the room.

Summary

As we have discussed in this chapter there are many different ways of delivering ACT to working populations, and the ACT model and technology may be used to achieve various training objectives. Our most common approach has been to deliver ACT as a generalized skills training program, designed to enhance employees' psychological health, flexibility, and behavioral effectiveness. The three-session training protocol described over the next three chapters is presented in this format. However, we encourage readers to look for the flexibility in this approach and find ways to adapt it to suit their own style of delivery and the particular context in which the program is being delivered.

CHAPTER 5

Training Session 1: Opening Presentation and Introduction to Mindfulness and Values-Based Action Skills

The opening training session is particularly important, as it sets the stage for the entire program and begins socializing participants into the ACT stance on well-being and behavioral effectiveness. The main aims of session 1 are to offer participants an initial overview of the training and to provide a conceptual and experiential introduction to mindfulness and values-based action skills. Session 1 also serves a number of other important functions, including establishing rapport with the group, cultivating a group climate of warmth and safety, and presenting of the summarizing tools (such as the two-skills diagram) that will be used throughout the program to help organize the training material.

Our description of this first session is divided into three parts to represent key training phases. The first part of this chapter illustrates the opening presentation and shows how the trainer describes the basic nature and aims of the training. Part II covers the introduction of the first mindfulness and values-based action interventions. Part III shows how the trainer communicates the rationale for the program and describes the home practice assignments participants are invited to complete during the week between the first two sessions. The table below offers an overview of this first session.

Training Phase	Key Interventions
PART I	
Welcome and introductions	Mindfulness or values warm-up exercise
Overview of the training	Presentation of two-skills organizing diagram
PART II	
Introduction to mindfulness	Raisin exercise; brief mindfulness of body and breath
Introduction to values-based action	Values card sort; Compass metaphor; define one value and translate into specific actions for the next week
PART III	
Presentation of rationale for the program	Two sheets of paper technique
Discussion of home practice assignments	Home practice handout; environmental reminders

Part I: Welcome and Introduction to the Training

Session 1 commences with the trainer and participants introducing themselves, and with the provision of some basic information about what the training involves. The more specific aims of this opening segment are as follows:

- Develop rapport with (and between) group members and create a climate of safety and warmth.
- Describe the basic format, content, and aim of the training.
- Instill hope that the training has the potential to be unusual, interesting, and effective.

Welcome and Introductions

The trainer begins by warmly welcoming participants to the training and by introducing himself or herself to the group. As part of this introduction, trainers might also want to provide some brief information on their area of expertise, professional background, and previous experience.

The trainer can then invite participants to introduce themselves to other members of the group (we still conduct these introductions even if participants know one another). It is worth designing the participant introductions in a way that is rapport building, engaging, and "ACT-consistent." A tried and trusted method is to invite participants to get into pairs, with each participant asked to introduce his or her partner to the group. The pairs of participants can then be asked to reflect on a particular question or topic that is directly related to the content of the training.

We show an example of this in the extract below, in which the trainer invites participants to share some mindfulness-oriented personal information that is relevant to one of the main themes of the first session (increasing present-moment awareness):

Trainer: To make your own introductions to the group more interesting, I'd like you to get into pairs so that you can introduce each other. Your partner will introduce you to the group, and you will introduce your partner. So, in your pairs, I'd first like you to share your first name, what job you do, and which department you currently work in.

I'd then like you to share the following information [the following points are summarized on a slide, flip chart, or handout]:

- <u>Two activities</u> that you personally perform while on "automatic pilot"—without being very aware of what you are doing as you are doing it
- <u>Two activities</u> you personally perform with more psychological awareness—activities that give you a sense of being more "in the moment"

As well as encouraging participants to begin reflecting on a process that is targeted during the training, this type of warm-up exercise usually helps to cultivate a sense of group cohesion, warmth, and safety. A few participants will inevitably share a couple of humorous or unusual examples that elicit some laughter and camaraderie within the group.

The above warm-up exercise is related to the mindfulness skills that will be cultivated during every session. An alternative option is to design a similar exercise that is oriented toward the values components of the program. In the following extract, the trainer is using an abbreviated version of a more elaborate values clarification exercise (the eightieth-birthday exercise) that is often used in ACT interventions:

Trainer: To make your own introductions to the group more interesting, I'd like you to get into pairs so that you can introduce each other. Your partner will introduce you to the group, and you will introduce your partner. So, in your pairs, I'd first like you to share your first name, what job you do, and which department you work in.

The other thing I'd like you to do is to share with your partner your initial response to the following scenario [this scenario can be summarized on a slide, flip chart, or handout]: Jump ahead and imagine that it is now your eightieth birthday party! All your friends, family, colleagues, and loved ones are there. It's a good turnout—imagine that all the people you've ever cared about in your life are able to attend. The cake has arrived. After you blow out the eighty candles, your loved ones, friends, family members, and coworkers take turns talking about your key strengths and personal qualities.

Your task is this: Share with your partner three things you would most want these people to say about the kind of person you have been in your life—whatever you would most want them to say about your key strengths and personal qualities. And remember: it's your imaginary party, so please feel free to share what you would really want to hear people say about you on your big day.

Gathering Hopes and Expectations

It can also be informative during this opening phase for the trainer to gain some insight into participants' initial hopes and expectations about what the training might offer. If the group is quite large (ten or more participants), the trainer might ask generally if anyone would like to share hopes and expectations or invite participants to discuss their hopes and expectations in pairs before feeding back to the group.

From the outset, the trainer should be seeking to utilize people's contributions to promote psychological flexibility. Here's an example of how such dialogue might unfold.

Trainer: Given the information you've seen so far, would anyone else like to share any hopes or expectations about what you might gain from this type of training?

Participant: I guess I'm here looking for the best way to handle stress. I stepped into a new job at the start of this year, and I also have a toddler at home, so life is suddenly pretty hectic!

Trainer: Wow, it does sound like a very exciting time of your life, Alex. Just out of curiosity, how does stress manifest itself in your life? I mean, what sort of impact does it have on you?

Participant: Usually it's difficulty sleeping, and then feeling tired the next day. As soon as my head hits the pillow you can bet I'll start going over all the things I haven't done or need to do.

Trainer: Thanks, Alex—a very useful example. And you know what? My mind likes to do that to me as well. [Trainer now expands his glance to the whole group.] Can anyone else relate to Alex's experience? [After eliciting a similar example from another member of the group, the trainer sums up as follows.]

Trainer: Great stuff. Noticing some of these shared experiences will be useful for what we'll be doing in these sessions. The human mind does tend to give us an almost constant stream of chatter, whether we like it or not! One important part of this training is to develop the skill of untangling ourselves a bit from our mind's output when it helps us to do so.

In this extract, it is worth noting how the trainer's language is already deliberately oriented toward one or more of the processes that combine to produce psychological flexibility. For example, the trainer's response to Alex's example includes an element of self-disclosure and the elicitation of similar experiences from other members of the group. The trainer uses similar strategies throughout the program, with the aim of normalizing participants' experiences, and gradually modeling and cultivating a more nonjudgmental or accepting stance toward internal events. The trainer also seizes an early opportunity to begin undermining experiential avoidance, simply by throwing open the possibility that we do not have much control over the mind's "chatter." Finally, notice how the trainer refers to the mind as though it is a somewhat separate entity. This way of speaking is deliberately designed to promote cognitive defusion by highlighting the healthy "psychological distance" that exists between the person *having* thoughts and the thoughts themselves (we will show further examples of this type of defused language in due course).

In sum, even during these opening introductions and exchanges, the trainer is looking to model, cultivate, and reinforce ACT's core processes. The training has begun.

Describing the Basic Format and Content of the Training

Once the introductions have been conducted, the trainer can describe the basic nature and format of the training. The bullet points below indicate the sort of information the trainer might convey:

- It is important to attend every session.
- Each session will include a mixture of presentation from the trainer, group and pair discussions, and skill practice.
- This is a psychological and behavioral skills training program—it is training, not therapy!
- Research evidence [which the trainer can mention briefly] demonstrates the impact of this type of training on people's psychological well-being and behavioral effectiveness.
- The training is not limited to work-related well-being and effectiveness, but instead offers general psychological and behavioral skills that can be applied in all areas of life
- Group and pair discussions will focus on people's experiences developing and using two key skills (mindfulness and values-based action).
- Practicing skills between the sessions is an essential part of the training and is supported by a series of exercise handouts.

Providing this sort of information serves a number of purposes. It highlights the skills-based nature of the program and emphasizes the importance of practice and between-session assignments. In addition, providing such information often helps to address some of the concerns employees might have about engaging in a psychological intervention alongside others working in the same organization.

As indicated in the bullet points above, we also typically use this overview to begin "selling" the training to participants; this can be done by briefly mentioning the evidence base underpinning the program and by emphasizing that participants will be learning generalizable skills that have the potential to improve psychological health and behavioral effectiveness across various life domains. The intention is to capture participants' interest as soon as possible and leave an early impression that the training has something valuable and interesting to offer.

Presentation of the Two-Skills Organizing Diagram

The final phase of this introduction offers participants an overview of the program's skill components and summarizes the central aim. To facilitate this presentation, the trainer can utilize whichever organizing framework is being used to summarize the interrelated training components. In the present protocol, we describe the framework that we have used to good effect over the past few years, which focuses on the development of two broad (and intimately related) skills, mindfulness and values-based action, and present the two-skills diagram we discussed earlier (figure 5.1).

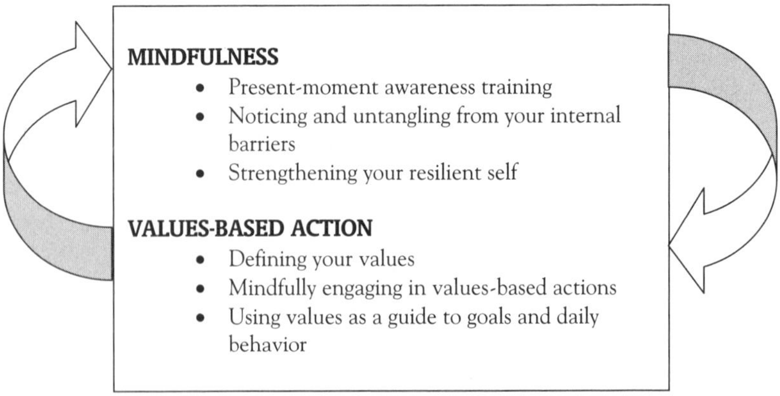

Figure 5.1. The Two-Skills Diagram

In relation to our two-skills diagram, the trainer might say something like this:

Trainer: This diagram offers us an overview of the entire training. The training has been specifically designed to help you develop these two related skills: mindfulness and values-based action. We focus particularly on combining these two skills because they have consistently been found to improve people's well-being and behavioral effectiveness. You'll see that I've included some more specific things underneath the two skills. So, under mindfulness, we have present-moment awareness training, noticing and untangling from internal barriers, and strengthening the resilient part of yourself. This might all sound like some strange psychobabble at the moment, but you'll find that these things will make much more sense as we progress through the training. I'm going to come back to this two-skills diagram regularly throughout the three sessions, just to remind you what we are doing and to help you organize the different exercises we'll be using.

Just out of curiosity, has anyone heard of mindfulness before? [Any experiences are briefly explored and acknowledged.]

Even on its own, mindfulness is one of the most useful skills we know of for improving self-awareness and psychological health. There are various ways of developing basic mindfulness skills, which we'll cover in these sessions. The most powerful techniques are kind of like mini-meditations, which strengthen our ability to focus on the here and now, to be psychologically present. Another technique involves simply practicing becoming more aware of your present-moment experience at regular intervals throughout your day. Developing mindfulness does take some practice, so please forgive me if I nag you a bit during these sessions about the importance of practicing the exercises at home!

The second skill, values-based action, may have some elements you are already familiar with. I often refer to this skill as "goal setting with a difference." The difference is that I'll be encouraging you to define your more general purpose in different areas of your lives—or what we call "values" in my area of psychology. I hope to show you how making our personal values a more prominent guide to daily action is a powerful way to reignite our sense of purpose and improve effectiveness.

You can see I have these large arrows linking the mindfulness and values-based action skills. An important part of my role is to show you how these two skills are closely related to each other. I plan to show you how developing greater mindfulness can in turn help us become more effective at pursuing our most important values and goals.

It's not necessary to be experiencing high levels of stress to benefit from this training. We know from the research that these two skills are among the most useful when we're experiencing things like stress, worry, anxiety, low mood, self-doubt, and loss of life purpose and direction. However, these skills are also designed to help you improve effectiveness and performance in many different areas of life—at work, in your personal and family relationships, in relation to your health and well-being, and in your leisure time. That's why we offer these skills in the workplace—there will hopefully be something for everyone here. My job is to help you develop the skills; it's then up to you where and how you apply them.

I've tried to capture the whole purpose of this training in a nutshell, and this is what I've come up with …

Mindful and values-based living.

[This statement is written in a large font on a board or flip chart and handout.]

As indicated in the dialogue above, the trainer is using the two-skills organizing framework to offer a simple overview of the skills that will be cultivated during the sessions and give an initial indication of the types of exercises that will be employed. The trainer might conclude this introductory presentation with a simple check-in question such as "How does all that sound?"

In our experience, employees will generally respond to this type of overview with an encouraging degree of interest, intrigue, and even some excitement about what is to follow. However, please don't be fooled into thinking this must be due to our expert presentation skills! The simple truth is that ACT-based training tends to "sell itself" to most of our workplace participants. We suspect this is because the skill components and overarching aim being presented reflect some fundamental aspects of the human experience.

Establishing Ground Rules for the Group

At some point during the opening presentation it is important to establish any ground rules for the group—particularly regarding the confidentiality of any personal information that might be shared during the sessions. This is part of creating a safe group context for cultivating and discussing ACT-based psychological and behavioral skills. We have found it most useful to discuss such issues after providing the group with some initial information about what the training will involve. Regardless of the level of familiarity between group members, we tend to set out the same expectations:

Trainer: During these sessions, I'll be inviting you to discuss the training material and exercises in pairs and as a group, as it's important for you to reflect on how you might use these skills in your own lives. Let me say from the outset that you are under no obligation to share any personal information in these sessions that you would rather keep private. Given that the training focuses on things like our personal goals in life and the thoughts and feelings that can impact our well-being and effectiveness, it is important that we agree as a group that any information we discuss in here remains confidential. I would request before we continue that you do not discuss any personal information that others have shared outside of this room—what we discuss in this room stays in this room. Of course, it is absolutely fine for you to discuss the training in general, and anything that you personally have shared, but other people's information should remain private and confidential. Is everyone happy to abide by this rule?

> [The trainer now adopts a more lighthearted tone]. Now, I don't mean to freak you out by saying this! I'm hopeful that you're going to find the exercises interesting and personally valuable, and I'm also hopeful that we'll have some useful group discussions about the human experience. I just want us to create a safe and confidential environment for developing what I think you will find some useful skills. Before we go on, does anyone have any immediate questions or concerns about confidentiality or that sort of thing? . . . Okay. Please feel free to grab me at the break or at the end, or send me an e-mail after today's session, if you would like to discuss any concerns.

Despite delivering ACT training within a wide range of organizations over the years, we can recall no significant problems associated with breaches of confidentiality. Occasionally, a participant has discussed difficulties with a coworker or manager who is not in the training but whom another member of the group recognizes from the participant's description. In such cases, we would reiterate the importance of confidentiality to ensure that information about the discussion is not communicated to the person in question, or indeed to anyone outside the room.

Expectations regarding the sharing of personal examples in the sessions may also need to be tailored to the particular organizational context and target population. Our default approach, indicated above, is to communicate that sharing personal experiences is welcome and useful, while at the same time ensuring that participants do not feel pressured into discussing issues they would prefer to keep private. The message to convey is that any group discussions can focus on issues related to the development of the two core skills.

The nature of this training certainly seems to encourage people to share examples from their own lives, which the trainer can use to help normalize the human experience and illustrate the nature of psychological flexibility. We generally find that workplace participants choose for themselves what to (and what not to) disclose. For example, when discussing personal values, a participant might be willing to share a value in relation to health and exercise while choosing not to share his or her values and desired actions around parenthood. We recommend that trainers have a good stock of hypothetical examples just in case (for whatever reason) most members of a particular group seem reluctant to share examples from their own lives.

The stance being modeled by the trainer inevitably has an influence on this group process. By exhibiting a warm, open, and nonjudgmental posture, the trainer can help to create a space for reflecting on (and indeed discussing) experiences with thoughts, feelings, behaviors, goals, and values (see chapter 8 for a more detailed discussion of ACT trainer skills).

Provision of Information on Other Sources of Support

Even when it has been translated into a workplace skills training program, it is important to be aware that ACT is a potentially powerful psychological intervention that invites people to make room for what might be difficult cognitive and emotional material in the service of building a value-guided life. As a result, it is critical that trainers delivering this type of intervention are able to provide details about additional sources of psychological support, should it be required. For example, when working in large organizations, we seek out details of any in-house occupational health services and employee assistance programs. We leave any leaflets or contact information in the training room and communicate to participants that we have done so (we also invite participants to approach us after the training if they would like to discuss additional sources of support). If the host organization does not offer such services, we ensure we also have information on local mental health services and details on how to access support through one's primary health care provider.

Over many years of delivering this type of training, we can recall only one or two occasions where we sensed the need to take a participant to one side to discuss accessing such services. Nonetheless, the provision of such information is an important safety mechanism, both for the trainer and participants, and should be viewed as a routine ethical requirement when delivering psychological interventions in nonclinical settings.

Troubleshooting

During the early interactions, it is not unusual for participants to begin discussing ongoing organizational issues or dissatisfactions—perhaps related to unpopular changes to working conditions, reductions to staffing or budgets, and so on. We often take it as a compliment on our ability to create a safe context that employees use the sessions to air such grievances! However, these discussions can sometimes take on a life of their own (particularly when they impact most members of the group), and the trainer needs to bring the focus back to the training in a skillful and respectful way. Our usual approach is to step in at an opportune moment to acknowledge the difficulties being faced and remark that the training is designed to develop skills to keep us psychologically healthy and functioning well even during challenging times. It can be helpful for the trainer to list the key exercises or material he or she hopes to cover in the session on a whiteboard or flip chart. Then, if the group discussions are digressing into areas that are difficult to link to the training, the trainer can politely suggest moving on to ensure there is enough time to cover the material scheduled for that session.

Part II: Introduction to Mindfulness and Values-Based Action Skills

The opening phase of the program is designed to provide participants with an early sense of the content, format, and purpose of the training. Given that some elements of the opening presentation are didactic, the most useful next step is to invite participants to engage in some introductory experiential practice. Indeed, the primary purpose of the remainder of this first session is to offer participants an experiential introduction to mindfulness and values-based action, and for the trainer to begin illustrating the functional links between these skills. The learning that takes place during the session is then designed to be transferred to participants' daily lives in the form of two home practice assignments.

The trainer begins this more experiential segment of the training with a couple of brief mindfulness practices. The main aims of this introductory mindfulness segment are twofold: to highlight the benefits of increasing present-moment awareness and to lay the basic foundations for subsequent mindfulness exercises.

Introduction to Mindfulness

It is sensible for the trainer to commence the skills practice as simply as possible by helping participants establish heightened contact with their present-moment experience (beginning with the mindful eating exercise described below). In the two-skills diagram, we refer to the opening mindfulness practices as present-moment awareness training. We explain to our participants that this is the best place to start the skills practice and describe the ability to contact one's present-moment experience as a fundamental psychological skill that is essential to the development of both mindfulness and values-based action skills. There are two experiential exercises typically introduced during this phase of the training: the raisin exercise and a brief mindfulness of body and breath exercise.

Here's an example of how the trainer might introduce this work:

Trainer: I'll provide a bit more rationale for the training as we progress today, but I figure it's about time now for us to begin some skills practice! My aim for the rest of this morning is to offer you a decent introduction to both of these two core skills: mindfulness and values-based action [the trainer is again referring to the two-skills diagram]. I'm then going to give you a couple of important exercises to practice at home before we come back together next week to work on these skills further.

We're going to begin this morning with some basic mindfulness skills. I have a couple of exercises that should give you an immediate sense of what mindfulness is, what it involves, and how it can be developed. The first thing we're going to do is present-moment awareness training. Becoming more aware of our present-moment experiences is one of the most fundamental psychological skills—a widely recognized way to begin improving well-being, self-awareness, and effectiveness.

Raisin Exercise and Discussion

Eating a raisin with heightened awareness is perhaps the most widely recognized practical introduction to mindfulness (Kabat-Zinn, 1990; Segal, Williams, & Teasdale, 2002). We have adopted this exercise from other mindfulness programs, as it helps participants discover for themselves the potential benefits (as well as the challenges) of strengthening present-moment awareness and offers a suitably gentle introduction to the experiential nature of the program. During the conversations immediately following this practice, we seek to ensure that participants have gained some of the insights usually associated with this practice, such as a realization of how much time is spent on automatic pilot. Consistent with the way this experiential work is structured in other mindfulness-based training programs, we employ a brief preamble prior to conducting the raisin exercise and then gather participants' observations and experiences afterward (Segal et al., 2002).

Trainer: Before saying any more, I'd be delighted if you would join me in a mindful eating exercise. I'll guide you through the exercise, which only takes a few minutes, and we can discuss it afterward. Please help yourself to just one of the tiny food items from the bowl, and let it sit for a moment in the palm of your hand. During this exercise, I'm simply going to ask you to use all of your senses to explore this object, first paying attention to the feel and look of this item and then being very aware of its taste and texture.

[The following instructions are adapted from Segal et al. (2002) and Stahl & Goldstein (2010); each [. . .] designates a brief pause; the instructions are delivered at a slow pace to give participants time to connect with each experience; the trainer also participates in the exercise.]

> First of all, see if you can become aware of the slight feel of this object that is sitting there in the palm of your hand [. . .]. Perhaps noticing the slight sensation of having this small object in the palm of your hand [. . .]. Now, pick up the object in the tips of your fingers and take a close look at it [. . .]. Focus on this object as if you've never seen anything like it before. Bring some curiosity and interest to the object. Explore it very closely, noticing all the tiny folds on the surface [. . .]. Noticing any dust or residue that has collected in the folds of its skin [. . .]. Turn the object slowly in your fingers, and notice any changes in color as it catches the light in the room [. . .]. Noticing the feel and texture of the object as you hold it there in the tips of your fingers [. . .]. If thoughts pop up during the exercise, just acknowledge these thoughts; let them be, and return your awareness to your object. Give your object a little squeeze to get a sense of its internal texture [. . .]. Recognize that this is a *unique* object—there is no other one exactly the same anywhere in the world, as far as we are aware. It's really rather

> precious when you think of it in this way [. . .]. Now bringing the object up to your nose and noticing whether it has any particular smell [. . .]. Hold the object close to your ear; give it a little squeeze and notice if it emits any sound. [Participants can be invited to close their eyes at this point in the exercise.] And now, placing the object in your mouth, on your tongue, but without biting into it. Simply noticing any sensation of having this small object resting there on your tongue [. . .]. Perhaps noticing whether your mouth has begun to salivate in anticipation. Your job here is simply to pay attention to the sensations you're experiencing *right now*. Now, moving the object around in your mouth and letting it settle wherever it feels most comfortable [. . .]. And now, staying fully aware of the sensations, take one slow bite into the object, becoming fully aware of any taste it releases into your mouth [. . .]. Just noticing the taste [. . .]. And take a second slow bite and notice whether the taste changes in any way [. . .]. Now go ahead and *slowly* chew your object, noticing the movement and feeling in your jaw and teeth as you chew, noticing the texture and taste as you chew [. . .]. When you are ready, feel free to swallow the small pieces of your object, all the time noticing the physical sensations you are experiencing in your mouth and throat [. . .]. Finally, just sitting here for a moment paying attention to any aftertaste this food item has left you with [. . .]. Just *being aware* of your current experience. Paying attention to what's happening for you in the here and now [. . .]. And, whenever you are ready, slowly open your eyes and come back into the room.

During the postexercise discussions, the trainer should encourage participants to share their direct sensory experiences of the exercise (Crane, 2009). We typically ask participants to discuss their experiences in pairs before feeding back to the group. As with the warm-up exercises, inviting participants to reflect on the training in pairs helps to create rapport among members of the group and is a useful way of generating a sense of shared human experience.

When feeding back experiences and observations, a few participants will usually spontaneously reflect on how this more mindful experience differs from their default way of eating without much conscious awareness. If such reflections are not forthcoming, the trainer can elicit them more directly.

As recommended by Segal et al., when gathering participants' feedback, the trainer models genuine openness, nonjudgment, and a gentle curiosity toward *all* experiences, whether those experiences happen to be pleasant or unpleasant, unusual or mundane. The following extracts illustrate some fairly typical examples of these postexercise discussions.

Trainer: Would anyone like to share with the group anything they noticed during the mindful eating exercise?

Participant 1: I was amazed at how tasty it was!

Trainer: Great. What did you notice about the taste?

Participant 1: It was when I bit into it—there was like this explosion of sweetness that I haven't noticed before. It tasted more like a piece of candy than a raisin!

Trainer: Excellent. It sounds like you were really aware of your experience in those moments. I'm interested that you say you haven't really noticed the sweetness in this way before. What was different this time?

Participant 1: Well, I eat quite a lot of raisins—I buy those little packs for my daughter and I'll often eat them myself. I just don't usually pay attention to what I'm doing, you know . . . I just scarf down handfuls of them without really thinking much about it!

Trainer: Good stuff. I'm delighted that you've been able to notice that experience. Eating is just one of the many things we humans often do on "automatic pilot"—without really being fully there. Anyone have a similar or different experience with their raisin?

In the next example, a participant reports an unpleasant experience with the raisin. This is also a valuable response, as it allows the trainer to make the important point that becoming more mindful involves being open to, and noticing, all types of experience.

Participant 2: I didn't much like the taste of it.

Trainer: So not such a positive experience for you, Colin. Could you describe what the taste was like?

Participant 2: I'd describe it as quite sour. I can still taste it in fact. To be fair, I've never been a big fan of raisins. I wasn't sure what this was. It's not even just the taste, it's the way they sort of feel in your mouth when you eat them. Euurgh!

Trainer: Right. Some really useful observations there. And how did the raisin physically feel in your mouth during the exercise?

Participant 2: It was all like . . . grainy and chewy; and all the little bits got stuck in my teeth!

Trainer: Thanks for sharing your experience. Funnily enough, it's useful for this training that you've been willing to practice *noticing* your current sensations and reactions to the raisin—even though they weren't pleasant for you. Your experience actually raises an important point about these exercises we'll be practicing. I hope to show you that mindfulness is not a skill that you only develop around pleasant experiences. The secret is practicing becoming more aware of *whatever* is here to be experienced—for example, just noticing whatever physical sensations you happen to be experiencing in *this* moment.

Once a few such examples have been shared, it is helpful for the trainer to briefly summarize the key learning points usually associated with the raisin exercise (the key points might also be listed in a flip chart or participant handout). These include some recognition of the experiential distinction between automatic pilot and present-moment awareness; a realization of the many daily activities we perform with little conscious awareness; and the notion that bringing greater present-moment awareness to an activity can sometimes transform the experienced nature of that activity (Crane, 2009). The trainer will often be able to elicit such insights from the group with a simple question such as "What do you think this type of exercise is designed to show us?"

It should be noted that other food items can be used instead of raisins. For example, two of our fellow ACT practitioners, Joe Oliver and Eric Morris, use mandarin oranges in their workshops with young adults, and we have ourselves sometimes used small sweets, such as M&Ms or jelly beans.

Discussions following this mindful eating practice do not have to be lengthy. The main aim at this stage of the training is to use people's experiences with the exercise to extrapolate some of the broader benefits of cultivating present-moment awareness. Essentially, we are hoping that participants emerge from this initial experiential work with a sense that contacting the present moment is a desirable and useful skill that can be developed and honed through the various exercises that will be introduced. Because of the brief nature of this program, the trainer is communicating this purpose of mindfulness in a fairly direct and simple fashion. Hence, the trainer may say something like this:

Trainer: [referring to the "present-moment awareness training" subheading in the two-skills diagram] So, we've already taken a first step in this training—practicing strengthening our present-moment awareness. This really is one of the most fundamental psychological skills, because we humans have this tendency to become very wrapped up in what's going on inside our heads. As a result, we can spend a pretty large chunk of the time in automatic pilot mode. As we heard during the introductions, our routine activities, like getting ready in the morning, eating, traveling to work, even driving our cars, are often performed in this mode. It's like we're not really fully "there." This ability to step out of automatic pilot and become more present in life is like a "psychological muscle"—it naturally develops with repeated practice.

One useful way of rounding off this practice is to ask participants to select one routine activity (one that they would normally perform on automatic pilot) that they would be willing to perform with greater awareness over the next week. We ask each of our participants to make a public commitment in the group to his or her chosen activity, and we distribute small colored stickers to act as an environmental cue. For example, if a participant commits to being more aware of the experience of the morning shower, the trainer might suggest placing a sticker on the bathroom mirror.

Brief Body and Breath Awareness Exercise

After the raisin exercise, the trainer carries the same theme straight into another brief mindfulness practice, which shows that present-moment awareness can also be strengthened by bringing awareness to current physical sensations in the body. To help organize participants' experience and learning, the trainer emphasizes that mindful eating and mindfulness of the body are two ways of developing the same basic mindfulness skills.

We might convey the natural link between these two practices by saying something like, "Of course, you won't always have a raisin handy to bring yourself into the present moment; but you will always have your body." In this way, we are essentially replacing the raisin with the body as the focus for fostering the same quality of mindful (that is, present-focused and nonjudgmental) awareness. Next to come is the following mindfulness of body and breath exercise.

First, we encourage participants to adopt an upright posture, with the back straight and dignified but not too rigid, and spine infused with energy. We say that by doing this we are "doing what the meditators do." We invite participants either to close their eyes or allow the gaze to become unfocused and directed downward.

We then invite participants to pay mindful attention to current sensations in their feet and toes, perhaps noticing any tingling or throbbing in feet or toes; noticing whether different parts of the feet feel warmer or colder than other parts; noticing the sensations of their feet encased within their shoes; and exploring any areas of pressure in the soles of the feet where they contact the floor. After a few moments, we invite participants to shift the "spotlight of their attention" to current sensations in the hands and fingers—just noticing, without judgment, whatever sensations are there in this moment to be noticed; exploring with gentle curiosity and interest any tingling or throbbing in the hands and fingers; noticing the position and temperature of their hands and fingers. While focusing on hands and fingers, we encourage participants to notice how easy it is to drift away into thoughts and lose awareness of current physical sensations. Each time participants notice they have drifted away into thought, they are asked to return attention once again to sensations in the body. We then invite participants to shift their attention to the abdomen for a minute or so, noticing the sensations and movement in the tummy with each breath. Finally, we end this brief exercise by inviting participants to expand their awareness from the abdomen to notice sensations throughout the entire body—to gradually develop a "strong sense of the entire body" sitting here in this chair, in the here and now. We then ask participants to open their eyes and return to the room.

Following the exercise, we again invite participants to share their experiences in pairs for a few minutes. After some pairs reflection, the trainer might briefly gather some group-level feedback by asking suitably open questions, such as "What did you notice during this brief exercise?" or "What was it like bringing your present-moment awareness to what's happening in your body?" Such questions will tend to elicit a range of responses. In any one group, it is typical for some participants to report finding it relatively easy to direct attention to different sensations or areas of the body while others will find this practice more difficult. More often than not, participants will share experiences (such as having attention captured by thoughts or sounds) that help the trainer highlight the nature and challenge of strengthening mindful awareness.

On the whole, we find that these brief introductory mindfulness practices serve a useful function in our worksite programs. They provide participants with an insight into the experiential nature of the program, generate some relevant discussions and observations, and ensure that some skills practice occurs at an early stage of the first session. Busy employees certainly seem to recognize (without much prompting) the potential benefits of spending more time in contact with their present-moment experience.

Introduction to Values-Based Action

As discussed at the end of the previous chapter, this program offers a series of values-based action exercises that span all three sessions. As discussed at the end of the previous chapter, this program offers a series of values-based action exercises that span all three sessions. We tend to kick-start this process in session 1 with a values card sort exercise (described below), and employ the same two handouts to support values-clarification and action planning in all three sessions (Handout 1, "Define Your Values," and Handout 2, "Values, Goals, and Actions

Worksheet"). The first of these handouts is designed to help participants define personal values for five life areas (health, relationships, work and career, leisure time, and personal growth). The format of this handout has been borrowed and adapted from other values clarification exercises found throughout the ACT literature (with the instructions on the first page and the guidance for each life area borrowed and adapted from a values questionnaire developed by Russ Harris, 2007, pp. 193–195). The handout encourages participants to construct an initially more detailed value statement for each area, then to capture the "essence" of that value in a handful of about three to five key value reminder words. The purpose of the reminder words is to make values more "portable" and psychologically present as an increasingly prominent guide in daily life.

The second handout, Handout 2, "Values, Goals, and Actions Worksheet," is a values-based goal and action planning summary handout with a section where participants can record their value reminder words and fill in a section for capturing a series of values-consistent goals. The time frames we have attached to each of these goal sets (e.g., next four weeks for short-term goals) are fairly arbitrary and are provided only as a rough guide. The handout includes space to record three value-based actions that could be performed over the next week. The three actions that are recorded on this handout form the basis of the home assignments that participants are invited to complete after each session. Finally, at the bottom of the handout there is a section for participants to record any potential "internal barriers" to value-based action (that is, unhelpful thoughts, feelings, moods, urges, and so forth that might interfere with participants engaging in value-guided behavior).

In this first session, our primary aim is to introduce participants to the basic nature, function, and benefits of behavioral values from an ACT perspective and invite them to translate one or maybe two values into more specific actions. This introduction to values in session 1 tends to proceed over the following four steps (each step is described in more detail in the following sections):

1. Provide participants with a practical definition of values from an ACT perspective, highlighting the distinction between behavioral values (desired life directions, personal strengths, or qualities of action) and goals (specific outcomes). We tend to initiate this first step with a values card sort exercise to help participants get a sense of some of their most important values.

2. Communicate the potential benefits of allowing personally chosen values to become a more prominent guide to daily behavior.

3. Encourage participants to translate one chosen value for one life domain and translate that value into a series of specific actions for the next week.

4. Help participants anticipate the thoughts and feelings that might function as internal barriers to valued behavioral activation.

Practical Definition of Values from an ACT Perspective

For many people, the notion of a value can at first seem rather elusive. Participants are usually much more familiar with the notion of concrete outcomes than they are with constructing and utilizing statements about a longer-term life direction or purpose. When delivering ACT in the workplace, we have found it most useful to describe values as "the personal strengths or qualities a person most wants to express in his or her goals and daily patterns of action." This definition of values seems accessible to most people and seems to cut through a lot of the initial confusion that values work can create.

It is important for the trainer to emphasize that values reflect personally desired qualities of one's *own* behavior. As Russ Harris notes, if it's not something a person can actually "do," then it's not considered a value from an ACT perspective (Harris, 2009). Hence, *feeling*-oriented desires such as wanting to be happy, feel more confident, be less anxious, or have better moods are not considered workable values because they do not reflect behavioral strengths or qualities of action. Likewise, statements about desired reactions or behaviors we want from others are not considered workable values from an ACT perspective.

Let's look at the type of terminology that helps to capture the essence of values. Being loving, generous, patient, physically affectionate, caring, enabling, nurturing, available, and attentive are just some of the qualities a person might value in the area of personal relationships. Such statements help to capture what we mean by behavioral values in this training because they point to behavioral strengths or qualities of action that have the potential to function as an intrinsically motivating and overarching guide to one's own behavior. Similarly, being hardworking, committed, productive, dedicated to continuing professional development, and an inspiring and supportive mentor are just some of the ways of capturing personal strengths or qualities of action an individual might wish to manifest on an ongoing basis in the domain of work and career. In short, values statements from an ACT perspective should reflect what an individual most wants to work toward in different areas of his or her life (Dahl et al., 2009).

The ACT literature offers various ways to kick-start values-clarification work. Such methods include imagining jumping ahead in time and being at your own 80th birthday party and writing down what you would most like to hear from your guests about how you lived your life. Another example is writing a brief epitaph that captures what you most want your life to be about (Hayes & Smith, 2005).

When first introducing values we particularly recommend the use of existing values tools—such as the Survey of Life Principles (SLP) developed by Ciarrochi and Bailey (2008)—which tend to work well in group training settings. The SLP includes over fifty value-oriented statements, such as "Being creative," "Being ambitious and hard working," printed on wallet-sized cards that participants are invited to sort into three piles: 1) Not very important to me; 2) of moderate importance to me; and 3) of the highest importance to me. When using these cards we remove a handful that we find less useful for our purposes, including some cards that might offend or embarrass some of our participants (e.g., "being sexually active." "being sexually desirable," "being wealthy") as well as those that tap into experiential control more than behavioral values (e.g., "experiencing positive moods states"). There are also some blank cards so participants can construct their own brief value statements and add them to the pile. Once our participants have sorted the cards into three piles, we ask them to identify their "top 5 values" (that is, out of those selected as the most important). Participants are invited to share their experiences of the exercise, but are not required to reveal specific values to others in the group unless they want to. Following a group discussion of the exercise, we encourage participants to brainstorm a series of small actions that could help to bring one or more of their top 5 values to life before the next session, and then to choose three of these values-based actions they would be willing to perform as part of the home practice (these actions can be recorded on the "Values, Goals, and Actions

Worksheet," Handout 2). To facilitate the values work conducted in later sessions, participants are encouraged to keep their top 5 values cards in an accessible place, such as in a wallet, purse, cell phone case, or calendar.

As part of the group discussions following the card sort, the trainer can begin to present some of the distinctive features and functions of using personally-chosen values as a more prominent guide to behavior. Here, values might be defined as: our deeply desired life directions; our chosen guide to action or guiding principles; the personal strengths or qualities we most want to exhibit in our actions and goals; what a person wants his or her life to be about. An important message to be conveyed from the outset is that values are never actually "achieved." Instead, personally-chosen values provide the guiding and motivating principles or purpose, while value-based goals provide specific and achievable outcomes as one actively pursues a valued life path. Value-based actions are the more immediate next steps that are chosen for their potential to "manifest" or "express" a value, which we often describe during the training as "bringing a value to life." We highlight these distinctions again when introducing the compass metaphor.

The Compass Metaphor

A useful way to illustrate the active nature of valuing is by using the metaphor of a compass (Hayes et al., 1999). Similar to the points on a compass, values help us to navigate in a particular life direction, providing a sense of whether our ongoing patterns of behavior are value-consistent.

It can be useful for the trainer to provide participants with a visual or physical demonstration of this useful journeying metaphor. One strategy is to provide each participant with a small pocket compass. Alternatively, each participant can be provided with a picture of a compass. In the following extract, the trainer has distributed pocket compasses to the participants. In this example, the trainer is using the metaphor to illustrate the aforementioned distinctions between values, value-based goals, and value-based actions and to make the important point that values are not off "in the future," but are instead available as a potential guide to action in each and every moment:

Trainer: A common way to illustrate the nature of behavioral values is to use the idea of a compass. I've given you all one of these little compasses just because it can really help to bring this stuff to life. Also, you get this nice little gift to take home with you!

It goes something like this. When we navigate on a journey using a compass, the first thing we need to do is choose the direction in which we want to head. Just to illustrate, imagine that for this part of my journey I'm choosing to head west. Having chosen my direction, I now just have to glance at my compass and orient myself in a westerly direction [trainer does so while standing in front of the group, orienting his or her body to face west on the basis of his or her compass reading]. Once I have a good sense of my chosen direction, I can identify some key landmarks or destinations up ahead that I can aim for to help me pursue my westerly path. These landmarks and destinations are useful because they'll help me to stay generally oriented in my westerly direction, and I can get a sense of progress and accomplishment as I reach some of the places dotted along my westerly path.

Some of the destinations I want to head for might be pretty close. So, as I'm choosing to face west from this point, I might set myself the goal of reaching [trainer names a nearby town that is west of the training location] by a certain time. I could also aim for some more major landmarks and destinations that are much farther into the distance—like aiming to reach Ireland by a certain date, and then after that New York. Now, notice that I can actually *reach* these destinations—I can cross them off my itinerary. But notice that it would make no sense for me to say that I have reached "west." West is not an end point that I'll ever get to; west is the direction I'm personally choosing to pursue.

And there's something that's more immediate than the destinations and landmarks up ahead. As long as I'm aware of my chosen westerly direction, each and every small step I deliberately take in that direction has meaning and purpose. Why? Because these small steps I'm taking from one moment to the next are all about heading west. I take *this* step [trainer takes a step with one eye on his or her compass] and I'm in this moment moving myself in a direction that I personally care about. And the same with *this* step [trainer takes another step]. There's a sense of direction and purpose even in these smallest steps, and that direction and purpose is west. Do you see what I'm getting at?

And here's the most interesting thing about all this: learning to make our *values* a more prominent guide in our lives is just like this! It's just like navigating on a journey by compass. The first and perhaps most important thing we need to do is define our personal values for different areas of our lives—that gives us the all-important purpose and direction. As we've just seen, our values are the personal qualities or strengths we most want to express in our actions in different areas of our lives. The landmarks and destinations up ahead—well, they're just like the short-term and longer-term goals we can set for ourselves to help us keep moving in a valued life direction. And value-based actions—they're the next small steps that I can take to bring my value to life right here, right now. It's like, what could I actually *do* today/tomorrow/this week that will be consistent with one or more of my values?

Now, one of the reasons we focus so much on values in this training is this: It has been suggested that many of us living in Western societies don't do nearly enough of this. We're well trained in how to be goal-focused—we focus mainly on the specific outcomes or end points we want to achieve. And that's fine up to a point. But we can easily lose sight of the values that give the sense of direction and purpose to our goals and actions. This is a shame, because we can miss out on obtaining a stronger sense of direction in life by not connecting to our values.

So, all the values exercises I'll be showing you are designed to help you notice what it's like to more clearly define your behavioral values—and what it's like to deliberately use those values on a daily basis as a guide to action.

Communicating the Benefits of Values-Based Action

Suggesting there are life benefits to be gained by allowing values to become a more prominent guide to action is part of a more general strategy aimed at increasing participants' motivation to reflect on values during and after the first session, and to practice bringing one personally chosen value to life during the next week. The benefits listed below can be highlighted by the trainer as a natural part of group discussions after the values card sort or used as a more structured summary at the end of this initial presentation of values.

Benefits of Values-Based Action

- Becoming more aware of values "reenergizes" our sense of purpose, life direction, and meaning.
- Values can be a powerful guide to life goals and daily actions.
- Values can work like an "inner compass," helping us navigate through challenging times and providing guidance for important decisions.
- Being guided by values means our actions will be less influenced by our sometimes "unhelpful" thoughts, feelings, moods, and behavioral habits.

Of course, talking about potential benefits is not the same as actually contacting these benefits! As the training unfolds, we see it as essential that participants be given sufficient opportunities to make experiential contact with values-based behavioral reinforcement. The values exercises in this program have been designed to help create such opportunities by encouraging participants to perform value-consistent actions outside of the sessions and to notice what happens when they do so. Describing the potential benefits just helps the trainer communicate that there is something to be gained by engaging in this values-based action process.

Helping Participants Define a Value and Translate It into Action

Depending on how the session is unfolding, it may be sufficient to employ the card sort mentioned above, encouraging participants to select and write down three small actions that are consistent with one of their "top 5" values. However, if sufficient time is available, participants can be invited to engage in further reflection in session 1 to identify values for different areas of their lives. Whichever initial values-clarification strategies are used, we always work with participants in the session to translate one value into a series of more specific value-inspired actions. The actions identified in the session then form the basis of the home practice assignment designed to be completed between sessions 1 and 2.

Handout 1, the "Define Your Values" handout is used to help participants construct value statements for different areas of their lives. In this first session, participants are invited to select any one of the five life areas and begin writing out the personal strengths and qualities they most want to pursue in that area of life. Some participants work faster than others, in which case it is fine for them to begin working on values in additional life areas. However, it usually pays to start small to ensure that all participants are able to contact one personal value and get the gist of the values-based action process. We would typically allow around fifteen to twenty minutes for this personal reflection on one value, moving on only when we sense that most participants have had time to engage with each step of the exercise.

The instructions for this entire exercise proceed as follows:

- Choose one of the five life domains. It doesn't matter which area you choose—just choose one area that you care about and would like to work on over the next week. You'll get the chance to work on other life areas and values in later sessions.

- Write out, in as much detail as possible, the personal strengths or behavioral qualities (values) you *ideally* want to express in this area of your life. You are constructing a value statement about the type of person you most want to be in this area of your life. Your "top 5" values (as identified in the card sort) can help you with this.

- Boil down that statement even further, to get a handful of three to five key words that will serve as a useful reminder for this value (to make the value more accessible and "portable").
- Brainstorm a range of specific value-based actions that you could perform over the next week to "bring this value to life." List as many relatively simple valued actions as possible. The size of the actions is unimportant—the most important thing is that the actions are consistent with the value you are working on.
- Select any *three* of your value-based actions that you are willing to perform before we meet again for session 2 (the home practice assignment).
- Turn to the blank values, goals, and actions summary worksheet handout and record your value reminder words and the selected actions in the relevant boxes. When it comes to the actions, be as specific as you can: What are you going to do? Where will this action take place? When (day/time) do you intend to do it? Who else will be involved?

These instructions can be delivered by the trainer in discrete steps to make things simpler and to have participants working through the exercise at about the same pace. The trainer can also pause at opportune moments to take questions. While facilitating this exercise, it can be helpful for the trainer to be working through each step on the board or flip chart to reveal (and draw up an action plan for) one of his or her own values. Alternatively, the trainer can demonstrate the key features of each step by using a hypothetical example, like those provided on Handouts 2a and 2b. These are made-up examples that can be used to illustrate some of the key features of this process. For example, the trainer might point out that the three value-based actions in both examples are relatively small and "everyday." This helps to convey the idea that valuing is not primarily about setting heroic goals or making sudden leaps of achievement; it is much more about gradually building patterns of daily action that are consistent with a valued behavioral quality or strength a person wishes to manifest in his or her life. The message is to start out small in order to get the gist of the values-based action process and progressively build up from there.

Although participants may also identify some value-based goals as part of this values exercise, we tend not to spend a great deal of time on goal setting in the first training session. Instead, we focus on the process of goal setting in more detail in session 2, where participants develop a values-based goal and action plan for the longer practice period scheduled between sessions 2 and 3.

In this first session, the emphasis is on the process of defining a value and translating that value into some fairly immediate action steps. As noted above, we employ this strategy mainly because we want participants to identify some relatively small value-based actions that could be completed as part of the home practice assignment between sessions 1 and 2. Values clarification and translating values into action can be viewed as mutually reinforcing processes (Hayes et al., 2012). That is, constructing a value statement encourages participants to think about concrete patterns of behavior that are likely to embody that value, and value-guided action planning in turn helps participants construct and further define personal values.

Anticipating Internal Barriers to Values-Based Action

By this point in the exercise, participants will have hopefully identified and recorded three value-consistent actions they are willing and motivated to perform over the next week. Prior to shifting into preparing for the home practice assignments, the group is encouraged to consider any barriers or obstacles that have the potential to interfere with actually engaging in the specified actions.

A simple and efficient way for the trainer to initiate reflection on barriers to valued action is to elicit examples from the group and write them up on the board or flip chart. For this part of the exercise, the trainer draws a line down the center of the board or flip chart. On one side the trainer writes **external barriers to valued action**, and on the other side **internal barriers to valued action**. External barriers can be described by the trainer as anything in the external environment that could interfere with participants engaging in their three chosen value-based actions. Internal barriers are described as any unhelpful thoughts, moods, feelings, sensations, or urges to do other things that have the potential to interfere with personally valued action.

At this point, it is useful for the trainer to communicate to the group that unhelpful thoughts and feelings are not always our most negative or undesirable ones; everyday and seemingly innocuous thoughts and moods may be just as likely to function as barriers to personally valued action. The trainer asks group members to provide examples of each type of potential barrier that might inhibit their own ability to engage in value-guided actions over the next week.

The distinction between internal and external barriers is not always clear cut. For example, while participants will very often suggest "lack of time" as an external barrier, some participants may suggest that *thinking* one doesn't have enough time represents an internal barrier. The most common private events offered for the internal barriers column are things like embarrassment, feeling unmotivated/tired/lethargic when the time comes, guilt, procrastination, excuses, and so on. From this first session, we are explicit that the program focuses particularly on reducing the impact of such *internal* barriers on people's ability to engage in effective and value-consistent patterns of action. We suggest that it is our internal experiences that often have the more subtle yet powerful influence over our behavioral effectiveness.

Part III: Demonstrating the Program Rationale and Preparing for Home Practice Assignments

We have now reached the final phase of the first training session, having introduced participants to some of the core features of both mindfulness and values-based action skills. At this juncture, it is useful for the trainer to offer participants a straightforward summary of the overarching purpose of the entire program in a way that begins to illuminate the link between the program's mindfulness and values-based action skill components. One method we have found useful for this purpose is to employ a visual presentation that we refer to (rather unglamorously) as the two sheets of paper technique.

Two Sheets of Paper Technique

As its name indicates, this technique requires just two pieces of paper! On one sheet, the trainer has the word **VALUE** written in large font. The other sheet states **"UNHELPFUL" THOUGHT/MOOD/FEELING**. Here's an example of how the trainer shifts into this visual demonstration:

Trainer: So, we've done some great work today. I'm delighted that I've been able to introduce you to these two core skills in this first session. [Trainer is pointing to the two-skills diagram.] That was my main goal for today, and it means

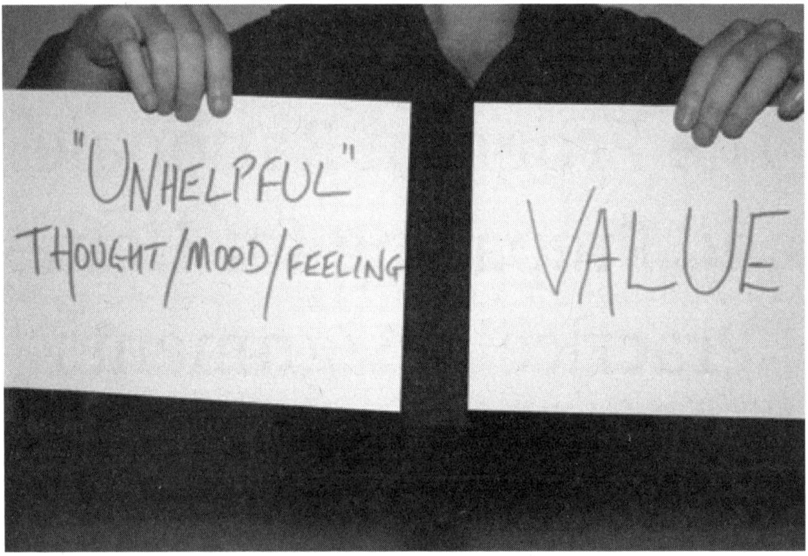
"UNHELPFUL"
THOUGHT/MOOD/FEELING
VALUE

VALUE

we can really hit the ground running next week. Before I give you some recommendations about practicing these skills over the next week, I just want to offer you a simple summary of what this training is all about. I particularly want to send you away today with a sense that these mindfulness and values-based action skills are intimately related. [Trainer is referring to the arrows linking the skills in the two-skill diagram.]

So, here's what we're doing. [The trainer is holding up his or her two pieces of paper (see photographs below).] Our daily actions and behavioral effectiveness are influenced by different things. On the one hand, we have our values. As we've discussed today, these are the personal strengths or qualities we would personally choose to guide our own behavior. On the other hand, we humans have a whole bunch of internal stuff to contend with—our frequently changing thoughts, feelings, and moods that might show up at any moment. Often this internal stuff also has a strong influence on our behavior. As you see on my sheet here, in this training we'll be looking particularly at the *unhelpful* internal stuff—the thoughts, feelings, moods, and sensations that have the potential to interfere with our day-to-day ability to pursue our personally valued goals and actions. You've already given some good examples up here on the board.

So, the move we are making in this training is essentially this ...

[The trainer now shifts the **VALUE** sheet of paper further toward the front and keeps the **UNHELPFUL THOUGHT/FEELING/MOOD** sheet where it is, now slightly in the background.]

Basically, this entire program is geared toward helping you make your personal values a more prominent guide to daily actions and life goals. Now, as I do this, notice that I am not removing this unhelpful internal stuff. That stuff is still right here. Trying to get rid of or change this stuff is typically ineffective and tends to be a waste of our valuable energy. What we'll be doing instead is becoming more mindfully aware of this internal stuff so that it becomes less

> of a barrier to values-guided action. [The trainer now continues playing with the two pieces of paper, alternating between having the "values" and "unhelpful thoughts/feelings/moods" sheets at the front.] Anyone have any comments or questions about this little demonstration of what this training is about?

Despite its simplicity, we have found this two sheets of paper technique to be surprisingly efficient and tend to utilize it in every session (often more than once per session) as a reminder of the general purpose of the training. The simple, visual demonstration serves some useful functions. First, when used at this particular point in the training, it offers the trainer another summarizing tool that helps to consolidate the learning that has taken place during the first session. The take-home message is that the training is designed gradually to increase the prominence of personally chosen values as a guide to effective and meaningful behavior. In addition (and as illustrated in the extract above), the trainer can use this technique to begin undermining experiential avoidance, simply by intimating that trying to control or remove unhelpful internal barriers is unnecessary. Finally, the trainer uses this strategy to communicate that mindfulness skills have the potential to reduce the impact of unhelpful internal states on value-guided behavioral effectiveness—thus highlighting the link between the two skills being targeted.

Preparing for Home Practice Assignments

As we approach the end of session 1, we outline the mindfulness and values-based action exercises we would like participants to practice over the next week (before session 2). We keep things as simple as possible in our workplace programs to increase the likelihood of participants engaging in some home practice. Handout 4a, "Home Practice 1: Between Sessions 1 and 2," summarizes the home practice assignments and encourages participants to record their experiences in preparation for pair or group discussion the following week. While we emphasize the importance of practicing these skills outside of the session, we will at the same time encourage participants to return for session 2 even if they have not completed the suggested tasks.

The first home practice assignment extends naturally from the values exercise that has just been completed. Specifically, we invite participants to engage mindfully in the three values-based actions they identified during the session. We inform participants that the values-based action home assignment has two main purposes:

1. To notice what it is like deliberately to take actions that are guided by a personal value.
2. To become aware of any internal barriers that actually or almost interfere with value-directed action.

To this end, we offer the following instructions:

Trainer: Your first task is this: Deliberately and purposefully perform your three value-based actions before we meet again next week! There is a bit more to it than that. It is important to practice being *mindful* while you engage in these actions. So, pay close attention to what happens. Notice any thoughts, feelings, or moods that show up before, during, and after you engage in each of your value-based actions. No need to wrestle with any of this internal stuff—the task for now is simply to observe and record. Notice whether your valued actions are easy, difficult, embarrassing, pleasant, neutral, or unpleasant. Notice anything that happens in the world around you when you engage in these actions. If other people are involved, notice how they respond to your value-based behavior.

Even if you are unable to perform one or more of your value-based actions, an important task is to become more aware of any thoughts, feelings, or moods that might be operating as internal barriers to valued action. Keep your eye out for any internal stuff that sort of hijacks your behavior. This information will be useful for some of next week's exercises.

Thus, we stress the importance of participants being mindful (or *psychologically present*) before, during, and after engaging in valued actions. We adopt this strategy for the following reasons. First, these instructions encourage participants to cultivate present-moment awareness during the week, thus building on the mindfulness exercises we introduce during this first section. Second, the instructions again highlight the reciprocal links between mindfulness and values-based action skills that lie at the heart of this program. Finally, encouraging participants to be psychologically present before, during, and after performing personally valued actions increases the chances that they will come into contact with some values-based behavioral reinforcement. Participants are encouraged to complete Handout 4b, "Home Practice 1: Record of Mindful Engagement," as a way of charting their progress on this assignment.

The other home practice assignment, also included in the handout, is a ten-minute mindfulness of breath exercise, which we encourage participants to practice at least three times before the second session (as noted earlier, participants receive digital recordings of the guidance for this and other mindfulness home practices). The exercise opens with some brief bodily awareness, followed by a longer period of mindful breathing, with attention focused on the sensations and movement in the abdomen occurring with each breath. The guidance includes typical mindfulness instructions:

- Becoming aware of current physical sensations (focusing on different areas of the body and then settling on the abdomen)
- Noticing when you have drifted away into thought
- Each time you find that you have drifted away, returning the spotlight of attention to the sensations and movement of breathing
- Cultivating an attitude of curiosity, interest, and nonjudgment during the practice—a stance of "just noticing" whatever shows up
- Allowing thoughts and feelings to come and go while repeatedly bringing attention to current physical sessions

We remind participants of a point we made earlier: these meditative-type exercises are among the most recognized and powerful ways of developing mindfulness. We also suggest that mindfulness is akin to a "psychological muscle" that will inevitably develop with repeated practice.

Setting Up Environmental Cues

As part of preparing for the home assignments, the trainer can advise participants on the utility of setting up reminders on one's person or in the external environment to act as cues for the suggested practices. Most of the participants we train in workplace settings are leading extremely busy lives, and it is not uncommon for participants to simply forget to engage in recommended assignments outside of the sessions. The following resources are placed in a pile in the center of the group:

- Sticky notes of different colors and sizes
- Colored stickers small enough to be placed on a cell phone, wallet or purse, computer screen, or mirror
- Silicone wristbands to be worn during the week as a reminder to perform valued actions or engage in mindfulness practice
- Small plastic key fobs with blank stickers for participants to write their value or value-based actions; each participant can be given three of these key fobs—one for each value-based action to be performed over the next week

Participants should be encouraged to take away a selection of these resources to set up visual reminders at work, home, and/or on their person. In addition, the trainer can suggest other useful tools and strategies, such as making diary notes on specific days to perform valued actions, using electronic calendar reminders, or setting cell phone alarms. If there is enough time, participants are invited to get into pairs and share one valued action they intend to perform over the next week, and also to discuss the particular reminder strategies they think will be most useful.

Ending the Session

Once the home practice assignments have been clearly communicated, the trainer can bring the session to a close. This might be done by thanking participants warmly and sincerely for their willingness to engage in the session 1 exercises, and perhaps with a final visit to the two-skills organizing diagram. Participants should be given the opportunity to raise any final questions, comments, or concerns about the material and exercises presented in this first session. The trainer might also look ahead to session 2, communicating to the group that the next session will include a number of mindfulness exercises that help us untangle from internal barriers that might otherwise interfere with our ability to pursue valued actions and goals.

Summary of Session 1

Session 1 is, not surprisingly, designed to get the program off to a good start! The trainer has offered an ACT-congruent rationale for the program and facilitated some relatively gentle experiential exercises and initial reflection on values. One of the key aims is to capture participants' interest in what the program has to offer so that they are motivated to try out the home practices and then return for the next session. We have found that in the workplace training context, a fairly direct approach is efficient and well-received. That is, explaining the skills that are going to be taught in the program and providing some examples of how those skills are to be practiced. When the first session has gone well, the foundations are set for the somewhat more intensive work conducted in session 2, which offers strategies to help people "untangle" from internal barriers to values-based action.

CHAPTER 6

Training Session 2: Untangling from Internal Barriers to Values-Based Action

In the second session (which usually occurs one week after the first), the trainer employs a range of intervention strategies aimed at helping participants develop the mindfulness and values-based action skills that were introduced in session 1. The experiential exercises, metaphors, and group discussions found in session 2 target a number of ACT's core processes, including contact with the present moment, cognitive defusion, acceptance, values clarification, and committed action. While session 2 sees the introduction of some new techniques (such as thought-defusion exercises), there are also opportunities for participants to repeat some of the exercises that were practiced during session 1, including mindful breathing, defining values, and translating values into specific actions. As noted in chapter 4, we view the provision of such opportunities for behavioral rehearsal to be an important feature of the skill development process.

An important task for the trainer in session 2 is to illustrate further the intimate functional links between mindfulness and values-based action. From an ACT perspective, it is the experiential combination of these psychological and behavioral skills that will ultimately lead to increased psychological flexibility. Accordingly, the link between the two skills is made explicit in the central theme running through session 2: untangling from internal barriers to values-based action.

It is worth noting that session 2 includes a number of potentially powerful interventions. Participants are invited to become more aware of what might be difficult (or at least self-limiting) psychological content and to reflect on the thoughts and feelings they experience as psychological barriers to personally valued behavior. Hence, at various points in this chapter we will be considering the role of the trainer in delivering these interventions in a validating, normalizing, and ACT-consistent manner.

The table below presents an overview of session 2.

Training Phase	Key Interventions
PART I	
Opening mindfulness practice	Mindfulness of breath; noticing thoughts and feelings and allowing them to come and go
Home practice review	Pairs and group discussion
Presentation of training rationale	"Passengers on the bus" metaphor
PART II	
Untangling from thought barriers to valued action	Self-reflection on unhelpful thought content; cartoon voices technique; physical demonstration of fusion/defusion; thoughts on screen exercise
Mindfulness of mood/emotion	Physicalizing exercise
PART III	
Defining values and values-based goal and action planning	Construction of four-week values-based goal and action plan
Discussion of home practice assignments	Home practice handout; environmental reminders; public commitment to one value-based goal

Part I: Opening Practice and Review of Home Assignments

At the beginning of the second session we open with a brief welcome back, offer a quick and simple reminder of the two skills being targeted (referring to the two-skills organizing diagram), and then facilitate a mindfulness of breath practice that lasts for approximately ten minutes. Consistent with our strategy of offering a progression of mindfulness exercises, the session 2 opening practice places somewhat greater emphasis on cultivating nonjudgmental awareness (noticing and allowing) of any thoughts, feelings, and sensations that arise during the exercise. These acceptance-oriented instructions sit well with the content of the second training session, which includes interventions designed to (1) reduce excessive entanglement with unhelpful thought content (2) undermine experiential avoidance; and (3) cultivate acceptance skills.

Mindfulness of Breath Practice

We prepare participants for this mindfulness exercise in the usual way by suggesting an upright and dignified posture, eyes closed or unfocused and cast down toward the table or floor, hands resting comfortably in the lap or on the arms of the chair. Participants are first invited to become aware of physical sensations in different parts of their bodies, before settling attention on the sensations of movement in the abdomen as they breath in and out. The basic instructions are the same as those listed toward the end of session 1. The guidance for this exercise includes an emphasis on the following type of instruction:

> "As you focus on the current physical sensations and movement in your tummy, allow any thoughts and feelings just to come and go as they please."

> "Practice noticing any thoughts that arise simply *as thoughts*, without getting overly entangled in them ... No need to push any thoughts away; just noticing the natural ebb and flow of thinking as it happens."

> "Still bringing the spotlight of your attention on current sensations in your tummy, and practicing simply acknowledging any thoughts, feelings and sensations that show up during the exercise."

During the postexercise discussions, participants often share experiences related to the nonjudgmental posture being targeted by this type of guidance. The trainer can harness and summarize these contributions to help reveal a key aspect of mindfulness—taking a more nonjudgmental (or "just noticing") stance toward fluctuating private events.

We have included below some fairly typical participant experiences with this type of exercise, along with examples of how the trainer might respond:

Trainer: Great. Thanks for participating in this opening mindfulness practice with me. Maybe have yourselves a little stretch ... Would anyone like to kick us off today by sharing their experiences of this exercise?

Participant: How long was that one?

Trainer: It was about ten minutes that time. What did you notice during this practice?

Participant: That time seemed to go very quickly for me. I still find a load of different things go on for me when I'm doing this. It's really quite strange, isn't it? Some of the time I was here focusing on my belly; but then the next minute I'd be off again. Who knows where I went. It's like I'm drifting off, but when I come back I might have no idea what it was I was just thinking about!

Trainer: Thanks, Ahmed—some really useful observations there; and I really like the way you describe the drifting off into thoughts and coming back. I notice some others were nodding there—I think in recognition of that type of experience. Barbara—did you notice something similar during the exercise?

With this fairly simple response to Ahmed's experience, the trainer is deliberately looking to tap into the group process. Specifically, instead of exploring this one individual's experience any further (which is also an option here), the trainer immediately brings other members of the group into the interaction, eliciting some shared experiences. This is a simple strategy that can increase the level of interaction within the group; with this style of group facilitation it is not unusual for participants to start sharing experiences with each other rather than simply reporting back to the trainer or tuning out of the dialogue while "waiting their turn" (Bieling, McCabe, & Antony, 2006).

Here's another fairly common response to the same exercise:

Participant 2: I like being able to let go of my thinking for a while. Everything always seems so urgent and so important all the time; so much to do; rush, rush, rush; never-ending lists of things to do. Taking a break from that is refreshing for me or something … I feel like I've just had a power nap!

Trainer: Thanks, Maria. It's quite common for me to hear people saying this sort of thing after some of these practices. I love the term you used there—"letting go." That's a term that sits really well with these mindfulness exercises. Practicing this perspective of not being so wrapped up in our thoughts—just noticing them as thoughts, and letting them come and go while *we* reside here in the present moment. As you heard in the instructions, it's important to remember that we're not trying to avoid any thoughts or to push them away; instead, these practices are about becoming mindfully aware—just noticing with gentle interest and curiosity whatever shows up during the practice.

At some point during these discussions it is useful for the trainer to communicate that it is perfectly normal for less desirable thoughts and feelings to show up during some practices. The message is that noticing such experiences contributes to a useful and insightful practice.

Troubleshooting

It is important for the trainer to remain on the lookout for what may be very subtle "misuses" of mindfulness exercises. Given the strong cultural endorsements of experiential avoidance, it is perhaps inevitable that some participants will initially and unwittingly utilize these practices in an attempt to control, avoid, distract themselves from, or "fix" unwanted cognitive and emotional content (see Segal et al., 2002 for some useful reflections on this phenomenon). This issue is further complicated by the fact that many participants report positive (and in some cases even slightly euphoric) experiences following their first encounters with mindfulness. Participants also often find the meditative exercises relaxing and can easily fall into the trap of thinking that relaxation is the goal. Thus, given the relatively brief nature of this program, the trainer needs to become skilled at exploring and recognizing how participants are viewing and using such practices. We find this becomes somewhat less of an issue during and following the second training session, as all of the interventions introduced during this session convey the message that we are looking to cultivate a more aware and accepting posture even toward unhelpful psychological content.

Home Practice Review

We cannot emphasize enough the value of conducting a detailed review of the home practice assignments. The function of such a review should go beyond merely checking in on whether or not participants have completed the recommended extracurricular tasks. Indeed, a well-conducted home practice review supports the following training goals:

- Clarify understanding of the key features of mindfulness and values-based action processes
- Emphasize the importance of generalizing mindfulness and values-based action skills from the sessions to daily life
- Provide further reinforcement to participants who have engaged in mindful and values-based action exercises outside of the sessions

Mindfulness Home Practice Review

Gathering participants' experiences with the opening in-session mindfulness practice tends to extend naturally into the home practice review (as participants will often spontaneously reflect on the difference between practicing mindfulness in the session and practicing at home). The trainer might spend a few more minutes capturing participants' experiences with the mindfulness home assignment. This will often involve discussing some of the challenges of practicing such exercises on a regular basis (lack of time, falling asleep, finding it boring, distractions at home, and so on).

The trainer can use this opportunity to highlight other ways of practicing mindfulness throughout the day, for example, by stepping out of automatic pilot mode and becoming aware of current physical sensations and movements in the body during the morning routine (showering, brushing teeth, drinking tea, traveling to work). Participants can be reminded of the raisin exercise and encouraged to practice in a similar way by eating one meal or snack more mindfully each day. The message is that it is useful to practice some form of mindfulness every day (even if it's only for a few minutes). The more formal meditative practices, like mindfulness of the breath, are offered to participants as the most powerful training methods for developing mindful awareness, but there are multiple opportunities throughout the day to strengthen basic mindfulness skills. We have found simple bodily awareness instructions to be particularly useful for building participants' everyday present-moment awareness, that is, helping them get into the habit of bringing awareness to the body at frequent intervals during the day as a way of "waking up" from automatic pilot mode.

Toward the end of this review of home practice, the trainer can take another opportunity to reiterate briefly why developing mindfulness is considered such a useful skill for improving psychological well-being and behavioral effectiveness. As we noted in session 1, we find it useful to suggest that mindfulness is akin to a "psychological muscle" that naturally develops through repeated "mental training."

Values-Based Action Home Practice Review

While the cultivation of some basic mindfulness skills is an important part of this workplace program, we are most interested in utilizing the various mindfulness practices to help people become better at engaging in personally valued actions in the presence of unhelpful thoughts, moods, urges, and emotions (that is, to promote psychological flexibility). Hence, we tend to spend a greater portion of time reviewing people's experiences with the values-based action home assignment. Recall that participants were invited to engage purposefully and mindfully in three value-based actions during the week between sessions 1 and 2. The simplest way for the trainer to shift the focus to values is by referring again to the two-skills diagram.

We tend to invite participants to discuss the values-based home assignment in pairs in the first instance, or in small groups of three or four people. Before doing so, it is worthwhile for the trainer to get a sense of how many participants within the group have deliberately taken some valued action over the past week. Here the trainer might ask, "Just out of curiosity, how many of you were able to mindfully engage in at least one of the value-based actions you identified last week?" Participants can be asked to indicate this with a show of hands. If everyone in the group completed at least one valued action, the trainer can ask how many engaged in two and then all three of the specified actions. The trainer should always adopt a nonjudgmental and curious stance when inquiring about home practice assignments. The aim is to recognize the challenge of making time for extracurricular practice and offer a suitable level of appreciation for any practice that has occurred.

As long as adequate attention was paid in session 1 to preparing for the home practice assignment (encouraging participants to set up reminders on their person or in the external environment and so forth), there is a good chance that a majority of participants in any one group have engaged in some purposeful value-guided action over the past week. However, it is sensible to assume that not all participants have completed this assignment. The home practice review should be designed in a way that will be useful regardless of whether the home practice was completed. Working together in pairs or small groups, participants can be asked to reflect on and discuss the following points:

- The ease or difficulty of performing three value-based actions
- Any consequences of taking or not taking value-based action—any impact on yourself or others
- Any internal barriers (unhelpful thoughts, feelings, urges, or moods) that almost or actually got in the way of your taking value-based action this week
- Any external barriers that almost or actually got in the way of your taking value-based action this week
- Your general impression of this practice of deliberately using a value as a guide to action

Once participants have spent some time discussing their experiences, they can be asked to return to the main group. As usual, the trainer can elicit some further group reflection with a question such as, "Would anyone be willing to share their impressions of this home practice?" or "So, I'm curious about how you found this values-based action home assignment?" The trainer might then gather a few participant experiences and address any questions in order to reiterate the key features of this behavioral process.

The trainer should be looking to explore and reinforce any expressions of an increased sense of vitality, motivation, or purpose derived from value-guided behavioral activation. As we are aiming to increase psychological flexibility, it is particularly useful when participants share accounts of following through with valued behavior even though they didn't much feel like it at the time. By highlighting these contributions, the trainer can communicate that the presence of unhelpful internal states does not have to be a significant barrier to valued action. Similarly, if a participant reports that his or her valued action was in some way "hijacked" by momentary thoughts, moods, or urges to do other things, the trainer might use this to highlight the often subtle power of our internal states to function as barriers to action and to underscore the considerable benefits of becoming more aware of what is influencing our behavior.

The following interaction involves a participant (we'll call her "Poppy") who identified going swimming as one of her value-based actions. Poppy went swimming during the week, attributes this valued behavior to the exercise, and makes some other useful observations that the trainer picks up on.

Participant: Forgive me for being so blunt, everyone, but I'm looking at this as a really useful exercise for getting me off my butt!

Trainer: [Chortling] You can be as blunt as you like in here, Poppy! Could I pry a little more into what you mean by that?

Participant: Sure. I had going for a swim as one of my health and fitness actions. I'd actually like to go much more than I do. I used to swim competitively a few years back, and I'd really like to get into training semiseriously again. But I'm good at putting it off. I don't really have the excuse of having a lot of those external barriers, but I am easily put off as soon as I start thinking about the hassle of getting to the pool; finding somewhere to park; getting changed and dressed again; having to wash my hair to get rid of the smell of chlorine. All that. It seems pretty lame really when I look at what I've written down here! But this week I stuck a sticky note on my front door on Tuesday night straight after the last session. All I wrote on it was "GO SWIMMING!!" So I went. And this time I made sure I would remember how good I felt after. I think I just need to keep reminding myself of that; when I do get up off my butt and go, it's going to be worthwhile.

Trainer: Thanks, Poppy—that is a splendid example for this training! And great work making use of a sticky note reminder to engage in your valued action. These little tricks can seem simple, but they are often surprisingly effective. [Trainer is now addressing the whole group.] Can others relate to Poppy's experience? We can choose some value-based actions and might have every intention of making them happen. And here's the rub—we humans may *also* have a whole bunch of less helpful thoughts and feelings that have the potential to stop us from doing these things. That's what we mean by having *internal* barriers to action. Poppy's example is great, because she took the opportunity to notice some of her unhelpful thoughts and still engaged in the value-based action of going swimming. And, in a nutshell, that's what these two skills are designed to help you do more of—noticing your internal stuff, without necessarily letting that stuff guide your actions, while gradually allowing your values to become a more prominent guide to daily action.

Did any other pairs discuss a similar—or perhaps very different—experience with this values-based action home exercise?

Poppy's example provides a nice illustration of the experiences the values-based action exercises are designed to promote. What is particularly useful from our perspective is that Poppy seems to be reporting heightened contact with how she felt after she went swimming. It is conceivable that because the exercise explicitly asked her to engage mindfully in valued actions (to *notice* what happens when bringing a value to life), Poppy was better equipped to contact this potentially important source of reinforcement (Dahl et al., 2009).

Moreover, Poppy's example suggests that she gained some additional insight into the internal events that threatened to "override" or "hijack" her valued action of going for a swim. Taken together, these experiences will hopefully function to increase the probability of Poppy behaving in a similar way again in the future—that is, by going swimming while in the presence of various compelling thoughts about the hassle of getting there, finding a parking space, washing her hair, and so on. Poppy's generally positive experience with this exercise might also encourage her to define and use values as a guide to action in other areas of her life.

Of course, not every participant will have an experience as insightful (and potentially reinforcing) as we see in Poppy's example. Nonetheless, there are usually at least a few people within any one group who will have contacted some reinforcing consequences following engagement in values-guided action (such consequences can be as simple as the sense of satisfaction a person gets from doing something he or she had been meaning to do for a while). Moreover, even if valued actions were not performed during the past week, the home practice review and discussions can still help to raise people's awareness of what is influencing their behavior.

To help structure the home practice review, we have essentially considered mindfulness and values-based action practices separately. The next step is to offer some additional rationale for the program that is oriented toward the main theme of this second session and toward helping participants grasp how the two core skills are related. You may recall that we began this process in session 1, using the simple yet effective two sheets of paper technique. In the next segment, we often illustrate ACT's "passengers on the bus" metaphor, which can be used to deliver the same basic rationale.

"Passengers on the Bus" Metaphor

"Passengers on the bus" is one of the most well-known ACT metaphors. It appears in the first book-length account of the ACT approach (Hayes et al., 1999; and see Hayes et al., 2012, pp. 250–251) and has since been described (in one form or another) in many subsequent ACT texts. We have found this image particularly useful when delivering ACT-based training to working populations and employ it to present the training rationale and to portray the functional link between mindfulness and values-based action.

To launch into the "passengers on the bus" metaphor after the home practice review, the trainer might say something like this:

Trainer: I'd like to show you a rather neat way of looking at the basic rationale for this training. I particularly want to keep revealing this important link between mindfulness and values-based action skills. [The trainer is now pointing out the arrows in the two-skills diagram.] Strangely enough, one of the best ways of showing you the rationale is with the scenario of being the driver of a bus that is full of passengers! [The trainer reveals a large cartoon picture of a bus driver with a bus full of "monster" passengers (see figure 6.1) and provides each participant with a smaller copy of the same image.] And here it is!

Figure 6.1. Passengers on the Bus

So, you're the driver of this bus. Let's call it the bus of life! As with any effective bus service, you'll have a good collection of passengers. I want you to imagine that all these passengers are your thoughts, moods, feelings, urges to do certain things—basically all the internal stuff we humans experience. As the driver, you might choose a particular direction for your bus, start up the engine, and get your hands on the wheel. And your passengers will be constantly piping up. Some of them might be quite helpful—approving of the direction you've chosen, telling you you're doing a good job as the driver. Some of them will be less helpful—questioning the direction you've chosen for your bus, urging you to stop the bus or to take some other direction. And some of the passengers will be downright unpleasant: these might be the ones that criticize you, tell you you're actually a crappy driver, perhaps predicting all the things that could go wrong. This is essentially the human condition—we all have passengers aboard the bus. The passengers want the driver's attention—they want us to listen to them and take the bus in the directions they are suggesting. And here's the thing, the influence these passengers can have over the driver is often very subtle—we're often quite unaware of how they influence our actions. So a lot of the mindfulness exercises we use in these sessions are designed to help you become more aware of your passengers—to step back a bit so that you can see these passengers for what they actually are, and see that you as the driver can follow a direction of *your* choosing, whatever the passengers happen to be saying.

Before I go on, I'm rather curious about what you are all making of this bus scenario as a way of portraying the human condition. [Trainer elicits a few comments from the group.]

Okay. So, here's a question for you. If we as the driver find some of our passengers are having an unhelpful impact on our well-being and behavior, why don't we just pull over, go to the back, and toss them off the bus?

Participant 1: Well...it's not that simple, is it? Like you say, they're a part of us, part of being a human being.

Trainer: Right. It's part of the human experience to have this stuff. I certainly have plenty of these less helpful passengers, and I'm guessing you all do too from time to time.

Participant 2: And even if you did manage get some of these characters off the bus, there'll just be a busload more waiting to get on at the next stop!

Trainer: Super! I like that—a nice addition to our bus scenario. [Trainer takes a couple more comments from the group before continuing.]

Trainer: One thing we do know from a lot of psychological research is that trying to wrestle with our unwanted passengers is *not* the most effective strategy for us humans. Struggling

> with them, trying to get them off the bus, can have the surprising effect of making the unwanted passengers stronger, not weaker. It's odd, but they kind of thrive on the attention and power we give them. And struggling with them is essentially a waste of valuable energy that could be spent on making sure the bus is moving in a direction that we care about.
>
> The funny thing is this: although some of these passengers might seem unpleasant or unhelpful, just having them on the bus is not really a problem for us humans. When we take a proper look at them, even the most unhelpful passengers are just thoughts and feelings, at the end of the day. We don't *have* to do what they tell us to do. Sure, they can climb all over the seats and make their noise, and sure, they can shuffle up to the front of the bus and make us take a look at them—but that's about it. You might say their bark is worse than their bite.

In most of our workshops we present the bus metaphor in this format—that is, with a static visual representation and accompanying trainer dialogue. However, one of the advantages of delivering ACT in groups is that such metaphors can also be physically acted out, if it is deemed useful and appropriate to the particular group and context. For example, participants can be invited to play the role of particular passengers, such as "worry," "self-doubt," "anxiety," "fear of failure," "I'm not good enough," "can't be bothered," "I don't have time," and so on. Participants can even be given T-shirts with these roles printed on the front and back. The chairs in the room are laid out like the seats on a bus. The trainer coaches the passengers to stand periodically, expressing things in line with the role they have been given. Participants can then take turns sitting up front being the driver (perhaps using a toy steering wheel as a prop) and experience how responding to what the passengers are saying is likely to influence the movement and direction of the bus.

An alternative to describing or acting out the bus scenario would be to show a cartoon animation of this type of ACT-inspired metaphor. We can make two recommendations here: *Demons on the Boat*, an animation developed by Joe Oliver available at http://contextualpsychology.org/demons_on_boat, and *Struggling with Internal Hijackers*, available online at http://www.youtube.com/watch?v=NdaCEO4WtDU. If audiovisual equipment is available in the training room, showing an animated film offers a useful way of varying the delivery format.

Multiple Uses for the Bus Metaphor

One of the great strengths of the bus (or demons on the boat) metaphor is that it is able to illuminate all of ACT's core processes. For example, in the previous extract, the trainer was using the metaphor to foster defusion by objectifying psychological content (portraying one's thoughts as passengers on a bus). In addition, as part of the same dialogue, the trainer was looking to undermine experiential avoidance. He did this by asking participants to consider why we humans don't simply remove unwanted thought and feeling passengers from the bus and by suggesting that trying to control the passengers may not be the most effective strategy. The metaphor also naturally illuminates the important role of behavioral values by referring to the driver's chosen direction and potential for control over the progress and movement of the bus.

Following its introduction, the bus metaphor is regularly referenced by the trainer and participants. For example, internal barriers to valued action can now be simply referred to as "unhelpful passengers" on the bus. In the next section, we show how the metaphor can be extended to set the scene for the introduction of interventions designed to cultivate defusion and acceptance skills.

Part II: Untangling from Internal Barriers to Values-Based Action

At the heart of session 2 we find some important exercises that are primarily aimed at helping participants develop defusion and acceptance skills. Defusion and acceptance are captured together within the mindfulness component of our two-skills organizing diagram (under "noticing and untangling from your internal barriers").

One of the aims of the "passengers on the bus" metaphor is to provide the basic foundations and rationale for this next training segment. Specifically, the metaphor has been used by the trainer to convey the following key messages:

- The person driving the bus is to some extent distinct from her or his thought and feeling passengers.
- Some passengers can have an unhelpful influence over the driver's behavior—that is, they have the potential to interfere with the driver taking the bus in personally valued directions.
- Struggling to remove the unhelpful passengers is unlikely to be successful.
- The passengers often have a subtle influence over the driver's actions, suggesting that increased awareness of one's passengers is vital.

In the final stage of presenting the bus metaphor, the trainer can make the link to the two core skills that are being targeted (mindfulness and values-based action) and explain briefly how the next set of exercises is designed to help us to untangle from any unhelpful passengers:

Trainer: So, the skills you're learning in these sessions are not designed to help you toss any of these passengers off the bus, or even to keep them quiet. Instead, I aim to show you how strengthening mindfulness skills gives us a whole new perspective on even our most unhelpful passengers. Instead of struggling with any of the passengers or mindlessly letting them dictate our actions, we'll be learning today how we can *untangle* ourselves a bit from them. This in turn increases the driver's ability to take the bus in a valued direction, no matter what the passengers are doing.

At this point, we do not expect participants to know what we mean when we talk about untangling ourselves from unhelpful thoughts and feelings. As part of the bus metaphor, we have merely suggested that there is an alternative way of relating to the passengers that does not involve struggling with them or allowing them to dictate our actions. The experiential nature of defusion and acceptance skills will be revealed in the exercises that are about to be introduced.

We begin this next segment of the training by illustrating how one can untangle from unhelpful *thoughts* that would otherwise function as internal barriers to valued action (also called cognitive defusion). Staying with the same general theme, we then introduce an experiential exercise (the physicalizing exercise) designed to help participants develop a more mindful and nonjudgmental awareness of mood and emotion.

Untangling from Thought Barriers (Cognitive Defusion)

Defusion exercises essentially train people to: take unhelpful thoughts a bit less seriously; notice the ongoing process of thinking; and learn experientially that thoughts do not have to control action (Harris, 2009). It is important to note that ACT does not encourage participants to defuse from the content of *all* thoughts at all times—that would be pointless and potentially unhelpful. Instead, ACT's defusion strategies focus primarily on helping participants relate differently to thoughts that interfere with valued action. This is what we mean in the training when we talk about unhelpful thoughts. Hence, the defusion exercises used in this training do not occur in isolation—they are presented as techniques that are ultimately designed to help participants increase the value consistency of day-to-day patterns of behavior.

Although we are about to enter a phase of the training that explicitly targets defusion, this process has been cultivated by the trainer from the start of the program. For example, from the outset, the trainer has been referring to the "mind" as though it were a separate entity, that is, in a manner of speaking, distinct from the conscious person who is experiencing its output. This type of defused language is designed to establish some healthy psychological distance between the person having thoughts and the thoughts themselves.

Similarly, the mindfulness practice employed at the start of this second training session promotes defusion by encouraging participants to notice the process of thinking as it unfolds (and without becoming overly wrapped up in it). This type of metacognitive practice might be described as helping participants catch a glimpse of thoughts *as thoughts* as they arise in awareness. As noted already, the "passengers on the bus" metaphor also serves a defusive function through the objectification of private events (that is, by talking about unhelpful or self-critical thoughts as if they are the cartoon "monsters" at the back of the bus).

In session 2, we introduce some exercises that are more explicitly aimed at promoting defusion. The set of defusion techniques we often use begins with participants self-reflecting on any internal dialogue they find self-limiting or which holds them back in some way from more effective or consistent engagement in personally-valued action. As part of this exercise, we encourage participants to identify any particular theme (or themes) in their unhelpful mind chatter and to come up with a suitable label or nickname for the mind when its output seems to be particularly unhelpful, perhaps threatening to "hijack" the effective pursuit of valued action. This strategy has been adopted from a technique used with ACT clients in therapeutic settings (e.g., Luoma et al., 2007; Strosahl & Robinson, 2008; Zettle, 2007). We ask participants to select the most unhelpful thought identified during this exercise, then introduce a playful exercise that invites participants to experience that thought as if it were being spoken in the voice of a well-know cartoon, film, or television character. This type of technique often results in participants taking such thoughts a bit less seriously, thereby reducing the power of the thought to exert an unhelpful or automatic control over behavior.

We find that this set of exercises is often sufficient to cultivate a healthy degree of defusion in the second training session. However, we also offer readers some alternative defusion techniques that we have at times employed in our workplace programs. These include offering a physical demonstration of the distinction between being fused with cognitive content and cultivating some healthy psychological distance between thoughts and the person who is having those thoughts. We also outline a common type of defusion-oriented mindfulness exercise that encourages participants to practice "watching" the moment-by-moment flow of thinking as it unfolds.

Defusion Terminology

Prior to describing these techniques, it is worth noting some of the terminology used in ACT to capture the experiential distinction between fusion and defusion. As indicated throughout this chapter, we routinely use the term "untangling" from unhelpful thoughts to refer to the defusion process. Other ways of describing this same process are "getting some healthy psychological distance from our thoughts and feelings" and "taking a psychological step back to see the passengers for what they actually are."

ACT also makes a useful distinction between *buying* and *having* thoughts (Hayes et al., 1999). "Buying" a thought denotes fusion—a psychological context in which the person is firmly attached to and strongly influenced by particular thoughts. "Having" a thought, on the other hand, suggests a more defused stance toward one's inner experience, essentially by offering a reminder that there is a conscious human being present who is currently experiencing thoughts. Similarly, ACT portrays the experiential nature of defusion as looking *at* one's thought content, as opposed to looking out at the world *from* or *through* that content (i.e., fusion; Hayes et al., 1999).

Introducing Defusion

It is helpful for the trainer to provide a brief psychoeducative introduction that sets the scene for the defusion segment. The aim of this introduction is to communicate that the human mind is very good at comparing, judging, evaluating, criticizing, problem solving, anticipating all the things that could go wrong, and so on. This type of dialogue helps to normalize the mind's proclivity for negative content (Harris, 2009; Hayes et al., 2012).

Trainer: As we've discussed, some of the most powerful barriers to greater well-being and life effectiveness are internal—our own thoughts, moods, and emotions. We humans are dealing not only with the external world, but also this very strange internal world that's influencing our behavior, often in rather subtle ways.

Take the human mind, for instance. The human mind is a wonderful tool that has allowed our species to take over the entire planet in a very short space of time. Many people say the mind evolved in large part to keep us out of danger, so it's constantly offering predictions about all the stuff that could go wrong, looking out for danger, worrying about whether we're doing as well as others, and so on. Research shows that a large chunk of human thinking is like this—negative by its very nature. In our society, we often look at this as if it is a problem—that's why the self-help shelves are full of those books telling us we should be thinking more positively! But actually, the human mind is just doing exactly what it has been designed to do—doing its best to keep us out of trouble and constantly judging how well we're doing compared to others. The difficulty we humans face in the modern world is that because the mind is so useful for many things, we become overly entangled in its output. Thoughts can sometimes just pop up out of nowhere and completely control our actions. We can become so lost in what our thoughts are saying to us that we completely forget that we are in this moment a conscious human being who is experiencing some thoughts!

And this is where mindfulness skills come in. Because humans have always had this tendency to get unhelpfully entangled in thoughts, people have been practicing mindfulness for millennia. This is not some new technique or gimmick that you're learning here—it's thousands of years old. If we can develop more mindful awareness of our thoughts, we have more choice over whether to get wrapped up in them or not. We have more choice over how much the thoughts we are currently experiencing should dictate our actions. And that's what I want to show you now. I have a couple of techniques that are specifically designed to help us become more mindful of thoughts.

Capturing Unhelpful Thoughts and Labeling the Mind

To help promote defusion, it is important that participants have the opportunity during the session to reflect on any of their thought content that could potentially function as an obstacle to value-guided behavioral activation. To aid self-reflection on unhelpful thought content, we provide participants with Handout 5, "Untangling from Thought Barriers," the "thought bubbles" handout. As noted at the top of this handout, participants are encouraged to record any "thought barriers"—that is, any thoughts that have the potential to interfere with the person's engagement in value-directed action.

The focus here is not on whether these thoughts are deemed to be true, valid, or accurate. Instead, this exercise is designed to raise awareness of how particular thoughts *function* (and, more precisely, the extent to which some thoughts interfere with valued behavior). The trainer can again make good use of the bus metaphor when facilitating this exercise—describing the task as identifying the "thought passengers" that have the most unhelpful influence over the direction and progress of the bus.

To help normalize people's more troublesome thought content, the trainer should complete the same thought bubble exercise on the board or flip chart. It is worth communicating to the group that unhelpful thoughts are not always the most "negative" thoughts. For example, everyday thoughts, such as thoughts about putting things off until tomorrow, might not seem particularly troublesome, and yet when fusion is present, such thoughts can still exert an unhelpful influence over a person's effectiveness at pursuing valued work and life goals.

As noted above, there is an additional step to this defusion exercise. We ask our participants to look for any theme or themes running through their unhelpful thought content, and to give the mind a label or nickname for when its outputs seem particularly unhelpful. We treat this as a fairly lighthearted addition to the exercise by saying something like this:

Trainer: One way to help you become more mindfully aware of your less helpful thoughts is to give your mind some kind of label or nickname to help you identify when it's tempting you with unhelpful stuff. So, look at my example on the board here. Based on my most frequent and common unhelpful mind chatter [trainer is referring to his or her thought bubble exercise], I like to refer to my mind as "Mr. Cautious." And so, when I notice thoughts like these attempting to interfere with my taking valued action, I can now sort of recognize it and say to myself, "Oh hello again, Mr. Cautious, my old pal—are you up to your old tricks again?!" Although this might seem a little odd, it is a surprisingly useful way of ensuring we remain mindful of this stuff and the influence it can have in our lives. You don't have to label your mind as "Mr. (or Mrs. or Ms.) whatever"—you could also describe your mind as a thing. For example, if your mind likes a good worry it might be "The Worry Machine." So in a moment of mindful awareness, it's like, "Aah, there goes my worry machine again!"

Get the idea? We're not trying to make any of these thoughts go away—that's not the point. This is just what human minds are programmed to do. The aim is to become gradually more aware of this stuff and ensure we don't allow it to interfere too much with us taking effective action consistent with our values.

It is useful to allow some time for participants to discuss their experiences with this exercise in pairs and to share the labels they've chosen for their minds. When the trainer has shared an example on the board, participants are often willing to share their unhelpful cognitive content with other members of the group. This strategy supports the normalizing process, as participants learn that other people also experience thoughts that exert an unhelpful influence over behavioral effectiveness. However, to ensure that participants do not feel coerced into sharing, it is worth the trainer reiterating that they do not have to share any specific thoughts or labels they would prefer to keep private. The primary aim is for participants to discuss generally what it is like to self-reflect on the mind's "products" and whether unhelpful thoughts are elusive or familiar and readily accessible.

This process of recording thought content on the handout is itself likely to cultivate some cognitive defusion. The exercise naturally encourages participants to step back from their thought content and to see it "out there" on the page. Giving the mind a label further supports the defusion process by raising awareness of, and objectifying, unhelpful mind chatter.

Once participants have discussed experiences with the exercise in their pairs or small groups, the trainer can invite people back into the main group and pose a general question such as "So, what did you notice and discuss about this exercise?" Here's an example of a useful reflection on this exercise, along with the trainer's response:

Trainer: So, what did you notice during this exercise?

Participant: It's really quite revealing. I don't know about others, but it's rare to get the chance to stop and think about what's going on in my head.

Trainer: Sure. It is common for us to be quite unaware of how our own thoughts are operating in our lives. You know, a lot of what we're doing here is about becoming more aware of this stuff. Did you notice any sorts of themes lurking in your unhelpful thought passengers, and perhaps give your mind a label?

Participant: [laughing] I did actually. I was just telling Dave, I've called mine "Madame Procrastination"! A favorite of mine is telling myself I can put things off until tomorrow. It keeps me from getting more done and ends up causing me more stress in the long run. Things just tend to pile up.

Trainer: Splendid! Madame Procrastination. Love it. Thanks for sharing that one, Sue. So now you have a name to help you notice when your mind is delivering that particular script. Anyone else notice any themes in their less helpful mind-stuff that could be captured by a label or nickname, just like I call mine "Mr. Cautious" when it's giving me all this chatter about what might go wrong?

Cartoon Voices Technique

Following the above exercises and discussion, we introduce an exercise that encourages participants to experience one of their unhelpful thoughts in an unusual context: as though it were being spoken first by a cartoon character and then by a film or television character (Harris, 2007; Hayes & Smith, 2005). We ask participants to focus on what they see as the most unhelpful thought identified during the thought bubbles exercise. Participants are asked to focus for a moment on that thought and simply to notice its impact. In the next step, we provide participants with a list of well-known cartoon characters with strange or funny voices, such as Homer, Bart or Marge from The Simpsons; Peter or Stewie from Family Guy; Bugs Bunny, and so on. (Alternatively, participants can choose a different cartoon character they are familiar with.) We then ask participants to close their eyes and experience the unhelpful thought for few a moments, this time "hearing" the thought in the voice of the chosen cartoon character. Participants are then asked to open their eyes and once again look at the thought in its original form and notice any impact. At the end of the exercise, we might encourage participants to discuss their experiences of this exercise in pairs before discussing in the main group.

Following this defusion work, it is not uncommon for participants to report an immediate change in relationship to unhelpful or difficult cognitive material. For example, some report taking a thought less seriously than they did before. Others report that the thought loses some of its meaning, menace, or power. This type of silly voice exercise also tends to generate some humor in the group that often serves a defusive function, with participants finding themselves chortling at thoughts that may have previously looked rather unpleasant set out on the page. During the discussions, the trainer should reiterate that we are not trying to remove or reduce the frequency of such thoughts, but to show it is possible to alter the way we react or relate to such thoughts when they do happen to show up.

Having experimented with many different defusion techniques over the years, we have found this relatively simple set of exercises to be among the most efficient and effective for illustrating and promoting defusion in our workplace programs. It is fair to say that defusion can be a rather confusing process. When ACT is delivered in one-to-one in therapeutic settings, such confusion might itself be harnessed in the service of increasing the client's psychological flexibility, but in brief training programs it can prove frustrating and counterproductive. One of the advantages we have observed with the exercises described above is that they help participants "get the gist" of cognitive defusion and quickly grasp the basic function of this important ACT process. Moreover, our participants often report using the comic voices technique outside of the sessions when they notice themselves becoming influenced by unhelpful thoughts. Another advantage is the versatility of this practice. For example, in session 2, we focus on applying the cartoon voice technique to any thoughts that have the potential to interfere with valued action; in session 3 we might repeat the exercise, this time encouraging participants to practice the same technique with other types of cognitive material, such as worry or self-critical thoughts.

Physical Demonstration of Fusion/ Defusion and Watching Your Thoughts Exercise

Despite our preference for the defusion practices above, it is worth considering some other exercises that we have seen working well in ACT groups. The first involves the trainer taking participants through a physical demonstration of what we mean by "untangling oneself" from unhelpful thought content. Here we use a technique adapted from one described by Harris (2009). Participants are asked to write one or more of their unhelpful thoughts in fairly large letters on a transparent sheet (the ones that were used by university lecturers of a certain age before the emergence of PowerPoint. If transparencies are unavailable, a sheet of plain white paper can work just as well.). If the thoughts do not fill up most of the sheet, participants are asked to simply write the word "thoughts" in various places and sizes on the transparency (and should some participants prefer not to share specific thought content, it is fine to simply have the word "thoughts" written several times across the sheet).

To illustrate the experience of being fused with thoughts, participants are asked to begin by holding the thought transparency very tightly in both hands, right up close to the face, so that it's almost touching the nose (the trainer does the exercise at the same time to demonstrate). Participants are asked to peer out at the world and at each other *through* these thoughts. The trainer asks participants to describe what this experience is like. The trainer might highlight some of the costs associated with becoming so embroiled in thoughts:

- From this perspective, it's difficult to notice that we are simply having some thoughts; we lack that level of mindful awareness.
- The thoughts we become this entangled with are likely to automatically influence our behavior.
- It's more difficult to connect with other people or engage effectively with the world around us.
- We may miss many opportunities for pursuing valued goals and actions that are unfolding in the world around us.
- From this perspective we are looking out at the world *from* or *through* these thoughts.

The trainer then invites participants gradually to move the thought transparency away from their faces and to hold it a little less tightly and at a slight distance so that the contents can now be more clearly viewed, and the person is no longer so embroiled in whatever is written on the sheet. Participants are asked to notice and describe any difference between the two perspectives.

The trainer can then suggest that this is what it is like to develop mindful awareness of thoughts—creating some healthy psychological distance so that we can observe thoughts for what they are. The trainer might suggest that "this is some of the healthiest psychological space we know of." From this new perspective, it is possible to notice that we are in this moment experiencing thoughts and also have more awareness of the world around us. The thoughts are still very much there, only now they can be noticed as thoughts. In ACT parlance, strengthening mindful awareness gives us the ability to look *at* our thoughts more frequently rather than always looking out at the world *from* or *through* our thoughts.

Participants should be encouraged to make this shift a few times—holding the thought transparency up to their faces to portray themselves looking out from or through thoughts, and holding it at a slight distance to portray themselves looking at thoughts. A final point to make is that mindful awareness allows for greater personal choice and control over actions—when defused from thoughts, the person is able to choose whether or not to allow these particular thoughts to guide behavior.

In the final step of this demonstration, the trainer invites participants simply to allow the thought transparency to sit in their laps. This final move is designed to promote willingness to experience even unhelpful thoughts—a stance of allowing them simply to be present (Harris, 2009; Hayes et al., 1999). Participants can also be asked to notice how little effort and struggle is involved when "holding one's thoughts more lightly." We include this move to make it clear that untangling from thoughts does *not* mean trying to push them away or remove them. On the contrary, we are working here to foster greater metacognitive awareness of thoughts, no matter how undesirable or unhelpful they happen to be.

Thoughts on Screen Exercise

Various mindfulness exercises support defusion by inviting participants to notice the process of thinking as it unfolds in order to gain an experiential sense of the difference between this perspective and the more common experience of being wrapped up in thought content. These practices include watching each thought passing through awareness as if it were placed on a leaf floating gently down a stream or imagining thoughts on clouds as they drift across the sky (Hayes et al., 1999; Hayes & Smith, 2005; Zettle, 2007). Some participants will struggle with the imagery required for these practices, so in session 2 we sometimes introduce a similar "thought watching" exercise that invites participants to watch their thoughts as if they were being projected one after the other onto a blank screen—somewhat akin to being an audience member at the movies.

Prior to conducting this exercise we explain to participants exactly what is involved. Specifically, we say that the exercise will ask them to watch their thoughts for a few minutes—to take the stance of a curious and dispassionate observer noticing passing thoughts as if they were being projected onto the blank screen of awareness. Participants are informed that it is likely they will often find themselves being "sucked into" the content of their thoughts and will lose this perspective of being the observer. A key part of this exercise is to orient people toward noticing these two modes of relating to one's thoughts.

The trainer begins the exercise by asking participants to close their eyes and connect with sensations in the body (the usual introduction to a mindfulness practice). After a couple of minutes of body awareness, the instructions proceed as follows:

Trainer: What I'd like you to do now is to take the perspective of a nonjudgmental observer of your thoughts. Practice watching your thoughts as they arise, as if they are being projected, one after the other, onto the blank screen of your awareness [...]. Some thoughts might appear as words, some might appear as images; some thoughts might be clear; some might be vague. There's no need to try to control any of your thoughts, just sit back and notice whatever your mind happens to provide you with [...]. The aim here is simply to catch a glimpse of your thoughts *as thoughts* as they come and go in your awareness [...]. Sometimes you'll be sucked into the content of your thinking and lose the perspective of the observer. When that happens, just take a second to acknowledge what has happened, and then notice the next thought being projected onto your screen [...]. Practicing being aware of the flow of your mind's activity—as if your thoughts are being projected onto your screen [...]. You may even notice some thoughts about the exercise itself; and that is just the next thing your mind is giving you [...]. You may find that you drift off with thoughts quite often. That's absolutely fine. As soon as you notice you've drifted off, reassume the role of an observer, aware of your thoughts coming and going [...]. Just catching a glimpse of a few thoughts *as thoughts* coming and going in your awareness [...]. The aim here is to get a sense of what it is like to drift away with thoughts, and what it is like to take the perspective of an observer, just noticing thoughts coming and going [...].

This exercise may last for about five minutes or so. Participants will often report finding this type of thought-watching practice trickier than mindfulness of breath and body exercises. Nonetheless, even this brief practice will often have the desired effect; even when participants sense they were drifting away for most of the exercise, there are usually a few moments when they have caught a glimpse of the process of thinking and register the difference between the two experiences. Some participants find this mindfulness of thoughts exercise particularly powerful, and will be motivated to practice this as much as exercises that cultivate mindful awareness around breath and body.

During the exercise debrief, the trainer might make the link to the transparency demonstration of fusion/defusion, and particularly the distinction between looking at versus looking from thoughts. It is important to reiterate to participants that this type of practice is not designed to reduce, remove, or change difficult thoughts, but rather to strengthen the ability to notice thoughts *as thoughts*, without necessarily getting wrapped up in what they are saying or allowing them to dictate our actions. The trainer might also remind participants that mindful awareness of one's thoughts is a skill that develops with practice. The useful thing about this skill is that it can be developed by becoming the observer of *any* thoughts and at *any* time! That is, we do not have to wait for unhelpful or negative thoughts to show up to develop defusion. The message to convey here is that we cultivate this skill by becoming more mindful of thoughts in general, and we can then begin to apply the skill to reduce the extent to which unhelpful thoughts function as barriers to valued action.

Mindfulness of Mood and Emotion

The next training piece is aimed at enhancing participants' experiential *acceptance* skills. It is worth restating that these processes are not being targeted in isolation. Defusion and acceptance are functionally related processes within the ACT model, which is why we find it useful to organize them under the same theme of noticing and untangling from internal barriers to valued action. This in turn feeds into the broader purpose of gradually increasing the prominence of people's personally chosen values as a guide to goals and daily action.

The Physicalizing Exercise

We consider the physicalizing exercise to be one of the most important mindfulness practices in our ACT-based training. This exercise was originally borrowed from the Gestalt therapeutic tradition and was described in the first book-length account of the ACT approach (Hayes et al., 1999, pp. 170–171; or see Hayes et al., 2012, pp. 286–287). As our workplace program has evolved over the years, we have given this practice increasing attention and prominence. Although the physicalizing practice is likely to cultivate a number of ACT's processes (contact with the present moment, acceptance, self-as-context), we employ this practice primarily to help participants cultivate emotional acceptance skills. As with the defusion exercises described above, the physicalizing practice is presented to participants as an element of the ongoing mindfulness skills training, and as a method for reducing the extent to which momentary feelings and moods function as internal barriers to value-inspired behavior.

As you will see from the exercise instructions, the physicalizing practice explicitly aims at establishing a degree of psychological distance between the person and his or her emotions, sensations, and/or moods. The guidance we provide for this exercise has two steps. First, participants are asked if they are willing to elicit, and open up to, a slightly more difficult emotion, and to notice any emergent feeling as a cluster of physical sensations occurring somewhere in the body. Second, the exercise encourages participants to *objectify* the feeling/sensation they experience during the practice by imagining it as though it were a physical object "out there."

Physicalizing Exercise Instructions

Before conducting this exercise, the trainer explains what participants will be asked to do. Here's an example of this initial dialogue:

Trainer: The mindfulness exercises we've practiced so far have asked you to notice whatever thoughts and feelings happen to be showing up as you practice. For this next exercise, we actually need a little bit of feeling to work with. So, what I'll be asking you to do at the beginning of this exercise is to think of a situation, person, or event in your life that's a little bit stressful. This doesn't have to be a major life issue, just something that has been bothering you lately, something or someone that might bring up some feeling or reaction in your body when you think about it. So first of all, could you all take a moment to think about any slightly or moderately stressful event, situation, or person that you'd be willing to think about for this exercise? [Trainer gives participants a moment before continuing.]

Does everyone have something? ... Great. So, what I'm going to ask you to do for this practice is to close your eyes, get present in the usual way, and then think about this stressful event or situation that you've chosen. Then I'll ask you to practice using your mindful awareness skills to really notice what shows up *in your body*, particularly noticing any reactions in your body—noticing any mood or feeling as a physical sensation somewhere in the body. I'll ask you to pay attention to whatever shows up, without pushing it away or trying to make it feel any different. I'm then going to ask you to imagine any feeling/sensation you've noticed as if it were a physical object—as if it placed outside of you for a moment. Shall we give it a try?

[The trainer goes on to guide participants through the exercise itself.]

Trainer: Sit yourself upright in the chair. Nice and dignified, but not too rigid [trainer demonstrates]. Relax your shoulders and jaw. Gently close your eyes, and start becoming aware of the sensation and position of your body sitting here in the chair ... noticing your posture ... noticing the position of your head on top of your shoulders ... now broaden your awareness to notice all the many sensations throughout your entire body right now ... from the top of your head to the tip of your toes ... like developing a strong sense of your entire body sitting here in this chair, in the present moment ... and now narrow your awareness to your tummy as you breathe in and as you breathe out ... noticing the physical sensations in your tummy as you breathe ... each time your mind drifts away to other things, returning your awareness to current sensations in your tummy ...

I would now like you to think about the stressful event, situation, or person that you've chosen for this exercise; allow yourself to think about your challenging or stressful situation for a few moments ... really "go there" in your mind ... really put yourself in the situation ... and, as you do this, become aware of any changes in your body ... do you notice any particular physical reactions in your body as you think about this event or situation? ... If you do notice a particular reaction or feeling, become aware of it *as a physical sensation* ... become aware of exactly whereabouts in your body you experience this feeling or sensation ... perhaps draw an imaginary line around the sensation to identify exactly whereabouts in your body it sits ... even if the sensation or feeling is unpleasant, just notice it for a moment for what it *actually* is—a physical sensation—not something you have to get rid of or struggle with ... bringing some curiosity to your feeling or sensation, as if you haven't noticed it in this way before ...

Still thinking about the stressful event or situation you've chosen for this exercise, what I'd like you to do is imagine that your sensation or feeling is now a physical object that has popped out of you and is now sitting there on the desk in front of you ... if this sensation or feeling *were* a physical object, what kind of shape would it take on? ... what would it look like? ... What color would your feeling object be? ... What kind of texture would your feeling or sensation have if it were an object? ... If the object could move, how fast does it look like it could move? ... How heavy does it look? ... Just imagining for a moment this feeling or sensation as if it had physical properties ... What would this sensation or feeling look like if you could step back from it like this ... [slightly longer pause] and now I'd like you to *welcome back* your feeling object, back inside your body where it belongs ... and once again spend a few moments identifying whereabouts in your body you experience this sensation ... where is it in your body exactly? ... *what* is it exactly? ... just experience your feeling as a physical sensation, nothing more and nothing less ...

once again draw an imaginary line around the feeling you are experiencing to identify where it sits in your body ...

And now, shift your awareness back to current sensations and movement in your tummy as you breathe in and as you breathe out ... and then expand your field of awareness from the sensations in your tummy to the sensations throughout your entire body ... again developing a strong sense of your entire body in the present moment ... I'll bring the exercise to a close in a moment; before I do, take a moment to congratulate yourself on taking the time out today to practice being mindful of feeling and sensation ... and getting ready to come back into the room ... remember whereabouts in the room you are sitting ... and imagine what you will see when you open your eyes ... whenever you feel ready ... open your eyes and come back into the room ...

Physicalizing Exercise Debrief

It is common for participants to have an insightful experience during this practice. A few participants might report experiencing little or no reaction during the exercise. In response, the trainer should acknowledge this as a common experience as well, and remind participants that they can practice this same exercise again in the comfort of their own homes.

To open the postexercise discussions, the trainer might say something like this:

Trainer: Thanks for practicing this mindfulness of feeling and sensation exercise. Did anyone notice any reaction showing up inside their body when thinking about something a bit difficult or stressful? ... And perhaps even "see" that experience take on the form of some object?

Participant: I did. I'm angry about a work situation, and I could feel that anger as I started thinking about it.

Trainer: Good stuff, Pam. And whereabouts in your body did you notice your anger?

Participant: It was in a lot of different places ... but mostly right here in my chest. It felt like a burning and bubbling sensation here in my chest [participant indicates where the emotion was felt]. Like hot stuff trying to burst out. Then it crept up into my throat and it felt like my face was getting hot ... felt like my face was glowing bright red!

Trainer: Great. Sounds like you really noticed your feeling as physical sensations. And when I asked you to imagine this feeling or sensation as a physical object, did it take on any particular form?

Participant: That was weird because it looked like how it felt. I imagined this rapidly spinning ball of fire; it was like lava—you know, like you see in those films about volcanoes or close-ups of the sun? But quite tight and small and intense.

Trainer: This is really good. Anything else you noticed?

Participant: I wasn't happy with you when you asked us to take it back inside! I wanted to leave it out there! [Other participants chortle and nod in agreement.]

Trainer: Yes, that's never one of my most popular instructions! What was it like inviting it back inside?

Participant: I suppose it wasn't that bad in the end. I still felt it at the end when you asked us to refocus on our tummies. I can still feel it now sort of around here [Pam indicates the part of her body where she feels the sensation] ... like there's some of it left over.

Trainer: This is great. Thanks, Pam, for sharing that interesting experience—very useful. Just becoming a bit more mindful of an emotion or feeling—noticing it for what it actually is, noticing in the body. Even if a feeling is a bit unpleasant, not fighting with it; just noticing where in our bodies we experience it. Anyone else notice their body reacting when thinking about something a bit stressful?

It is worth noting how the trainer is responding to Pam's experience with this exercise. Pam is describing an internal state she finds somewhat undesirable, and the trainer is responding with some gentle yet unmistakably positive comments such as "Good stuff," "Great," and "This is really good." On the page, such comments might suggest that the trainer is lacking in empathy! However, these responses make sense within the context of this type of training. The trainer is generally looking to cultivate a stance of willingness to experience even difficult private events in the service of actively pursuing values. The trainer's positive responses are not directed to the content or tone of the emotion being experienced—that is, the trainer is *not* saying to Pam, "Good stuff, I'm glad you're angry!" but rather responding appreciatively to the way Pam was relating to her emotional material as part of the exercise. Because these responses are consistent with the general theme of the training, Pam instinctively knows that's what the trainer is referring to.

When gathering people's experiences with the part of the exercise that invites participants to imagine a feeling as a physical object, the trainer might refer to the distance that is being cultivated between the person having the feeling and the feeling itself. A visual demonstration usually works better than a purely verbal description. Thus, the trainer might this time simply use his or her hands to represent an emotion being experienced. The trainer holds both hands so that they are covering his or her entire face. This posture indicates how we often become embroiled or entangled in emotional content. The trainer then explains that the physicalizing exercise helps us to cultivate some "healthy psychological distance" between the conscious person here experiencing this emotion and the emotion itself. The trainer illustrates this distance by gradually moving his or her hands (i.e., the emotion) to a comfortable distance from his or her face. The emotion is still there (the trainer wiggles his or her fingers); it's just that the person now has a different, more mindful, perspective on it. Now the person notices the emotion for what it is (a cluster of physical sensations unfolding somewhere in the body), and the emotion is less likely to have an automatic or unhelpful influence over that person's behavior. Just to reiterate, we are not trying to dampen or change undesirable emotional content with the physicalizing exercise, but rather encourage our participants to adopt a more mindful and accepting perspective on their emotional material.

Before taking the group into some further values-clarification work, it is useful for the trainer to offer a straightforward summary of the mindfulness and acceptance practices that have just been completed. Although we have introduced a number of experiential exercises in this segment, they are organized together within the mindfulness skills training component. Becoming more mindful of thoughts and feelings has been pitched as a general skill that can be employed more specifically to notice and untangle from internal barriers to values-based action. To organize these exercises and consolidate learning, the trainer can refer again to the two-skills diagram and/or employ the two sheets of paper technique to remind participants that these exercises are ultimately designed to enhance our ability to use personally chosen values as a primary guide to action.

When using the two sheets of paper technique in session 2, the trainer might emphasize that the skills being cultivated are designed to increase our ability to engage in personally valued behaviors *while in the presence of* a range of unhelpful thoughts, feelings, moods, and sensations. Stated another way, the combination of mindfulness and values-based skills helps us to act on our values even when the mind is giving us reasons not to, and even when we don't feel much like it. In this way, the propensity for the passengers to have an unhelpful influence over the movement and direction of the bus is diminished.

Part III: Values-Based Goal and Action Planning and Preparing for Home Practice Assignments

In the final phase of session 2, we encourage participants to define personal values and identify a series of values-based goals and actions, using the same handouts that were used in session 1 (we leave out numerous copies of these handouts in each session for participants to work on and take away). The set of values-based exercises found in this segment of the training includes the following three steps:

1. Define values in at least two areas of life (preferably different areas from the value that was defined in session 1).

2. Set some suitably specific short-term, medium-term, and long-term goals that would help to bring one or two values to life. Participants are particularly encouraged to set four short-term, value-based goals they are motivated to achieve over the next four weeks (part of the home practice assignments).

3. Select a further three value-based actions that can be performed mindfully over the next week.

We aim to allow around twenty to thirty minutes during session 2 for participants to self-reflect on personal values, capture one or two values in a few key reminder words, and identify value-consistent goals and actions. As we discuss further below, this work naturally feeds into the home practice assignments recommended for the practice period between sessions 2 and 3.

Defining Values

To prepare participants to construct additional personal value statements, the trainer can again provide a brief overview of some of the distinctive features and potential benefits of the valuing process. Participants might be asked to revisit their top 5 values identified during the card sort described in session 1. As in the previous section, participants are then encouraged to construct a longer value statement that details the personal qualities and strengths they most wish to express in their behavior over the long term, and then to identify a smaller number of perhaps three to five value "reminder" words.

Perhaps the most commonly expressed confusion about the values exercises relates to the distinction between values and goals. It is therefore often helpful for the trainer to show some examples, or go through the goal and action plan process with one of his or her own values on the board or flip chart. When referring to presented examples, the trainer can continue to highlight important aspects of this behavioral process. It is useful to convey the message that values are effective and empowering when they are *personally chosen*. Values are less likely to be personally meaningful and motivating if they reflect what a person feels he or she "has to" do because other people demand or expect it. The trainer might also take participants through an example that demonstrates well-constructed goal and action statements. Goals and actions should be designed to bring the value to life. They will also ideally be time-bound, situated, and specific (Hayes & Smith, 2005). We say a bit more about this further below, once participants are ready to shift from defining values into values-based goal and action planning.

It is recommended that the trainer also take steps during this phase of the training to manage participants' expectations about pursuing values. For instance, it is worth communicating to the group (if it hasn't already come up) that no one is expected to be value-consistent all of the time. Rather, the cultivation of values-based action skills is designed to help participants gradually increase the prominence of values as a guide to daily action and ensure that one's life goals are linked to some overarching purpose and are personally meaningful. Part of this process involves learning to notice when one has strayed from a valued path and—without becoming embroiled in self-criticism—becoming adept at regularly reorienting oneself in a valued behavioral direction (Luoma et al., 2007). One of the originators of ACT, Kelly Wilson, describes valued living as a "lifetime of many gentle returns" to a valued behavioral path (Wilson & DuFrene, 2010, p. 133). Managing expectations in this way helps to ensure that participants do not start feeling "oppressed" by their values or give up on the valuing process as soon as they notice they have engaged in some value-inconsistent behavior. The hope is that participants will come to experience values as a flexible, always available, and empowering guide to behavior and life goals (and not as a set of rigid rules or "commandments" about how they should or shouldn't behave; Harris, 2009).

As noted above, it is useful if participants are able to define values for a different life area than the one they focused on during and after session 1. However, there is no need to be prescriptive about this; it can be equally useful for some participants to take another opportunity to define and manifest the same value (or another value in the same life area) that they were working on in the first session. While expanding valued behavioral activation across a range of different life areas is a desirable outcome, the main priority at this stage is for participants to make contact with one or two motivating values and to become aware of what it is like to use a value as a behavioral guide outside of the sessions.

Translating Values into Goals and Actions

Once the trainer senses that everyone in a group has had time to define at least one value, participants are encouraged to begin translating one or two values into a series of goals and actions (again using Handout 2, "Values, Goals, and Actions Worksheet," presented in chapter 5). The central message to be conveyed is as follows: To bring personal values to life, it is essential to translate them into specific goals and actions.

We spend a bit more time focusing on the process of effective goal setting in this second section (we skipped over this process in session 1 to concentrate on ensuring participants were able to translate a value into three fairly immediate actions). The key piece of advice is to make sure goals and actions are value-consistent, sufficiently specific, achievable, action-oriented, and time-bound. To support this process, the trainer might also mention the widely used SMART acronym for goal setting. The acronym encourages goals that are Specific, Measurable (or Meaningful), Achievable, Realistic, and Time-bound. To ensure that more immediate actions are adequately specified, we adopt a technique from behavioral activation that encourages participants to detail the *who* (or with whom), *what*, *where*, and *when* of each valued action—captured by the simple acronym *wwww* (Kanter et al., 2009).

For some participants, there may only be enough time to complete this goal and action planning process for one value within the session. This is not a problem, as the trainer is focused on ensuring that participants get a good sense of the key features of this process. Once participants have got the gist of the steps involved in values work, they can be encouraged to complete these same exercises on their own to clarify additional values and sets of goals and actions. As noted previously, we find it is sensible to start small so as not to overwhelm participants.

Handout 6, the "Values, Goals, and Action Map," conveys the essence of this behavioral process in a visual format. In this map, the value is represented by the squiggly line running diagonally up the center of the page. The twists and turns in the value line are deliberate, as they illustrate that actively pursuing a valued direction is not always a straight path. Sometimes, the person might have to double back or take a little detour. However, when stepping back and looking at larger patterns of action and goals over time, it is easy to see the general direction being pursued. The rectangular boxes on the map are designed for participants to record their individual valued actions—each box could contain another small step along the valued path. The empty "scrolls" are designed for participants to record value-based goals they wish to aim for along the way. Participants can be encouraged to divide this map into time segments of their choosing. For example, three evenly spaced vertical lines drawn down the page creates four sections to represent (say) the next four weeks.

The map can be used to convey a number of relevant points. The value is the central feature—it is the guiding principle that serves as the basis for generating meaningful and purposeful goals and more immediate actions. Once a value has been adequately defined, the setting of specific and attainable goals will help to initiate and maintain a person's movement in the valued direction. The actions (and the broader patterns of value-linked action created over a period of time), whether small or large, pleasant or unpleasant, easy or more challenging, are likely to possess greater meaning and purpose by virtue of being guided by the underlying value. In line with the ACT approach, it is the ongoing process of pursuing values that is the primary focus. In this way, goal achievement is not viewed as the be-all and end-all, but rather as a pleasant by-product of pursuing a valued life direction (Dahl et al., 2009). To put that another way, valuing from an ACT perspective is much more about the journey than the destination.

It is not essential that every participant complete one or more of these value-based action maps during the session. We tend to present this type of handout to the group as an alternative that might prove useful to those who prefer a pictorial overview of the behavioral skills that are being cultivated. Some of our participants have indicated that a visual representation of valuing provided at this point helped everything "fall into place."

Home Practice Assignments

As noted in chapter 4, we have designed the program to leave a break of a few weeks between the second and third training sessions. This time interval is designed to give participants the opportunity to begin transferring the two skills to daily life before returning for the final session to discuss and consolidate any progress.

The values-based action exercises described above are designed to lead naturally into a discussion of the home practice assignments for the period between sessions 2 and 3. The first home practice assignment is a repeat of the value-based action exercise participants were encouraged to complete after session 1. Specifically, participants are invited to engage mindfully in three value-based actions over the next week. These actions should be selected by the participant from those identified in the preceding exercise.

As shown on Handout 7, "Home Practice 2: Between Sessions 2 and 3," the instructions for this practice are the same as before, with emphasis placed on mindfully performing personally valued actions. Specifically, participants are asked to notice what happens before, during, and after engaging in valued actions, and to notice any internal barriers that show up in the form of unhelpful thoughts, feelings, sensations, urges, moods, and so on. Hence, even if an intended value-guided action is *not* performed on schedule, participants are encouraged to become aware of any private events that seem to be influencing their behavior. This ensures that the suggested home assignment has a "win-win" quality. If participants actually engage in value-derived actions, they are invited to notice the experience and consequences of that process. If participants do not complete actions, it is another useful opportunity to become aware of any "passengers" that are having an unhelpful influence over behavior.

The second recommended home assignment is for participants to achieve four value-inspired short-term goals that have hopefully already been recorded on the earlier goal-setting handout (and perhaps also on the value-based action map shown earlier in the chapter). In addition to these specific recommendations, participants should be encouraged to continue working on each step of these exercises on their own, constructing value statements for all five life areas detailed in the handouts, identifying key value reminder words, and translating all values into specific goals and actions. It is useful to provide each participant with a pile of blank values-based goal and action planning handouts for this purpose.

At this point we would also offer advice to participants on other more informal mindfulness techniques. These techniques include becoming more mindful of eating, drinking, walking, driving, and other routine activities, and the useful practice of bringing mindful attention to the body at frequent intervals throughout the day.

The third home assignment is for participants to continue practicing the guided mindfulness exercises. The specific recommendation is for participants to practice one of the two "core" exercises (mindfulness of breath or mindfulness of body and breath) at least three times per week before the final session. In addition, we encourage participants to practice the cartoon voices and physicalizing techniques outside of the session and to bring mindful awareness to various routine activities.

When discussing these exercises, it is useful for the trainer to reiterate some of the key features of mindfulness practice. This summary could include a reminder that the exercises are not designed to change or avoid unwanted thoughts and feelings; it might also include encouragement to keep practicing even if they don't find some practices enjoyable and regardless of whether they notice any change or benefits. Mindfulness is again described by the trainer as a "psychological muscle"—it develops naturally with repeated practice.

Setting Up Environmental Reminders

As in session 1, participants are encouraged to set up reminders for home practice. The aim is to have some kind of sensory cue that will help to elicit value-guided action and offer a regular reminder about engaging in mindfulness practice. The same set of resources are made available. The trainer can offer some suggestions here, such as writing value reminder words, goals, or actions on the colored key fobs and attaching them to one's keys; placing small stickers on a cell phone or bathroom mirror as a reminder to practice; or wearing one of the silicone wristbands as a frequent reminder to use values as a more prominent guide to behavior over the next few weeks. If there is time available, participants can be invited to get into pairs to make a public commitment to achieving a value-consistent goal they hope to achieve by session 3, and also to share the reminder strategies they intend to use.

Ending the Session

The trainer brings the session to a close by warmly thanking participants for their willingness to engage in the various exercises that have been introduced and by expressing appreciation for the progress that is being made. To help participants organize the training material, the trainer can refer once again to the two-skills diagram. Participants should be strongly encouraged to use the period between now and session 3 to try out these skills in daily life. Finally, the trainer might emphasize the importance of returning for session 3, which focuses on further strengthening the same two skills, and on ensuring that any progress continues after the training has been completed.

Summary of Session 2

Session 2 of this program includes some important defusion and acceptance interventions that help to reveal how ACT's mindfulness and values-based actions processes are related. We have included a number of different intervention options in this chapter. It is not essential that all of these strategies be covered in the session; in fact, trying to squeeze in too much will only overwhelm participants, even if there are up to three hours available for this work. What is most important is that key interventions are being woven together to produce a coherent theme that emerges out of the sessions. Hence, in this session, we offer defusion and acceptance exercises as ways of helping us untangle ourselves from internal barriers to valued action. By the end of session 2, we hope that participants have been able to identify at least a couple of motivating behavioral values. The home practice assignments are then set up in a way that encourages participants to explore the experience of using those values as an increasingly prominent guide to daily action over the next few weeks.

CHAPTER 7

Training Session 3: Consolidating Mindfulness and Values-Based Action Skills

The third and final session in this protocol might be described as a "booster" session. As discussed in the program overview in chapter 4, we have found that varying the timing of the final session has little impact on the overall improvements in mental health, behavioral functioning, and psychological flexibility that employees obtain from this type of training. The longest gap we have left between sessions 2 and 3 is three months. We have also successfully delivered the same training with shorter gaps of one month, six weeks, and two months and have to date observed no significant impact on participants' experiences of the program.

The final training session serves a number of useful functions. By this stage of the intervention, many participants will already have made good progress toward developing a combination of mindfulness and values-based action skills, and the third session helps to consolidate and build on that progress and encourages participants to generalize the skills to additional life areas. Similarly, for participants who have lost experiential contact with the purpose of the training since the second session, the final session typically provides a well-timed opportunity to reconnect with ACT's core processes.

The third session is designed mainly as an opportunity for further rehearsal of exercises that have already been introduced, such as basic mindfulness training, the physicalizing exercise, defusion exercises, mindfulness of thought, and values-based goal and action planning. As participants are by now usually familiar with the program's basic rationale, we tend to use session 3 to provide one final "dose" of experiential practice. Hence, session 3 usually contains less didactic presentation from the trainer. Instead, the session is made up of a series of experiential practices linked together by the prominent organizing tools—the two sheets of paper technique, "passengers on the bus" metaphor, and the two-skills overview diagram. In this chapter we also consider some other ACT intervention options (such as the milk exercise and taking the mind for a walk) that might be employed in this final session.

Training Phase		Key Interventions
PART I		
Welcome back		Two-skills diagram
Opening mindfulness practice		Mindfulness of body and breath
Home practice review		Pairs and group discussion
Assessing value consistency		Self-reflection on value-consistent and -inconsistent actions over the past two weeks
PART II		
Mindfulness of thought and feeling		Thoughts on clouds exercise; physicalizing exercise; contacting the resilient "observer" perspective
PART III		
Values-based goal and action planning		Short-term, medium-term, and long-term values-based goal-setting exercise; value-based action map
Recommendations for continued practice		Home practice handout; top tips for building a valued life
Final personal reflections on the training		

Part I: Opening Practice and Review of Home Assignments

Session 3 begins with the trainer warmly welcoming participants back to the training. The trainer refers to the two-skills diagram to remind participants of the two interrelated skills that are being targeted. The trainer might also communicate the importance and general aim of this final session:

Trainer: I'm delighted you've been able to come back for the final session. It is such an important session because it will give you an opportunity to reflect on any impact the training has had so far and hopefully help you further integrate these two core skills into your everyday lives. We'll use the time today to try some of the key exercises again, and we can also discuss some useful strategies for keeping things going once the training has ended.

Mindfulness of Body and Breath

Following the opening introduction, the trainer guides the group through a mindfulness body and breath practice. We tend to employ the same exercise that was employed at the beginning of session 2: beginning by cultivating mindful awareness of the body, anchoring awareness to the sensations and movement in the abdomen with each breath, and noticing and allowing the rise and fall of thoughts and feelings during the practice. Following the practice, participants can be invited to share their experiences with the exercise and reflect on any practice that has occurred over the last few weeks.

In this final session, we find it useful also to provide participants with a much briefer mindfulness practice that takes just one or two minutes (or less) and can be performed "anytime, anywhere." The brief exercise we offer our participants is adapted from the three-minute breathing space found in MBSR and MBCT programs (e.g., Chaskalson, 2011; Segal et al., 2002). We refer to the exercise as "three quick steps to mindful awareness" and provide participants with the following instructions (we usually practice the exercise once in this final session, and provide these instructions as a handout):

Step 1: Pull yourself out of automatic pilot and contact the present moment

Take a moment to check in. How are you feeling right now? What sensations are you experiencing in your body right now? What thoughts are you having right now?

Step 2: Narrow your awareness to your breathing

Bring the spotlight of your attention to the physical sensations and movement in your tummy as it rises and falls with each breath.

Step 3: Expand your awareness to the entire body

With a broader awareness, notice all the sensations occurring throughout your entire body; develop a strong sense of your entire body in the here and now.

Home Practice Review

As in session 2, the trainer should facilitate a review of the mindfulness and values-based action home assignments. In the final session, this often takes the form of a more general discussion of how things have been progressing in relation to the training over the past few weeks. It is not uncommon for participants to report some notable and "ACT-consistent" benefits at this stage, as they get the gist of combining mindfulness and valued behavioral activation processes in their daily lives. We begin with a focus on the extent of mindfulness practice outside of the sessions before reviewing people's experiences pursuing value-guided goals and actions.

Mindfulness Home Practice Review

This review tends to extend naturally from the discussion of the in-session mindfulness practice. By the third session, many participants will be reporting that they have been getting into the habit of practicing guided mindfulness exercises a few times each week or using some of the briefer mindfulness exercises to contact the present moment on a more frequent basis. It is usual for participants to report noticing some benefits as a result of continued practice. One of the most commonly reported changes we hear in session 3 takes the form of reduced "reactivity" to undesirable inner events. It is useful when participants share such experiences with the rest of the group, as those who have practiced less (or not at all) get to hear that it is still worth making the time to do so.

The trainer's task is to offer some reinforcement for any informal or formal home mindfulness practice that has taken place and reflect on the benefits being reported. As before, a useful strategy for the trainer is to harness contributions from the group to reiterate the key features and functions of mindfulness skills. The trainer should also emphasize the importance of continuing to practice after the training has ended. Participants are encouraged to keep practicing and applying the skills in daily life, regardless of whether they've already noticed any benefits, and regardless of whether they enjoy doing it. The trainer might also take this opportunity to remind participants of other ways of cultivating mindfulness, such as becoming more aware of one's daily activities and getting into the habit of using the three-step exercise described above to activate present-moment awareness several times during the day.

Values-Based Action Home Practice Review

For the values-based action home practice review, the trainer first invites participants to get into pairs to discuss the five reflection points listed below. These are similar to the points that were used for the same purpose in session 2. This time, the discussion is extended to valued goals as well as actions. Also, emphasis is placed entirely on *internal* barriers to valued goals and action, and participants are encouraged to reflect on these aspects of the valuing process over the last four weeks:

- Whether you were able to achieve the four values-based goals you set for yourself in session 2
- The ease/difficulty of pursuing values-based goals and actions
- Any consequences of taking or not taking values-based action—consider any impact on yourself or others
- Any internal barriers (unhelpful thoughts, feelings, urges, or moods) that almost or actually got in the way of your pursuing values-based goals and actions over the past four weeks
- Your general impression of this practice of deliberately using behavioral values as a guide to life goals and daily action

Once participants have had the chance to reflect on these points among themselves, the trainer elicits a general group discussion with a question such as "So, I'm curious about your experiences using personal values as a more prominent guide to goals and actions. What sorts of things have you noticed over the past four weeks?" Although one can never predict exactly what will come up, it is common in the final session for participants to report the following types of experiences:

- Not being so reactive to difficult internal states
- Increased motivation to engage in actions that have been put off or procrastinated over

- Greater engagement in activities that were previously deliberately avoided
- Clearer sense of the personal importance of particular life areas and activities

Here's an example of a participant ("Sophia") reporting a change in behavior in session 3 that has been noticed by others in her life. In this extract, we haven't included all the dialogue but instead have highlighted the participant's report of an apparently psychologically flexible response in a difficult situation. Sophia is describing how she responded during a difficult interaction with an extended family member at a recent wedding:

Participant: I sensed my husband flinch next to me when she said what she did. I felt the usual reaction inside, I was really seething, as I think anyone would. But for a change that was okay. It didn't ruin the day for me. I didn't let that take over. I sat there sort of serenely noticing what this person does to my insides but not engaging with her. I hardly said anything—just looked at her, hardly even nodding; then I changed the subject and said something about how nice the hotel was........And the funniest thing was my husband sitting there staring at me openmouthed! He couldn't believe I didn't do my usual thing of taking the bait and then getting upset for ages afterward. I told him it was because I'd been doing this training!

Trainer: Thank you for sharing that example with us, Sophia. It's like music to my ears hearing this sort of thing in the final session! The key thing for me is that you say you *noticed* that you were seething inside, yet chose not to act on that on this occasion. Sounds to me like you employed a nice combination of mindfulness and valued action skills.

We include this extract because it reveals a frequent and important facilitation task for the ACT trainer. During group discussions, it is not unusual for participants to provide a lot of background detail about situations in which they have been applying these skills. The trainer's task is to spot elements within each contribution that suggest a degree of psychological flexibility. As in the example above, the trainer can draw the group's attention to that particular part of the contribution while at the same time reinforcing the participant's psychologically flexible response.

Other comments we hear in the final session indicate that the training has successfully reduced experiential avoidance. Consider these two comments that came from different participants. In both cases, the participants were talking about activities that had previously been avoided because of their anxiety-provoking potential:

> "I've started drinking coffee again."

> "I was able to watch a film at the cinema with my boyfriend for the first time in a long while."

Assessing Value Consistency

An important part of values work involves asking people to reflect on the value consistency or inconsistency of their recent patterns of behavior. ACT's values exercises and rating scales typically ask people to rate: (1) the importance they attach to a particular value in their life at this moment in time (say, on a scale of 1 to 10); and (2) how effective, successful, or consistent they have been at pursuing that value over the last week or few weeks (e.g., Wilson, Sandoz, Kitchens, & Roberts, 2010). A high discrepancy between value importance and value consistency can indicate a particular value or life area that is being neglected.

We employ a similar strategy in the final session of our workplace program. Handout 8, "Assessing Value Consistency," has been adapted from one developed by Kirk Strosahl and Patricia Robinson for their ACT workbook for depression (Strosahl & Robinson, 2008). We have made some minor changes to their original handout to reflect the language we use in our training and to extend the focus to the five life areas found in our other values exercises.

We particularly like this exercise because it goes beyond a simple numerical self-rating of value consistency and invites participants to think about and record specific patterns of action that show the most consistency with a value and specific patterns of action that are less consistent with that same value. This approach is useful for raising participants' awareness of which actions are serving their values and which are not. From an ACT perspective, an awareness of discrepancy between a personal value and behavior may itself motivate participants to take steps toward greater value consistency (Dahl et al., 2009).

It should be noted that this is not necessarily an easy or comforting exercise for participants to complete. Some participants will feel satisfaction while completing the handout as they become aware of a degree of congruence between their values and behavior. However, the exercise also confronts people with the fact that many habitual behavioral patterns can be incongruent with personally chosen values. It is not uncommon for participants to report feeling sad, shocked, or disappointed that they spend a lot of time doing things that are not in line with important personal values.

Thus, part of the trainer's role when facilitating this exercise is to normalize such experiences. Our own approach has been to use the exercise to further manage people's expectations about valued living. We reiterate the point that no one can be value-consistent all of the time. Rather, the aim of the training is to become gradually more effective at using values as a guide in daily life. The trainer can encourage participants to view valuing as a way of living a vital, meaningful, and purposeful life—as an ongoing process rather than as an outcome.

It is recommended that the trainer work on the exercise at the same time as the group. At the end of the exercise, the trainer can hold up his or her completed form to show that it is normal (and indeed useful) to notice patterns of action that are less consistent with values. The trainer can highlight the benefits of becoming more aware of which of our daily actions are serving our values. With this awareness, a person can deliberately and gradually expand patterns of personally valued action while reducing those patterns of action that are less consistent with values.

We have found it most useful to employ this value consistency assessment to wrap up the review of values-based actions and goals home practice in session 3. Toward the end of the review, we encourage participants to complete this assessment for one or two of the values they defined and worked on during and after the last session. The trainer can be explicit about what the exercise is designed for. The specific aim is to become more aware of behavioral patterns that are consistent or inconsistent with personally chosen values. The broader purpose is gradually to increase the prominence of values as a guide to daily action.

Another tool for assessing value consistency is the bull's-eye exercise (Lundgren et al., 2012), which gives a useful visual representation (with participants making marks on a target) to indicate how consistently a person has been pursuing values. A version of the bull's-eye also appears in Harris (2007). It is a useful tool because participants get to see a representation of values in each area of life in the same figure.

Troubleshooting

One issue that often arises during values work involves participants reflecting on values conflicting or clashing—the difficulty of bringing all values to life when life is already full of other demands and activities. There are various ways to deal with this that have been discussed by ACT authors (we particularly recommend a book on how to navigate values conflicts by McKay, Forsyth, & Eifert, 2010). Our preferred response is not to encourage participants to rank values in order of importance, but to work on the basis that values may be equally important. The secret of building a valued-based life is then to skillfully and flexibly look out for opportunities to take action on other values in small ways, even when one particular life area, such as work or family, has to take priority during some periods. It is useful to remind participants that the size of an action is not the most important thing—it is the degree of value consistency that counts.

Part II: Mindfulness of Thought and Feeling

Following the home practice review, the trainer shifts attention back to ACT's mindfulness and acceptance processes. This next part of the session includes exercises designed to rehearse and strengthen acceptance and defusion skills, along with a practice designed to highlight a resilient and stable "observer" perspective on one's constantly changing inner experiences, or self-as-context. As in the previous session, these processes are presented to participants as psychological skills that can be cultivated and used to reduce the extent to which unhelpful thoughts, moods, and feelings interfere with the pursuit of personally valued goals and actions.

The trainer presents the rationale for this next phase of the session in the usual way—by using the two sheets of paper technique:

Trainer: [Utilizing the two sheets of paper technique. One sheet contains the word **VALUE**. The other sheet has the words **UNHELPFUL THOUGHT/MOOD/FEELING.**] So, let's touch base again with what we're doing here. Essentially, this whole training is designed to give you the skills to do this [trainer moves VALUE sheet further to the front]—gradually increasing the role of personally chosen values as a guide to goals and daily actions. We can't simply remove our unhelpful thoughts and feelings. What we can do is develop greater mindful awareness of the unhelpful thoughts and feelings and moods that can be powerful internal barriers to increasing patterns of values-based action. Essentially these skills give us the ability to engage in valued actions even while we are experiencing a range of difficult or simply unhelpful thoughts, moods, or feelings.

> So just like last time, I'd like us to practice a couple more mindfulness exercises today that strengthen our ability to untangle a bit from this internal stuff when it shows up.

In this final session, we typically extend the two sheets of paper technique to communicate the notion of *willingness* that lies at the very heart of ACT (Harris, 2009; Hayes et al., 2012). Hayes et al. (2012) define willingness from an ACT perspective as "a values-based choice to expose oneself to an unpleasant thought, emotion, memory or sensation or to feared situations." (p. 276). In other words, willingness refers to a person's propensity to engage in ongoing and increasingly expanding patterns of personally valued action, even when that action is eliciting a host of difficult or unpleasant thoughts, feelings, and other internal states. It is important to note that we are not referring here to some kind of passive resignation or "grin and bear it" toleration (Hayes et al., 2012). Instead, behavioral willingness and psychological acceptance should be viewed as active and empowering processes. These processes can, for example, allow a person to step into an anxiety-provoking situation in the service of pursuing a valued goal while relating to the unfolding anxiety in a mindful, defused, and nonjudgmental way.

We do not use such technical language when conveying this behavioral process in our group interventions. Instead, we simply extend the two sheets of paper dialogue to communicate that these skills are designed to help us remain open to whatever inner experiences show up during the process of living a value-guided life. In this final session, it is not unusual for participants to recognize the freedom and possibilities inherent in this approach. If difficult internal states no longer represent significant barriers to the pursuit of valued goals and actions, then many more behavioral choices and options become available to the individual.

Mindfulness of Mood and Emotion

The trainer begins this segment with the physicalizing exercise that was introduced in session 2 (see chapter 6). The exercise helps to convey the message that the training is not seeking to help participants control, change, or avoid difficult emotional experiences but rather to relate to emotional content in a more mindful way. The exercise is practiced just as it was in session 2, with participants first asked to think of a mildly stressful event, situation, or person that may elicit some feeling or bodily reaction. Participants are then invited to notice any emergent mood or feeling at the level of physical sensation within the body, fostering a more nonjudgmental stance on what may be a somewhat uncomfortable feeling or sensation. The exercise also invites participants to relate to an emotional experience as though it were an object, thus cultivating some healthy psychological distance between feeler and feeling. The exercise is debriefed as before, with participants invited to share their experiences and with the trainer offering a straightforward summary of the function of this type of practice.

Mindfulness of Thoughts

The same basic rationale—developing the skills that help us to untangle from internal barriers—is carried forward into the next exercise, which is designed to build on the defusion work conducted in the previous session. Whereas the physicalizing exercise was offered as a specific technique for developing mindful awareness of mood and emotion, the next exercise is offered as a way to develop mindful awareness of thoughts. At this point, we tend to employ another meditative exercise (observing one's thoughts as if they were placed on clouds drifting across the sky) that serves the same function as the thoughts on a blank screen exercise.

The thoughts on clouds exercise has two aims: (1) for participants to observe their thinking in the moment as an ongoing process, catching a glimpse of thoughts *as thoughts*; and (2) for participants to get an experiential sense of the shift between observing thoughts and becoming hooked by thought content. This exercise does not have to be lengthy (a five-minute practice is often sufficient). The preamble to the practice is important. It helps for the trainer to explain to participants what the exercise involves and what to expect (that is, that they will often drift off into thought content and lose the observer perspective and the flow of the exercise). The exercise begins with some brief awareness-of-body instructions before continuing with the instructions below. We have borrowed and slightly adapted these "watching thoughts on clouds" instructions from an exercise presented by Zettle (2007, p. 146):

Trainer: And now imagine that it's a lovely warm day. The temperature is just how you like it. Imagine that you are lying comfortably on your back in an open field watching soft white clouds as they gently drift across the blue sky. I want you to use this image to assume the role of an observer of your thoughts as they drift in out of your awareness. There's no need to try to control any of your thoughts, just sit back and observe whatever your mind happens to provide you with […]. As you lie there, imagine that each thought your mind gives you is being carried by its own cloud as it moves slowly across the blue sky […]. Catch a glimpse of your thoughts as they come and go, with each thought attached to a cloud that's drifting across the sky […]. From time to time you'll probably drift off into thoughts and lose the flow of the exercise. That's to be expected. Whenever that happens, just back up a little, return to your position lying in the field, and watch the next thought that comes up being carried by on a cloud. Simply observing the flow of your thoughts as they drift by on clouds […]. You may have thoughts about the exercise—just place those thoughts on clouds and watch them drift across the sky […]. Notice how easy it is to drift away *into* thoughts and lose that sense of being the observer of your thoughts as they come and go […].

Toward the end of the exercise, the instructions invite participants to bring their awareness back for a couple of minutes to their physical sensations and abdominal movement while breathing, and then finally to broaden awareness to sensations throughout the entire body. Right after the exercise, the trainer invites participants to share their experiences in pairs or small groups before eliciting a few examples from the group for discussion. The following extracts show how the trainer might respond to different experiences with this exercise:

Trainer: Would anyone be willing to share their experiences observing the flow of thinking?

Participant 1: I find that one a bit more tricky than focusing on what's happening in my body. I think I sometimes got to place a thought on a cloud; and then I'm thinking, "Oh, was that a thought?" "Is that a thought?" It's a bit of a mind twister! Then I had this ... almost like a revelation ... after something you'd said—where I was like, hang on, these are *all* my thoughts, I'm observing all these thoughts!

Trainer: Excellent stuff, Daniel. Thanks for that. I like the way you describe the watching your thoughts part of the exercise. It can be tricky to be mindful of our thinking, but I sense you've done exactly what the exercise asks. Just taking a slight psychological step back so that you observe the process of thinking as it happens. Did anyone else also find that one tricky?

Participant 2: I felt I was sitting here watching a film of the clouds and sky. I do like this one. I was a bit surprised by the thoughts that appeared on my clouds. At first, I saw some thoughts that were about the way I was breathing, and then for some unknown reason I was thinking about those long-life bags you get from the supermarket! So I put the image of one of those bags on its own little cloud! I have no idea where that came from ... I think I might have been reading about that the other day.

Trainer: Some great work there—stepping back a bit to observe your thoughts. I like the way you say it's as if you're here watching a film. Instead of always being so wrapped up in the content of our thoughts, just observing them as thoughts drifting in and out of awareness. The mind is like a "thought-generating machine"—pumping out all sorts of stuff all day long.

While many participants respond well to the image of clouds moving across the sky, some participants will find the imagery component much more challenging. It is not uncommon for participants to report struggling so much with the cloud/sky image that they didn't catch much of a glimpse of the flow of their thinking. In response, we would suggest that such exercises are tricky rather than effortful, purely because of our tendency to be hooked by thought content. We would also suggest that the observer perspective can be strengthened with regular practice. If a participant is clearly struggling with the imagery requirement, the trainer can suggest making more use of other mindfulness practices, such as just noticing and allowing thoughts while cultivating awareness of the body and breath, or using the somewhat simpler practice of watching thoughts being projected onto a screen introduced in session 2.

Despite the challenging nature of cultivating mindful awareness of thoughts, we find that the earlier mindfulness work has usually given participants sufficient grounding to benefit from this exercise. In fact, as noted earlier, some participants will show a preference for the "thought-watching" exercises and will continue to practice them on a regular basis.

Highlighting the Resilient "Observer" Perspective

There is one ACT process that we have not yet directly targeted: self-as-context. As noted in chapter 2, self-as-context (also referred to as the "observing self") refers to our ability to contact a somewhat transcendent sense of self as the stable observer of our constantly fluctuating inner experiences (Hayes et al., 1999). In a manner of speaking, the observing self refers to the conscious "space" or "place" from where we humans notice our experiences. Although we haven't explicitly cultivated this ACT process up to this point in the program, it's not difficult to see how it has been accessed through the mindfulness practices that are conducted across all three sessions. For instance, the thoughts on clouds exercise described above encourages participants to observe somewhat dispassionately the flow of thinking, and participants may come to learn that this is a perspective that is always available to them. In fact, most mindfulness exercises can be easily adjusted or extended to cultivate this observing sense of self simply by encouraging participants to notice that they are able to step back and observe their constantly changing thoughts and feelings ("notice that you are able to take this perspective of being the observer of your thinking"). While thoughts, feelings, and sensations are constantly changing, the observing self is a constant and unchanging aspect of our psychological experience.

During our workplace programs, we have taken to describing the observing self as a highly "resilient" perspective or aspect of ourselves.

We say this perspective is resilient because it is not in any way threatened or harmed by negative or unpleasant thoughts, emotions, moods, or sensations. There is always a danger that participants will attempt to overanalyze this process, so we find it useful to tack observing-self instructions on to the end of one or more of the other mindfulness practices. In fact, in session 3, we use the idea of the observing self to suggest that this perspective is gradually being strengthened by ongoing engagement in the various mindfulness exercises that have already been introduced. This perspective might be physically portrayed by revisiting the transparency exercise that was used to illustrate defusion in session 1. The trainer can show that cultivating mindful awareness of thought and emotion naturally encourages us to adopt more frequently the role of the observer of our fluctuating internal events.

We have also often employed an abbreviated version of one of ACT's meditative exercises (the observer exercise), which is specifically designed to help people make experiential contact with this resilient sense of self (Hayes et al., 1999; Hayes et al., 2012, pp. 233-237). This exercise can be employed as a one-off, or the basic instructions can be tacked on to the end of a couple of the other mindfulness practices (such as the one at the start of this session). We employ it as an augmented mindfulness exercise that encourages participants to bring awareness to body, breath, feeling, and then thoughts, and to assume the stance of the observer of these aspects of experience. Here's a sample of the instructions we use to cultivate this perspective (some of these instructions have been adapted from a version of the observer exercise developed by Harris, 2007):

Trainer: [continuing from an exercise that opens with the cultivation of mindful awareness of bodily sensation] And as you notice your body, also notice that there are two things going on here. There's your body with all its sensation; and, there *you* are, the conscious observer of your body. Your body is constantly changing. It started out as a baby and it will continue to change as you progress through your life. Yet despite all these changes to your body, the part of you that observes your body remains a constant presence. There's your body, and there *you* are, the observer of your body. Take a moment to notice that you have this perspective of being the observer of your bodily sensation...

These basic instructions are then extended to observing current feelings inside the body, and finally to observing the flow of thinking. At the end of the exercise, the trainer concludes with the following:

Trainer: So, you are much more than just your body, your feelings, your thoughts. These things are the content of your life, while you are the conscious observer of these ever-changing experiences.

The exercise can be debriefed in the usual way, by inviting participants to share their experiences with the practice. If we haven't used these observing-self instructions before now, we make a point of communicating that we are not introducing anything new, merely pointing out the resilient perspective that is already being cultivated. The rationale for this type of exercise is the same as before—helping participants build the skills that can then be applied to untangle oneself from internal barriers to the effective and consistent pursuit of personally valued goals and actions.

Alternative Options for Session 3

The final session we are describing here is weighted in favor of various mindfulness practices. There are, however, a number of other intervention options that could be used in place of some of these practices. Different techniques should be considered if the more meditative work seems in any way excessive, or if a number of participants in the group are falling asleep during the eyes-closed practices. As noted in the previous chapter, in this final session we often repeat the cartoon voice defusion technique, this time encouraging participants to practice the technique with other types of cognitive material, such as worry or self-critical internal dialogue. We also outline below two alternative defusion-oriented intervention strategies that we have used successfully in our workplace programs over the years. One technique offers an extension of ACT's well-known "milk, milk, milk" word repetition exercise, and the other utilizes the "taking your mind for a walk" exercise (both exercises can be found in Hayes et al., 1999, 2012).

Rapid word repetition has the effect of revealing the direct properties of a word (e.g., its sound), while the word's indirect properties (its literal meaning) dissolve into the background (Hayes & Smith, 2005). In ACT, the traditional word used for this exercise is "milk," but other words can be used with similar effect. Participants are first asked to say the word "milk" once, to report the meaning the word brings to mind, and to imagine some of the properties of actual milk (e.g., imagine how milk tastes and smells). Participants are then invited to repeat the word "milk" out loud fairly rapidly for about one minute. When we have conducted this exercise in groups it usually has the desired effect. That is, after repeating the word, participants often notice that the meaning of the word disappears (if not, the trainer can ask the group what happened to the meaning of the word). The trainer can point out that while words (including the things we say to ourselves) will always have meaning, they are also ultimately just words and sounds.

To make this exercise more personally relevant we sometimes follow up the milk practice by asking participants to record any unhelpful thoughts in one or two words, write those words on a sticky note, and place the folded note anonymously in an opaque bowl that we place in the center of the room (the "defusion bowl"). The trainer does the same. The trainer then takes out two or three of the sticky notes and conducts the group as they repeat each word (or words) over and over again, perhaps at different speeds. This tends to unfold into a rather lighthearted exercise, but it does need to be delivered with some care so that participants do not feel offended or ridiculed by the process. When conducting this exercise, we always explain at the outset what is involved and make it clear that placing a thought in the bowl is entirely optional. Also, we tend to use this practice only when training small groups (say, three or four people), and where we are sensing a good degree of group warmth and cohesion.

Another exercise that is well suited to groups (and also promotes defusion) is the "taking your mind for a walk" exercise (Hayes et al., 1999; and see Hayes et al., 2012, p. 259). For this exercise, participants are asked to work in pairs or groups of three. One participant assumes the role of the person, while the other participant plays the role of the person's mind. The person and the mind then take a stroll outside for a few minutes. The person chooses the direction and may be encouraged to take one of the pocket compasses that were distributed in session 1 (to get a sense of pursuing a particular direction). The mind is instructed to do pretty much what minds do—offering a fairly constant stream of predicting, evaluating, comparing, judging, problem solving, worrying, encouraging, and so on. It's good if some of the mind's chatter is unhelpful (questioning the route being taken by the person, worrying about what might be around the next corner). The person is instructed to be mindful of the mind's almost constant chatter without responding or engaging—simply taking a series of steps in a direction of his or her own choosing. After five minutes, the participants change roles, with the other participant assuming the role of the person. This exercise can be usefully combined with mindful walking (becoming simultaneously aware of the sensations in your body and of your surroundings as you walk—all the time noticing that the mind is chattering away in the background). As part of this exercise, we encourage participants to relate to the mind's chatter as if it were a radio playing in the background.

Part III: Values-Based Goal and Action Planning and Tips for Continued Progress

We have now reached the final phase of the final session. We take this opportunity to encourage participants to contact another value, preferably in a life area they haven't yet worked on. The procedure is the same as before, with participants first constructing a value statement and boiling that statement down to a handful of key value reminder words; participants are then encouraged to transfer the value just defined to the values, goals, and actions summary worksheet (see chapter 5). On this sheet, participants are guided toward capturing a series of value-consistent goals, along with three valued actions that would bring that value to life over the next week.

When facilitating this exercise, the trainer can take a final opportunity to communicate some of the key features of values-based action, ensuring that participants have grasped the distinction between values and goals and that the values being constructed have a personally chosen and motivating quality. The trainer might also reiterate the key features of effective goal setting and action planning to encourage participants to identify specific, situated, and time-bound goals and actions. If leaving a long gap between the second and third sessions, there is no harm in kick-starting this entire process by repeating the values card sort exercise described in session 1. This can be particularly useful if some participants are still struggling to define their values.

Tips for Expanding Patterns of Values-Based Action

At this point the trainer communicates that the valued living journey has only just begun! The aim now is for participants to start building increasingly larger patterns of values-based action across different areas of their lives. To this end, it is helpful for the trainer to offer some "top tips" for maintaining and expanding on any progress already made (some of these tips were inspired by Dahl et al., 2009, and are distributed as a handout):

Continue Defining Your Values

Defining your values is not a one-off exercise; make use of the program's handouts to continue constructing and clarifying your most important values in every area of your life.

Keep Your Values Close

Find ways to keep your values prominent in your mind; otherwise, values have a tendency to drift into the background.

Have a Value-Based Day

Every so often, dedicate a whole day to a particular value; look for opportunities in your normal routine to engage in a series of small value-consistent actions. Notice what happens when you do this.

Take Some Bold Steps

Step out of your comfort zone from time to time in the service of your values; notice the passengers that show up when you do so.

Take Valued Actions in the Presence of Unhelpful Thoughts and Feelings

Recognize that your own thoughts and feelings do not have to be barriers to effective and consistent action.

Know That You Can Reconnect with Your Values at Any Time

You can't be value consistent all the time! When you notice you've strayed from a valued path, simply reconnect with a value and identify the next small value-consistent step you can take. Do not be oppressed by your values—use them as a vital and meaningful guide.

Recommendations on Continued Practice

Handout 9, Home Practice 3: Ongoing, the home practice summary sheet for the final session, repeats one exercise from the previous home practices (three valued actions to be performed mindfully over the next week) and recommends that participants complete the entire values-based action process once again on their own (ensuring values are adequately defined; generating a series of more specific values-based goals and actions; continuing to use reminders until values-based action becomes a habit). The rationale for these suggestions is that with a bit more practice values-based living can gradually become a habit—something that happens more spontaneously and naturally as behavior becomes more frequently influenced by personal values and less by unpredictable and perhaps unhelpful internal states.

This final home practice handout also provides another set of recommendations on continued mindfulness practice from this point onward. If we haven't already provided a list of recommended readings, we distribute a list of ACT and mindfulness self-help books at this point.

Summary of the Program

Before closing the session, we find it useful to return again to where the program started—by referring to the two-skills diagram. The trainer might communicate that research has shown that developing a combination of these core skills has been found to improve people's psychological health, behavioral effectiveness, and general satisfaction with life. The trainer should drive home the point that these are psychological and behavioral *skills*—they need to be practiced and they need to be used. Finally, the trainer might again touch on the ultimate purpose—to increase the prominence of personally chosen values as a guide to life goals and daily behavior. This has been done by defining values and developing mindfulness skills that improve our ability to untangle from internal barriers to valued action.

Final Personal Reflections

One way to conclude the program is to leave enough time for all participants to share the following: (1) any impact the training has had on their work or home lives so far; (2) what they will take away with them; and (3) in which areas of life they would like to apply these skills. These three points can be noted on the board or flip chart.

We have seen a wide range of different responses at the end of this type of program. Some participants simply get up and dash out with hardly a thank-you or good-bye. Other participants will be visibly moved that the training has come to an end and by what it has revealed to them, and some participants will stick around to express gratitude for having been given the opportunity to attend.

Summary of Session 3

Session 3 is designed to provide skill consolidation, hopefully getting participants to a place where they will continue to develop these skills and build increasingly larger patterns of values-guided actions. We often find that session 3 can be a particularly enjoyable experience for the trainer, as participants will usually have a good grasp of the basic rationale for the training and are now familiar with how the session unfolds. The trainer's dialogue can therefore be reduced, and he or she can concentrate on providing participants with another opportunity to practice some key exercises and prepare for further integration of the two core skills into everyday life.

CHAPTER 8

ACT Trainer Stance and Skills

In this chapter, we consider the facilitation stance and skills that trainers are required to adopt to deliver this type of program in an effective and ACT-consistent manner. Although the various interventions described in this book might appear on paper to be ACT-consistent, they can easily be implemented in a way that is incongruent with ACT's underlying principles. This is likely to happen if the trainer lacks intimate and personal experience with the interrelated processes that combine to produce psychological flexibility. Thus, a large part of learning the ACT approach involves applying ACT processes in one's own life, and to all of the interactions and challenges that unfold when delivering this type of ACT-based training program in workplace settings.

Many of the books on the ACT approach include chapters on ACT's therapeutic stance (see for example Batten, 2011; Harris, 2009; Hayes et al., 2012; Luoma et al., 2007). Although this guidance is geared mainly toward those applying ACT in individualized therapy settings, the same relationship stance is required when delivering ACT to groups (Flaxman et al., 2011). Regardless of where and with whom its technology is being applied, ACT has the potential to be a powerful and moving experience both for participants and for the therapist or trainer. Many of the messages being conveyed in ACT go against the cultural grain by encouraging participants to open up to even the most difficult private experiences in the service of actively pursuing a values-based life.

Thus, at the most basic level, becoming an effective ACT trainer requires the following characteristics:

- An intimate, experiential, and personal understanding of ACT's six interrelated processes
- The ability and willingness to create a warm, compassionate, equal, open, and respectful relationship with all members of the training group

These qualities are related, in that a personal familiarity with ACT's core processes naturally supports the development of compassion for oneself and the human condition. The ACT practitioner takes on the role of a fellow human being rather than that of an "expert." That is, trainers will frequently find themselves caught up in the same thought and language traps that are interfering with their participants' ability to engage in personally valued patterns of action. This aspect of the ACT approach can be harnessed to create warm and effective working alliances with training groups.

In this chapter, we outline some of these issues, focusing particularly on how each of the six core processes applies to the trainer (and to each and every interaction in the training room) just as it applies to participants. We also consider the equalizing effect of ACT interventions, as trainers assume the stance of "being in the same boat" as members of their training groups. Toward the end of the chapter, we provide an overview of an evidence-based ACT train-the-trainer initiative developed in Sweden that has helped to cascade the ACT approach to significant numbers of people outside of the traditional clinical arena.

The Psychological Flexibility Model Applied to the Trainer

In chapter 2, we presented ACT's unified model of psychological flexibility (see figure 2.1), which is presumed to apply across most (if not all) areas of human functioning. This model is applied not only to enhance participants' psychological health and behavioral effectiveness, but also to ensure the effectiveness of the trainer's facilitation stance and skills. The ultimate aim of the training described in this book is to enhance employees' psychological flexibility. As well as being the desired outcome, psychological flexibility also provides the context for this type of training. A trainer using this approach should seek to become adept at noticing, modeling, and reinforcing the six core processes found in this model. In the following sections, we provide just a few examples of how each of the six processes applies to the trainer's own psychology and to the interactions unfolding in the training room. For the sake of clarity we consider each process separately. However, it is important to remember that these processes are in practice intimately and mutually related.

Contact with the Present Moment and Mindfulness

Life is always lived right here, right now; there is nothing that can be directly experienced but the present moment. The abilities to consider the past and plan for the future are essential for humans and extremely helpful most of the time. Difficulties occur for us humans when we become excessively engrossed in the future or past, perhaps lost in worry or rumination, and thus lose contact with the present and the natural contingencies that life is offering in the here and now. ACT suggests that the problem isn't that we need to eliminate past or future thinking, but rather that we need to help people become more flexible—to be in the present when a present focus works best, to be in the future when planning works best, and to be in the past when remembering works best. A focus on the present is particularly important because that is where new learning occurs and where the value-oriented opportunities afforded by the environment are discovered (Luoma et al., 2007).

Whether you are a relative novice or an experienced ACT trainer, there is always room for improvement. If you learn to become more psychologically present as a trainer, you will develop greater sensitivity to what actually works with the group in front of you in the given situation (and will be in a better position to adjust your behavior accordingly). When you are here and now, you can notice and make use of internal and external events. As an example, if you as the trainer start to feel sleepy, or the session starts to seem lifeless or dull, it might be the case that the group is feeling the same, and it might be a good idea to change pace, change tone of voice, facilitate an experiential exercise, check in with the group, or take a break. When the trainer has lost contact with the present moment—perhaps entangled in thoughts about which intervention might come next—then it is much more difficult to recognize such experiences unfolding within oneself and out there in the training room.

As outlined in the protocol, we implement a number of well-known mindfulness practices to increase awareness of present-moment experience. Many of these practices are formally built into the structure of the sessions, for example, by facilitating a mindfulness of breath/body practice at the beginning of sessions 2 and 3. However, it is also useful for the trainer to become skilled at shifting the group's attention to present-moment experience during the natural flow of the session. For example, during periods when the training has become a little too logical or "wordy," the trainer might pause and say something like this:

Trainer: I don't know about you, but I'm getting a bit lost in all this conceptual chatter. Let's pause for a moment and come back to our senses. So, take a moment now to become aware of the sensations in your body as you sit there in the chair ... notice for a moment any sounds that are unfolding right now here inside the room ... and any sounds reaching you from outside of the room.

Because participants are being asked to practice mindfulness exercises outside of the sessions, it is critical that the trainer also engage in the same amount of practice. This means that the trainer can share his or her own experience when reviewing participants' engagement in the recommended home practices. It is easy to forget how difficult it is to fit skills practice into a busy schedule if you are not doing the same yourself!

Acceptance

Acceptance is probably the ACT process that is most easily misunderstood—acceptance from an ACT perspective does not refer to passive tolerance, giving up, or resignation. One key distinction to convey when working with acceptance is that there are things that can, and maybe should, be changed, while other things it is wiser to accept. There are a lot of things in the external environment we can influence to varying degrees, like identifying work-related stressors and modifying them, requesting a change in workload, working to improve (or end) relationships that are not enriching life in important ways. And there are other aspects of our experience where we do best in applying a degree of open acceptance; those are usually things that happen inside our skin—emotions, thoughts, memories, and sensations.

One of the trainer's main tasks is to model acceptance throughout the program. Some key interventions are particularly useful in this respect—a good example is the physicalizing exercise, which clearly conveys the message that we are not looking to change or remove unwanted internal states. To conduct this type of work convincingly, the trainer must be able to model a stance of willingness to experience difficult emotional content that arises during the pursuit of valued behavioral directions. If the trainer is experientially avoidant, this may manifest itself in the training in subtle and unhelpful ways. For example, if something a participant is saying elicits an emotion the trainer is personally unwilling to experience, the trainer may quickly change direction, seek a distraction, or "rescue" the participant, when pausing for a moment to recognize that there is emotion in the room may be the more effective option.

It is also important that the trainer understand how acceptance is related to the other core processes (particularly values). Acceptance is not cultivated for its own sake but rather as a strategy for ensuring that people's fluctuating emotions and moods (or attempts to avoid them) are not functioning as significant barriers to valued action.

Self-as-Context

This process is relevant to training skills in many ways. Self-as-context enables or facilitates many different experiences, including theory of mind, empathy, compassion, self-compassion, acceptance, and defusion. Your ability as a trainer to take the perspective of your participants is a very useful skill. Contacting the viewpoint of "I/here/now" that is inherent in contacting the oberving self naturally leads to the realization that this same perspective is available to others.

One way that self-as-context can sometimes create an obstacle for trainers is if we become overly attached to (or fused with) a conceptualized self as the "effective trainer." As an example, I might be fused with thoughts like "I am the trainer and professional here; I should have answers to all the questions; and I am here to give my participants something they do not have." Such attachments may impact negatively on the training if the trainer begins to modify his or her behavior in ways that are not necessarily helpful to members of the group but are instead aimed at defending, reinforcing, or avoiding a particular conceptualized self.

It might be true that we sometimes take on the role of trainer, and it is also true that this is just one of our many roles in life. Through flexible perspective taking we can become more authentic by acknowledging to ourselves that as well as sometimes performing the role of the trainer, we are also fellow human beings, struggling with the challenges of life. And the same goes for our participants. We all have a lot to gain if we can stay open to the fact that they are not merely "participants;" they are so much more. An effective way to view our participants might be to see them as unlimited, capable, and conscious beings with their own keys to the future they want.

Defusion

Becoming personally skilled at defusion can help the trainer in various ways. Defusion can ensure the trainer does not get unhelpfully hooked by his or her own thought content during a session and also ensures that the trainer keeps the focus on the function of participants' thoughts rather than on their literal truth or content. In ACT we are usually not that interested in whether what a participant tells us is literally true or not; we are usually more interested in what *function* saying or believing this has for the participant in the given context. To continuously perform functional analyses of our own "languaging" and the "languaging" of participants is usually one of the trickier things to get the hang of in ACT—probably because we are so well trained in allowing our behavior to be influenced by reason-giving, and less well trained in looking at the function of the particular "languaging" we are being influenced by.

The same goes for the role of the trainer. Even if you have read all the ACT books in the world, and you know that what you are saying to the group is 100 percent true in the sense that it is ACT-coherent, this is not what is most central. What is important, again, is function: Is what I'm working with now of help to my participants in increasing life skills and helping them to live more in accordance with the life they want to live? If not, it's time to be flexible, dance between the core processes, and consider other ways of working with the group.

In ACT, trainers are strongly encouraged to avoid arguing with, trying to coerce, or trying to convince participants. This is because we want participants to do things because they choose to themselves, and let their own experiences be the teacher, and also because trying to convince is usually not effective in helping others. In this respect ACT is similar to motivational interviewing (MI; Miller & Rollnick, 2002). ACT and MI can both be considered "contextual CBT" (Hayes et al., 2011). Among the common features of ACT and MI are that they are both focused on behaviors, and both recognize that change takes place within the context of a supportive and empathic relationship (Miller, 1983). Both MI and ACT support autonomy and assume people have the ability to make sufficient and necessary behavior changes. Another shared feature is that MI is very much about the function of language; in MI, the therapist wants to elicit "commitment language" on behalf of the client, since this directly predicts behavior change. To give an example, in MI you are not primarily interested in convincing a client about the "truth," such as trying to convince a smoker of the actual facts about the dangers of smoking. What is of interest is *function*: How can trainer and client most effectively use language in the process of creating behavior change that might benefit the client? If you are trained in MI, it can be useful to use those skills in your role as an ACT trainer.

As we noted in our training protocol (chapters 5–7), facilitating defusion work can sometimes be challenging, and trainers need to be prepared for some participants to find the process confusing. We have included some structured defusion techniques in the protocol (see session 2), but there are other ways of modeling defusion at opportune moments during a session. For example, given our earlier point about being careful not to coerce or lecture participants, the trainer might model defusion by saying something like this:

Trainer: Right now I'm noticing that I'm having a bunch of thoughts urging me to try to persuade you about how this exercise works. However, I know from experience that acting on those thoughts is not the most effective way to convey these skills.

Here the trainer models the "I'm having" prefix designed to promote defusion and also communicates the stance of noticing thoughts as thoughts without necessarily acting on them.

Values

When trainers are clear about their values, it is likely that those values will shine through in many small behaviors. For example, imagine a trainer who chooses to be guided by the value summarized as "having a generous, offering stance." By ensuring this value is psychologically present, the trainer might be reminded to share some personal examples when appropriate, to make sure the training room is nicely lit and well laid out and that he or she is well prepared for the session, and so on. In short, by contacting the value, the trainer is reminded of what he or she wants to be about in the training room, and this helps to identify and motivate a series of value-consistent behaviors.

One way to model values is to share your aims or purpose with the group at the outset. This could include an expression of gratitude that people have given up their time for the training, and an explicit commitment to your purpose, for example, "I really appreciate your effort in coming here today; you probably have loads of things to do and still prioritized these sessions. My aim is to do everything in my power over these three sessions to make this a highly valuable use of your time."

The trainer can then revisit his or her values frequently when conducting the training. Values self-reflection might take the following form: What do I want my work today to be about? Why did I start working with people and helping others? What would I like to give and share with the group? What effects would I like to see from the work I'm about to do with this group?

Committed Action

Ultimately, all of ACT's processes are marshaled in the service of helping people build larger and larger patterns of action that are guided by personally chosen values. The trainer's commitment to act on his or her training-related values can imply either persistence or change in behavior, depending on the situation. Hence, once in contact with what you want to stand for in your role as a trainer, it is useful to get in the habit of identifying and pursuing specific patterns of action that will help to bring the underlying value to life.

Self-Disclosure

As indicated in the preceding discussion, appropriate and well-timed self-disclosure has an important role to play in ACT-based interventions. Self-disclosure can help the process of normalization and often has the effect of equalizing trainer–participant relations. The trainer can provide personal examples in various places, perhaps by sharing one of his or her own values and publicly committing to completing valued actions between the sessions (just as participants are asked to do). It is also helpful for the trainer to share examples of unhelpful thoughts that have been (and perhaps still are) experienced as internal barriers to greater engagement in values-guided action. As noted above, it can also sometimes be beneficial for the trainer to disclose that he or she is noticing private experiences unfolding in the moment. This is a useful way for the trainer to model the mindfulness, defusion, and acceptance skills that are being cultivated throughout the program.

Humor

Humor is a surprisingly useful tool for ACT-based training. Humor can be relevant in all aspects of ACT work. Although we are often discussing serious issues that can impact people's quality of life, our sessions are also characterized by a great deal of laughter, tomfoolery, and camaraderie. It is a wonderful moment when a person who has been troubled by a certain self-referential thought starts chuckling after repeating that thought out loud in a strange voice as part of the defusion work or peers out at others in the group *from* that thought written in bold font on a transparency sheet.

Of course, humor does need to be used with care and should be adapted to fit the trainer's own personal style of delivery and the organizational culture in which the training is being delivered. Although we generally adopt a lighthearted tone throughout the training, there are still moments when we sense we have misjudged things, perhaps adopting a lighthearted response to a participant contribution when a more serious and validating response was called for. The trainer's use of self-deprecating humor is usually a safe option—it will often help to show that the trainer is a fallible human being who is dealing with much the same work and life challenges faced by the group.

ACT Train-the-Trainer Program

For those readers who already have some experience with ACT, we would like to highlight a very successful train-the-trainer initiative, led by Fredrik Livheim, which has been implemented in Sweden since 2008. Using this approach, some 400 new ACT trainers have been prepared and supervised in delivering their own ACT interventions. The majority of those trainers are now regularly delivering ACT workshops to thousands of people every year.

This train-the-trainer program is usually delivered over four days, spread out across one semester. One feature of the program that has been found to be especially helpful is that the trainers are asked to facilitate their first ACT workshops at the same time they are attending the course, so they are learning by doing.

It is reasonable to ask whether trainers new to ACT can learn to deliver an ACT intervention that produces observable positive effects in only four days. To investigate this we have (so far) conducted five randomized controlled trials in Sweden, where we measure effects on participants receiving this ACT-based training from trainers who are relatively new to ACT but have received our four-day training (see, for example, Brinkborg et al., 2011; contact Fredrik Livheim for information on other as yet unpublished studies).

The results of these studies are very encouraging. The ACT workshops delivered by this new army of trainers have produced a range of beneficial effects even when delivered by facilitators with only four days of training. Effect sizes are comparable to observed effects when ACT has been delivered by Flaxman and Bond (Bond & Bunce, 2000; Brinkborg et al., 2011; Flaxman & Bond, 2010b). We have also investigated if there is a difference when ACT is delivered by fully licensed psychologists or by master's-level students in psychology. The data suggest that the same outcomes are achieved even when ACT workshops are facilitated by master's-level students in psychology (Brinkborg et al., 2011; see also Lappalainen et al., 2007).

Experience Required to Train Trainers

In order to ensure adherence to the ACT approach and to ensure quality interventions, we strongly recommend that trainers of trainers be highly skilled in ACT generally and have some experience delivering ACT in groups. In Sweden, we have also trained new trainers of trainers. Our recommendations are based on those experiences.

Trainer Level of Education

We recommend that those training others to deliver ACT interventions have a basic degree in psychology or a related behavioral health subject. Those we have trained up to this point have all held at least a master's qualification in psychology with extensive training in CBT.

ACT Experience

If you are to start training other trainers, it is of course critical that you have extensive ACT experience. You need to be thoroughly familiar with ACT's core processes, ACT research, ACT's links to RFT, and so on, so that you can communicate this information and experience to the professionals you are training. Without this experience, there is a risk that ACT will become a package of separate techniques, metaphors, and exercises that are not used flexibly and as intended. As a trainer of trainers, it is important to be updated on research in the area you are aiming to work in. And the research base for ACT is growing rapidly. At the time of writing, we understand that there have been more than sixty ACT outcome studies (including around thirty randomized controlled trials) published in peer-reviewed scientific journals.

It is difficult to give exact recommendations on how much ACT experience is required by those looking to train other potential trainers. As a rule of thumb, we recommend that before taking on the role of instructor, it is desirable to have (1) facilitated at least ten ACT workshops for groups; (2) attended four or more experiential ACT workshops by recognized ACT instructors; (3) attended a couple of full training rounds in the specific ACT intervention to be delivered, with an instructor who has experience training new trainers; (4) read relevant textbooks, including *Learning ACT* by Luoma et al. (2007) and *Acceptance and Commitment Therapy* (2nd ed.) by Hayes et al. (2012); and (5) be updated on relevant ACT research.

Overview of a Four-Session ACT Train-the-Trainer Program

We lack the space to give a very detailed account of this train-the-trainer program. Instead we provide an overview of the schedule of activities below; readers can contact Fredrik Livheim for further details on setting up a course.

We have found it beneficial to have two instructors when training other trainers. The advantages to this approach are that the participants have two models to observe, and it is also more interesting to listen to two people during the four days of training. Moreover, by using two trainers we find we can train and supervise twice as many participants within the same program.

If you are to start training new trainers and do not have a web page, it is a good idea to create one. A web page can be used to advertise the training and is also a useful hub for providing course-related information and material to your participants.

Schedule of Activities

The time line shown below gives an idea of the entire train-the-trainer process. In Sweden we usually offer at least two full ACT trainings per year, one in the spring and one in the autumn (the example below is a spring schedule). The training days usually occur every second week:

- Advertise the forthcoming training (previous November)
- Last day to apply for training (January 7)
- Information to participants (January 10): Participants are notified about acceptance and sent preparatory materials and information about recruiting their own groups.
- Training—Day 1 (February 20)
    - Sort out practical questions.
    - Participants hand in answers to questions in precourse packs.
    - Overview of ACT, using the "hexaflex" psychological flexibility model.
    - Overview of research evaluating ACT as a group training program.
    - Discuss general ACT stance and skills.
    - Practice experiential exercises.
- Training—Day 2 (March 5)
    - Go through session 1 of the ACT program as if the group were made up of "ordinary" participants.
    - Be sure to model effective facilitation behaviors.
    - Discuss rationale for exercises and how they relate to ACT processes; discuss common pitfalls when delivering ACT to groups.
    - Supervision in smaller groups; one hour of supervision is usually enough at this stage, as participants are not yet leading their own ACT groups.
- Participants present session 1 (between days 2 and 3 of training). The participants give their first session of ACT-based training with their own group.
- Training—Day 3 (March 19)
    - Go through session 2 of the ACT program as if the group were made up of "ordinary" participants.

    - Supervision in smaller groups (two hours).

- Participants present session 2 (between days 3 and 4 of training). The participants give their second session of ACT-based training with their own group.
- Training—Day 4 (April 2)
    - Go through session 3 of the ACT program.
    - Supervision in smaller groups (two hours).
- Participants present session 3. Participants facilitate their last session of ACT-based training with their own group. It can be a good idea to have them deliver the last session up to three months after session 2.

We have found this format a very useful way of increasing the number of mental health professionals who are able to deliver effective ACT workshops to Swedish workers and to the wider population. The initial research findings are encouraging, suggesting that even relatively novice ACT practitioners can develop expertise by receiving this training while at the same time delivering ACT to groups of their own. The supervision component allows the new trainers to discuss their experiences and hear ACT-consistent responses to the most common challenges that arise when delivering ACT in groups in nonclinical settings.

Summary

There is a particular stance required when delivering ACT interventions, characterized by a humble, equal, and validating relationship with clients and participants. Perhaps the most important qualification for delivering ACT is that potential trainers show willingness to apply the ACT model to their personal and professional lives. Only then does the challenge of increasing psychological flexibility reveal itself, allowing a person to effectively communicate this approach to others.

Given the number of employees who would stand to benefit from greater access to ACT interventions, it is important to recruit and develop new trainers to deliver these interventions. The train-the-trainer program developed in Sweden appears to be a particularly efficient and effective method of developing ACT trainers in a relatively short time. It is hoped that a similar approach will be adopted in other countries so that ACT can reach a much larger proportion of the working and general population.

CHAPTER 9

Research Review

In this penultimate chapter, we present a summary of the research that has: (1) examined links between psychological flexibility and employees' mental health and work-related functioning; and (2) evaluated the effectiveness of ACT-based interventions delivered to working populations. This chapter provides an updated version of a review we contributed to Ruth Baer's book on mindfulness and acceptance interventions (Baer, 2010; Flaxman & Bond, 2010c). Although we have not conducted an exhaustive review of the available literature, we believe the studies summarized in this chapter provide evidence that the worksite intervention approach described in this book is effective and illustrates why we view the promotion of psychological flexibility among working populations as an important endeavor.

We have organized this chapter into three main sections. We begin by briefly reviewing the most commonly used measure of psychological flexibility. We then review research from various countries, involving a number of different occupational groups, that has shown psychological flexibility to be an important predictor of both well-being and performance-related outcomes. In the third and final section, we review the intervention research confirming the efficacy of the "2 + 1" ACT-based training program described in this book, along with studies that have documented the beneficial impact of other ACT-based programs delivered to working individuals.

Measuring Psychological Flexibility and Its Facets

The principal instrument for measuring psychological flexibility is known as the Acceptance and Action Questionnaire (AAQ; Bond & Bunce, 2003; Bond et al., 2011; Hayes, Strosahl, Wilson, et al., 2004). The traditional version of this scale (the AAQ-I) had short (nine-item) and longer (sixteen-item) forms, both of which have been used in the occupational health research reviewed in this chapter. More recently, Bond et al. (2011) validated the AAQ-II, an updated and improved measure of psychological flexibility, which has been used in ten-item and seven-item formats. To reflect the nature of psychological flexibility, both versions of the AAQ include items that capture a person's willingness to experience unwanted internal events:

> I try to suppress thoughts and feelings that I don't like by just not thinking about them. (AAQ-I)
>
> I worry about not being able to control my worries and feelings. (AAQ-II)

Both versions of the AAQ also include items that capture a person's ability to take action while experiencing unwanted internal events:

> When I feel depressed or anxious, I am unable to take care of my responsibilities. (AAQ-I)
>
> Worries get in the way of my success. (AAQ-II)

AAQ items are rated on a 7-point scale, ranging from 1 (never true) to 7 (always true), and the responses are then summed to create an overall score. Some research studies refer to the AAQ as a measure of experiential avoidance (or its opposite, psychological acceptance). To avoid any unnecessary confusion, throughout this review we refer to the AAQ using the more recent term: psychological flexibility (or its opposite, psychological inflexibility).

Reflecting the global interest in ACT, the AAQ has been translated into several languages, including Italian, Dutch, French, German, Hungarian, Japanese, Norwegian, Portuguese, Spanish, Romanian, and Swedish. All versions are available to download from the contextual psychology (ACBS) website: http://contextualpsychology.org/act_measures_in_languages_other_than_english.

In addition to using the AAQ as the primary indicator of psychological flexibility, researchers have sought to measure its subprocesses. For example, cognitive defusion has been measured with scales that ask respondents to rate how much they believe in the content of particular thoughts. This approach is consistent with the idea that ACT helps to "deliteralize" unhelpful psychological content so as to reduce the extent to which it functions as a barrier to valued behavior (Hayes et al., 1999). Similarly, some of the research reviewed below includes established self-report measures of mindfulness; and a few studies have included measures of values-based action, which ask people to rate how effective they have been at pursuing personally important values.

The Role of Psychological Flexibility in Occupational Health and Performance

A growing number of studies have found significant relationships between psychological flexibility and various employee and organizational outcomes. For example, Bond and Bunce (2003) conducted a longitudinal study to assess the influence of psychological flexibility on the mental health and work performance of over four hundred customer service workers within a financial services organization in the United Kingdom. Questionnaires (including the AAQ-I) were completed by these employees on two separate occasions, with a one-year time lag between them. Performance was measured by obtaining company records on the average number of computer errors made by each employee. Results indicated that psychological flexibility longitudinally predicted both mental health and work performance. The beneficial effects of psychological flexibility were observed even after controlling for other potentially influential individual and work characteristics, including job control, negative affectivity, and locus of control (see also Donaldson-Feilder & Bond, 2004).

In addition, this same study tested the hypothesis that psychological flexibility would interact with job control to influence employee well-being and performance. Job control is defined as the perceived ability to exert influence over one's work environment in order to make it more rewarding and less threatening. There are sound theoretical reasons for investigating interactions between psychological flexibility and job control. Employees high in psychological flexibility are viewed as less likely to waste their limited attentional resources striving to avoid or control undesirable thoughts and emotions (by, for example, engaging in thought suppression or avoidant behavior). With greater attentional resources at their disposal, psychologically flexible workers should be better able to notice when they have job control in any given work situation and can therefore learn how to utilize this control to take action that is consistent with their core values and goals. This enhanced capacity for noticing, and responding to, the goal opportunities that exist in one's environment has been referred to as "goal-related context sensitivity" (Bond et al., 2008). In support of this theoretical reasoning, Bond and Bunce's (2003) study showed that employees with higher levels of psychological flexibility gained the most benefits from having higher control over their work.

Bond and Flaxman (2006) investigated the degree to which psychological flexibility and job control predicted employees' ability to learn new skills at work. In this study, a large group ($N = 448$) of call center workers in the United Kingdom provided data on three separate occasions. At Time 1, participants completed questionnaires (including the AAQ-I) and had their performance on a new computer software program assessed. Soon after Time 1, these same participants attended a five-day training program focused on the new software. After four weeks of using the new software (Time 2), the same employees completed a customer service test (scores on this test provided an objective indicator of work-related learning). Finally, a further two months after the test (Time 3), participants completed a measure of mental health, and their job performance was assessed for the period following the training program. The researchers found that employees who had higher psychological flexibility showed the highest levels of learning at Time 2, and they also had better mental health and performance at Time 3. As with the previous study, psychological flexibility was found to enhance the beneficial effects of job control.

These links between psychological flexibility, job control, and employee well-being were further examined within the context of an organizational change intervention (Bond et al., 2008). Employees of a financial services organization took part in an intervention that was designed to increase job control. Questionnaire measures were administered prior to the intervention (Time 1) and again fourteen months later (Time 2). Absence rates for each participant were obtained from organizational records. The workers who had higher levels of psychological flexibility perceived greater levels of job control as a result of the intervention, and this enhanced perception of control led to superior improvements in absence rates and general mental health. These findings are again consistent with the view that psychologically flexible individuals have a greater capacity for noticing, and responding to, control and goal opportunities that exist in the work environment.

Whereas the studies reported above focus on financial services workers, researchers have also investigated the benefits of psychological flexibility, mindfulness, and values-based action among various other working populations. For example, Mitmansgruber, Beck, and Schüssler (2008) administered the AAQ to a group of 134 experienced (mostly voluntary) paramedics working for the Austrian Red Cross. Psychological flexibility explained 39 percent of the variance in these paramedics' psychological well-being and 11 percent of the variance in their life satisfaction. It is notable that in this study, the AAQ explained unique variance in paramedics' psychological well-being beyond measures of mindfulness and various facets of meta-emotion (which assessed people's reactions and attitudes toward their own emotions).

McCracken and Yang (2008) found psychological flexibility, mindfulness, and values-based action to be a powerful set of predictors of stress and general life functioning among a group of ninety-eight rehabilitation workers in Singapore. Their participants were drawn from various occupations including nurses, physiotherapists, occupational therapists, physicians, and speech and language therapists. When examined as a set, these three factors explained between 13 percent and 61 percent of variance on a range of indicators of mental health and social functioning. The AAQ was found to be the best-performing predictor for six out of ten indicators of employee well-being.

Finally, Vilardaga et al. (2011) examined the extent to which psychological flexibility (measured by the AAQ-II), a measure of cognitive fusion, and self-rated success at pursuing personally chosen work values predicted levels of burnout. Their participants were a large group (N = 699) of addiction counselors working across the United States. In support of the ACT model, psychological inflexibility, fusion, and less successful pursuit of values-directed action were all significant predictors of employee burnout. It is notable that these predictive effects were found after the researchers had accounted for the effects of a range of potentially influential work-related factors, including job control, coworker and supervisory support, workload, salary, and tenure.

Psychological Flexibility: A New Approach to Reducing the Adverse Impact of Emotional Labor?

An innovative strand of research has focused on the potential role of psychological flexibility in reducing the impact of emotional labor on service sector workers' well-being. This research is being led by Michal Biron (University of Haifa, Israel) and Marc van Veldhoven (Tilburg University, The Netherlands). This work has great potential for the understanding and promotion of employee well-being, given the predominance of service sector occupations in most developed countries.

The term *emotional labor* refers to the need for customer-facing workers to manage the expression (facial, verbal, and bodily display) of emotions in accordance with the requirements of the job. Think of an airline cabin crew member greeting you with that warm and friendly smile as you board and disembark from the plane. Of course, while maintaining his or her smile for each and every passenger, it is possible that the crew member will not be, in that same moment, experiencing "warm and friendly" feelings. As a result, researchers have found that customer service workers adopt certain types of strategies to manage the tension between displayed and actual feelings (e.g., Grandey, 2003; Zapf, 2002).

One emotional labor strategy, known as *surface acting*, has been linked to reduced employee well-being and the development of symptoms of burnout (particularly emotional exhaustion). The airline employee example above is suggestive of surface acting, as the worker may feel the need to suppress his or her felt emotions in order to simulate a display that customers (and indeed the employing airline) expect from someone in that job role (Biron & van Veldhoven, 2012). Such internal affect regulation strategies require psychological effort, which may over time lead to overdepletion of energy or other valued personal resources (Hobfoll, 2002).

Biron and van Veldhoven hypothesized that service workers with higher levels of psychological flexibility might have an alternative, and potentially more adaptive, strategy at their disposal. Specifically, psychologically flexible individuals are less likely to engage in the internal suppression of emotions and may instead be able to "make room" for even the more difficult feelings that arise from job demands while redirecting their energy and attention toward the task at hand and pursuing valued work goals (Bond et al., 2008).

To test these ideas, Biron and van Veldhoven administered the AAQ-II to a sample of 170 Dutch service sector workers employed in various not-for-profit industries, including health, education, government, and leisure. These participants then completed measures of emotional demands and emotional exhaustion across three consecutive work days. Consistent with their theoretical predictions, the researchers found that psychological flexibility was not only associated with lower levels of exhaustion, it also offered workers some protection from the detrimental impact of emotionally demanding work days. In contrast, and consistent with previous emotional labor research, the use of surface acting was associated with higher exhaustion at the end of each day and served to exacerbate the link between emotional job demands and exhaustion. These findings suggest that workers in emotionally demanding roles would benefit from ACT-based training, which (as we document below) has been consistently shown to increase employees' psychological flexibility.

Research Examining the Effectiveness of ACT-Based Training for Working Populations

In the final section of this chapter, we review a series of studies that have assessed the outcomes of ACT interventions delivered to working individuals. This review includes research that has evaluated ACT-based training programs delivered using the 2 + 1 format described in this book, as well as ACT interventions delivered in other formats, such as one-day workshops or via self-help resources.

ACT for Improving Employees' General Mental Health

Bond and Bunce (2000) published the first evaluation of ACT as a worksite training program. The study compared ACT ($n = 24$) with a waiting list control group ($n = 20$) and an innovation promotion training program ($n = 21$) designed to teach workers how to reduce work-related stressors at their source. Both training programs were delivered to small groups of employees using a "2 + 1" format (Barkham & Shapiro, 1990) involving three training sessions: two on consecutive weeks, with a third session three months later. Each training session lasted approximately three hours.

The ACT intervention was an earlier version of the three-session program described in this book. Bond and Bunce examined change on measures of general psychological distress, depression, and propensity to be innovative at work. These measures were administered before the training began, three months after the two initial training sessions, and a further three months following the third and final training session. The findings clearly showed the benefits of using ACT to improve employees' mental health. Specifically, at both postintervention measurement occasions, ACT participants showed significantly lower levels of psychological distress than those in the innovation training and wait-list control groups. ACT even resulted in improvements in innovation potential that were equivalent to those found in the innovation training condition. Consistent with ACT's theory of change, mediation analyses revealed that the improvements in mental health and innovation found among the ACT participants were explained by increases in psychological flexibility (measured by the AAQ-I) but not by changes in dysfunctional cognitive content.

In a more recent study, we compared a group of UK public-sector employees who had attended two sessions of ACT-based training (using a number of the strategies and exercises described in this book) with another group of employees in the same organization who had attended training based on Donald Meichenbaum's (1985) well-validated stress inoculation training approach (see Flaxman & Bond, 2010a). Three months after two half-day training sessions, both programs resulted in significant reductions in participants' psychological distress. The two interventions did, however, appear to produce their benefits via different mechanisms. Similar to the Bond and Bunce (2000) study, we found that the beneficial impact of ACT on employees' mental health was significantly mediated by an increase in psychological flexibility, and not by a change in dysfunctional beliefs.

In a related study, we examined changes in mental health among a larger group of UK employees who had attended three half-day sessions of our ACT-based training, comparing them to a group of their coworkers who had been randomly allocated to a waiting list to receive the training six months later (Flaxman & Bond, 2010b). As with the studies reported above, three half-day sessions of ACT-based training resulted in significant improvements in general mental health across a six-month evaluation period. Because this study involved a much larger sample of employees than our previous studies, we were able to assess the extent of change over time as a function of employees' level of mental ill health before they started the program. By far the largest improvements in mental health were found among a subgroup of employees who had the highest levels of psychological distress at the beginning of the study. In fact, we found that a majority (69 percent) of these initially more distressed participants who completed our ACT program experienced clinically meaningful improvements to their mental health. This finding is important, as it shows that the ACT-based training described in this book can deliver significant benefits to the high numbers of working individuals who experience a common mental health problem such as anxiety or depression.

Brinkborg et al. (2011) delivered a group-based ACT training program to improve the mental health of social workers in Sweden. The trainers in this study had themselves been trained as part of the ACT train-the-trainer program, developed by Fredrik Livheim, described in chapter 8 of this book. The ACT intervention was delivered to social workers over four training sessions, which occurred every other week. Each session lasted for three hours. Session 1 focused on stress, acceptance, and language; session 2 targeted values; session 3 focused on obstacles to valued behavior and on increasing flexibility; and session 4 focused on the development of compassion and on maintaining improvements. Participants also completed various home practice assignments and practiced mindfulness exercises. As a result of this intervention, a group of initially high-stress social workers experienced significant reductions in perceived stress and work-related burnout and significant improvements in general mental health. In addition, 42 percent of these participants improved to a clinically significant degree over the course of the study. This study is useful because it offers a rigorous demonstration of the effectiveness of Livheim's train-the-trainer model. A number of other (currently unpublished) intervention studies have found similarly beneficial effects of this training program for other occupational groups (contact Fredrik Livheim for further details of this Swedish research).

A particularly promising development in the occupational health literature concerns the use of ACT to reduce work-related burnout, which is typically characterized by emotional exhaustion, an increase in depersonalization (or cynicism) toward the people one works with, and ultimately to a reduced sense of job-related efficacy and accomplishment. Recently, Joda Lloyd, a prominent member of our London-based ACT research group, has developed a strong theoretical argument for the link between psychological flexibility and the burnout syndrome. In a recent study led by Lloyd, a 2 + 1 ACT workplace intervention led to a reduction in emotional exhaustion, which in turn protected employees from experiencing depersonalization (see Lloyd, Bond, & Flaxman, in press). Some of the other studies reviewed below also report reductions in burnout as a result of ACT interventions, and we foresee this becoming an important focus for ACT researchers and practitioners in future years.

ACT for At-Risk Workers

Whereas the previously mentioned studies employed no participant exclusion criteria, Dahl, Wilson, and Nilsson (2004) delivered ACT to a selected group of Swedish health care workers who were at risk for long-term work disability as a result of stress and musculoskeletal pain. This ACT intervention was delivered in individual rather than group format. These researchers employed an additive treatment design, in which health care workers were randomly assigned to one of two groups: medical treatment as usual (MTAU) ($n = 8$), which included visits to physicians or other medical specialists and physical therapy interventions, or MTAU plus ACT ($n = 11$). The ACT intervention was delivered via four one-hour individual sessions, conducted weekly at the worksite or in employees' homes. Dahl et al.'s intervention was designed around four ACT components: clarifying values, promoting cognitive defusion, encouraging goal-consistent exposure, and committing to patterns of values-based action. To reiterate, the aim was not to reduce stress and pain symptoms, but to increase employees' ability to pursue valued behavioral goals in the presence of these symptoms.

The two main outcome measures in this study were sick leave utilization (number of sick days), which was measured objectively, and medical utilization (number of visits to a physician or other medical practitioner). At posttreatment, the workers who had received four ACT sessions had a mean of one sick day over the past month, while those in the medical treatment only group took an average of 11.5 sick days. By the six-month follow-up, the difference between the two groups had widened considerably, with the ACT group averaging just one-half of a sick day across the follow-up period, in comparison to an average of 56.1 sick days taken by the medical treatment only group. In view of these differences, it is perhaps not surprising that the ACT group also paid significantly fewer visits to medical practitioners, with ACT participants averaging 1.9 medical visits during the six-month follow-up, compared to 15.1 visits in the comparison group.

Consistent with ACT theory, the superior functioning found among ACT participants in this study could *not* be attributed to a reduction in the frequency or intensity of difficult thoughts, emotions, or physiological sensations. To elaborate, although ACT reduced employee absence and medical utilization to a much greater extent than treatment as usual, there were no significant differences between the two groups in terms of impact on stress and pain symptoms. This finding suggests that ACT principally changed the way these at-risk employees were relating to their symptoms of pain and distress (Dahl et al., 2004).

ACT for the Enhancement of Addiction Counselors' Well-Being and Performance

Other research has focused on evaluating ACT as a method for enhancing the psychological health and job performance of substance abuse counselors. Counselors have been targeted for psychological intervention because of their propensity for burnout and because of the difficulties associated with learning and implementing new treatments designed for substance-abusing clients (Varra et al., 2008).

Hayes, Bissett, et al. (2004) investigated the impact of ACT on stigmatizing attitudes and burnout among counselors in the United States. Counselors were randomly allocated to attend an ACT intervention (*n*

= 30), a multicultural awareness program (n = 34), or an educational control condition that provided instruction on factors linked to the use of methamphetamine and MDMA, or "ecstasy" (n = 29). All three training programs were delivered via one-day workshops. Measures of burnout and stigmatizing attitudes were administered prior to the one-day workshops (pre), immediately after the workshops (post), and three months later (follow-up). To measure stigmatization, the counselors responded to items such as "A person would be foolish to marry someone who had a drug or alcohol addiction." As an indicator of cognitive fusion, the counselors rated the extent to which they believed various negative thoughts about clients with substance abuse problems ("My client is not going to change no matter what I do").

Counselors in the ACT group showed no change in stigmatizing attitudes at posttreatment (immediately after the training), but by three-month follow-up, they experienced significantly more favorable attitudes toward their clients (less stigmatization) compared to the counselors in the educational control condition. The opposite pattern was found for multicultural training, which resulted in a significant improvement in attitudes immediately posttreatment, but not at follow-up. Additionally, by the final assessment point, ACT participants had significantly lower levels of burnout than those in both the multicultural training and control conditions. Consistent with the ACT model of change, the beneficial impact of ACT on both burnout and stigma was mediated by a reduction in the believability of negative thoughts about clients—an indicator of cognitive defusion.

In a similar study, Varra et al. (2008) examined the utility of ACT for enhancing addiction counselors' willingness to use evidence-based pharmacotherapy. The aim was to determine whether a one-day ACT workshop delivered prior to a workshop on treatments for substance abuse problems would enhance adoption in practice. Sixty counselors were randomly assigned to the ACT workshop or to an educational control condition that involved instruction on addiction prevention and a presentation on leadership styles. Measures included counselors' use of pharmacotherapy, willingness to use pharmacotherapy, perceived barriers to implementing new treatments, and psychological flexibility (AAQ-I).

At three-month follow-up, counselors who had attended the ACT workshop were more likely to refer their clients for pharmacotherapy, reported a greater willingness to use pharmacotherapy, and had higher levels of psychological flexibility than the counselors in the educational control condition. Interestingly, the counselors in the ACT group perceived more barriers to using new treatments than the controls but reported a significant decrease in the extent to which they *believed* that these barriers would interfere with using or learning new treatments (an indicator of cognitive defusion). The reduced believability of barriers and increased psychological flexibility mediated the greater use of pharmacotherapy found among the counselors who had received the ACT intervention. Thus, helping counselors to defuse from psychological barriers to learning and adopting new evidence-based treatments appears to facilitate the integration of those treatments into practice.

ACT in Different Delivery Formats

The intervention research reported throughout this section has focused on the delivery of ACT to employees at the workplace. Researchers have also evaluated ACT interventions that have been delivered using different methods, yet still with evidence of beneficial impact on working-age adults. In this regard, we would like to highlight the excellent research conducted by Marine Fledderus and her colleagues in Holland. Fledderus et al. (2010) evaluated a group-based ACT intervention that was delivered in a public health setting. Participants were individuals experiencing mild to moderate psychological distress, 53 percent of whom were members of the working population. Their ACT-based program (known in English as "Living to the Full") was delivered over eight two-hour sessions and was designed around ACT's six core processes. By a three-month follow-up, this group intervention resulted in significant improvements in emotional and psychological well-being and in psychological flexibility. Consistent with the studies reported above, the improvements in mental health were mediated by increases in psychological flexibility (measured with the AAQ-II).

In another study Fledderus, Bohlmeijer, Pierterse, & Schreurs (2012) evaluated the impact of an ACT-based guided self-help program for members of the Dutch general population with mild to moderate levels of depressive symptomatology (76 percent of whom were in paid employment). Participants in this study received an ACT self-help book (Bohlmeijer & Hulsbergen, 2008), which includes nine modules based on ACT's six core processes. Participants were instructed to complete one module per week for nine weeks and received varying degrees of e-mail support each week from counselors. The book included an audio CD with guided instructions for ten to fifteen mindfulness exercises. The intervention resulted in significant (and in some cases statistically large) improvements on a wide range of indicators of mental health and well-being. These beneficial effects were maintained at a three-month follow-up. In addition, the self-help program resulted in significant improvements in both psychological flexibility and mindfulness skills during the course of the study.

Summary

There is now a convincing body of evidence demonstrating that higher levels of psychological flexibility are associated with a range of favorable worker and organizational outcomes. Moreover, several published intervention studies have shown that ACT interventions are able to elicit significant improvements in employees' general mental health. ACT has also shown potential for improving work performance indicators (such as innovation potential) and rates of employee absence due to illness. The consistency of the mediation findings is noteworthy, with a number of studies demonstrating that ACT produces its beneficial effects by increasing people's psychological flexibility. The processes of change observed in these workplace studies mirror those found among clinical populations, providing further support for the breadth of ACT's underlying model of human functioning (Hayes, Luoma, et al., 2006).

In this chapter we have reviewed only a selection of the earlier and recent ACT and psychological flexibility research involving working populations. We are aware of numerous other studies that are currently under way or that will be soon be submitted for publication. The emerging research includes qualitative evaluations of people's experiences with ACT interventions in the workplace, investigations of the links between psychological flexibility and workers' ability to recover during their leisure time, and an encouraging number of new studies indicating that ACT is an effective approach for preventing and reducing employee burnout. Moreover, ACT researchers and practitioners continue to apply ACT's intervention technology in new and innovative areas including leadership development, workplace safety training, career coaching, and social skills training. We review some of these innovative applications of ACT in our final chapter.

CHAPTER 10

The Evolution of ACT in the Workplace: The Leading Edge and Beyond

This book is focused on using ACT in a group format to improve mental health and behavioral effectiveness in the workplace. These two targets are, of course, also the principal ones for which ACT is used in individual and group psychotherapy sessions; indeed, the ACT strategies and techniques that we have described in this book were originally developed for psychotherapy. We have selected and shaped those techniques that our research and experience have demonstrated are among the most effective in workplace settings. It remains true, though, that these techniques and their strategic aims are largely a facsimile of their therapeutic counterparts. This need not be the case, however. Both ACT and the theory of language and cognition upon which it is based, RFT, provide significant potential for developing new techniques and intervention targets specifically related to the workplace. Efforts to do this are largely just beginning. Here, we describe some of this innovative work and indicate potential new horizons for applying ACT and RFT to the world of work.

Theory and Practice: Back to Basics

ACT is one example of a technology that derives from the basic theory of language and cognition specified in RFT. Although research has shown that it is an effective one, we would limit our ability to maximize change in people and, indeed, in organizations, if we limited ourselves to that one technology. By going "back to basics" to analyze teams, workplace communication, culture, and other organizational contexts from an RFT perspective, we may be able to devise a wider range of methods for producing change. For example, the notion of deictic frames, which involves perspective taking—people recognizing that there is an "'I" and "you," a "here" and "there," and a "now" and "then"—led Bond (2012) to develop a technique to enhance people's transformational leadership (TL) skills (discussed in more detail later in this chapter). Transformational leaders are those who generate awareness and acceptance of their team and organization's mission, who broaden and elevate the interests of their employees and stimulate them to look beyond self-interest to the good of the team and organization. Overall, transformational leaders get people to expend great effort to accomplish their team's mission or vision. As can be seen from even this brief definition, transformational leaders need to motivate people to work beyond what they may think they are capable of achieving. A leader who cannot understand the needs and aspirations of another person is unlikely to excel at this crucial task. Worse, a leader who does not have compassion for another person is unlikely even to interact with, get to know, or show the degree of compassion needed to effectively motivate him or her.

Based upon RFT, Bond (2012) hypothesized that leaders who were more flexible in their perspective taking might be able to find more compassion for colleagues whom they may even dislike and, hence, be better able to successfully motivate and lead them. To this end, Bond has augmented a traditional TL training program with various ACT- and RFT-derived exercises, several of which are outlined in the discussion below. The one that stems most directly from RFT attempts to expand leaders' deictic frames involving colleagues that the leaders find hard to understand, appreciate and, hence, motivate. In this "Switching Perspectives" exercise, people are asked to:

- Think of a colleague who has annoyed or frustrated you, or for whom you have negative feelings.
- Write down five conceivable reasons for his or her actions and/or attitudes.
- How would you think and feel at work if those reasons applied to you, or if you had this colleague's history?
- How do you connect with and motivate someone who may potentially act for those reasons?

While thinking about RFT led Bond to develop this particular technique, one can see how, not surprisingly, it draws on processes described in ACT's hexaflex model. Self-as-context is the most obvious example, but acceptance, defusion, and contact with the present moment are also needed in order to get the "psychological space" required to effectively imagine reasons why another person might behave the way that he or she does. Even the values-based action processes of the hexaflex are required, if only to a small extent, to provide the impetus for fully engaging with what people could consider to be a silly, pointless, or boring exercise.

Clayton (1995) developed an organizational development (OD) strategy that is also based on RFT, yet is less readily understood from an ACT perspective. As recounted in Stewart, Barnes-Holmes, Barnes-Holmes, Bond, and Hayes (2006), Clayton demonstrated the use of this strategy, within a field experiment, in an organization that was undergoing change. As part of that change process, the chief executive officer of the company gave a speech to employees, saying that he wanted to develop a work environment that was creative and caring. In one experimental condition, the CEO gave a scripted speech in which he merely told the employees that he wanted to establish such a work environment; in the other condition, he conveyed this same message, but he linked the desired attributes of "creative" and "caring" to a negative attribute that prior research indicated his employees currently had about the organization: chaotic. To do so, he said, "This is a caring place, we care about our clients. And yes, it is a bit chaotic, but this gives us the freedom to be creative in meeting our clients' needs." Results showed that employee attitudes changed more when desired, positive organizational attributes were linked to an existing negative belief. RFT predicts such an outcome, in specifying that it is easier to elaborate an existing verbal network than to develop a new one, not to mention a new one that may actually conflict with the current network (Stewart et al., 2006). In addition, management communication that widely contradicts people's experiences of their work environment may activate (or, more technically, be in a frame of coordination with) other features of their verbal networks, such that they experience cynicism, ridicule, and counterproductive work behaviors (absences and lax working), in relation to their organization. We believe that this is a clever example of how people can bring to bear knowledge of RFT to develop new intervention strategies, and we predict that more work of this type will be appearing in the near future.

Identifying New Work-Related Intervention Targets for ACT

In this final section we consider some other innovative applications of ACT. We begin by providing an overview of some of our most recent work, which has seen the successful application of ACT principles to enhance a recognized leadership development program. We also reflect on how ACT and RFT principles might contribute to the theory and practice of organizational development. We then review the work of other innovative ACT practitioners who are employing ACT within the context of improving workplace safety, team development, and career coaching and enhancing work-related interpersonal skills and behaviors.

Enhancing TL with ACT

In a meta-analysis across eighty-seven studies, Judge and Piccolo (2004) showed that TL is associated with many criteria of leadership effectiveness, including job performance and employee attitudes. Not surprisingly, therefore, there is great demand for the development of TL skills, since both individuals and organizations can benefit from strategies for enhancing TL. Bond (2012) hypothesized that one such strategy may be ACT.

Unpacking our brief definition of TL in the preceding section, one can see how this conceptualization of leadership overlaps with the six processes that constitute psychological flexibility. For example, transformational leaders demonstrate the following skills:

- Through their actions they show consistent values, beliefs, and principles (*idealized influence*).
- They inspire and motivate others, in part, by creating a vision for the future and acting in a manner consistent with that vision, even if it is difficult to do so (*inspirational motivation*).
- They consistently and actively look for opportunities to innovate and make changes in order to move toward their team's values and goals (*intellectual stimulation*).
- They work to establish a rapport with all members of their team so that they can more effectively motivate and develop them (*individualized consideration*), for example, by using the perspective-taking exercise discussed above.

As can be seen, these four TL characteristics very much center around identifying and moving toward the values and goals of a team and its organization (idealized influence, inspirational motivation), even when it is difficult to do so or one has to establish a rapport with a challenging colleague (individualized consideration). In addition, TL emphasizes a type of behavioral flexibility similar to that at the core of psychological flexibility: the need to consistently examine if change, or innovation, is required in order to better pursue the team's goals and values (intellectual stimulation). Due to this conceptual correspondence between TL and psychological flexibility, Bond (2012) hypothesized that increasing people's psychological flexibility would allow them to become better transformational leaders.

To test this hypothesis, he selected various ACT techniques that he thought could be offered to leaders going through the TL training specified in Bass and Avolio's (1999) detailed manual, which is widely used by both practitioners and researchers. The structure of this one-and-a-half-day training program involved a half day of ACT training followed by one day of TL training. We have emphasized in this book the need to adapt ACT to the work environment so that the training will attract participants and, even more important, not frighten them off. To this end, the half day of ACT training was packaged as learning an "Essential Leadership Stance" (ELS). The rationale is that as athletes, musicians, or dancers need a particular physical stance in order to succeed in their endeavors, leaders need a psychological one. Only from a particular psychological stance (the ELS) will people be able to lead effectively. Thus, the connection between the ACT skills and TL training is literally reflected in the name "ELS": one needs an effective leadership stance to use TL skills effectively.

Being branded as ELS was not the only way the ACT training was tailored to the work environment. Bond (2012) also selected ACT techniques that were likely to be both powerful and acceptable (or at least not off-putting) to a wide range of workers. With the exception of one technique, all of the ones Bond selected have been discussed in this book:

- Experience a raisin
- Mindful breathing as an anchor (creating a breathing space)
- Physicalizing emotions and physical sensations
- Passengers on the bus
- Having a thought as opposed to buying a thought
- Switching perspectives: "What is he thinking?"
- Take five (establishing values and goals every day while mindfully breathing)

We have not discussed the final technique, "Take Five." Here, participants are asked to spend five minutes at the beginning of the day, perhaps while traveling to work, mindfully breathing, identifying key goals for the day, and then linking those goals to various values toward which they are working. Creating this linkage not only reminds people of their values, but it also serves to motivate them to achieve their goals, as they can see the reason they wish to accomplish them.

Using a randomized controlled trial, Bond (2012) tested the impact of this ACT-enhanced TL (or ACT+TL) training among team leaders of financial traders in an investment bank. The effectiveness of ACT+TL was tested against the same one-day TL training preceded by a half-day training in negotiation skills. Results indicated that teams whose leaders were trained in ACT+TL made approximately £17 million ($27 million) more over the eight months following their training than did teams whose managers received training in negotiation skills instead of ACT. In addition, members of the teams whose leaders received ACT+TL had better mental health after eight months than did the negotiation skills group. Results indicated that both of these outcomes were largely mediated by an increase in the TL ratings of leaders by their followers (team members); that is, it appears that the ACT+TL teams made more money and improved their mental health primarily because they perceived that their team leaders became better transformational leaders.

This is the only study of which we are aware that has investigated the application of ACT to leadership development. We believe this represents just the beginning of a fruitful area of research and practice. Over the past thirty years, research has clearly indicated that TL skills help to improve productivity and effectiveness in the workplace; however, while those skills are well established and well known, they are also very difficult to practice. They involve complex psychological processes, such as consistent, goal-committed actions, that difficult thoughts and feelings can easily undermine. ACT offers tools that can help leaders navigate those difficult internal events so that they can effectively deploy TL skills. Future research and practice can help to identify which specific tools are most efficient in doing so.

Organizational Development and ACT

OD is defined as the application of behavioral science theories to the planned change of workplace processes, structures, and strategies in order to improve organizational effectiveness (Cummings & Worley, 2009). Psychology has been at the heart of the systematic study of OD from its inception, but it has been psychodynamic theories that have overwhelmingly represented the field of psychology in OD (e.g., see de Board, 1978). We believe, however, that ACT and RFT have the potential to make an important contribution to OD, as organizations, and attempts to change them, rely on rules, values, and other types of verbal behavior. ACT, and RFT in particular, focuses, of course, on understanding how verbal events relate to each other and how those relations can transform the function of other events; thus, we believe that ACT and RFT have the potential to help organizations in planning OD interventions. Bond et al. (2006) began a brief discussion on how this may be accomplished, but, in truth, very little has been done to further those initial thoughts.

One exception, however, is an effort by Steven Hayes (2010) to scale up the six processes of the hexaflex to the level of the organization. To do so, he gave each of the six psychological processes that constitute psychological flexibility a corresponding process at the level of the organization (or, indeed, it could be at the level of the team or department) (see Table 10.1).

Table 10.1. Translating the six processes of psychological flexibility to the organizational level.

Psychological process	Organizational characteristic
Acceptance	Openness to distress, problems, and conflict
Defusion	Multiple views, filtered by workability
Contact with the present moment	Good monitoring, flexible attending
Self-as-context	Aware of perspective, context, and those of other people's departments and other organizations
Values	Clear values and goals, chosen by the group
Goal-committed actions	Active steps, linked to values and goals

The goal of an ACT-enhanced OD intervention would be to ensure that structures, processes, and strategies are in place in order to maximize the six organizational characteristics that constitute its "operational flexibility." We are not aware of any OD intervention that has been based on this organizational hexaflex, but, as with the individual-level one, it may serve as a useful road map for guiding one. Certainly, we would find it interesting to see an OD outcome study that tests the effectiveness of attempting to enhance a company's operational flexibility.

Selecting and Assessing Workers

Research by Bond and colleagues shows that psychological flexibility predicts productivity measures such as absence rates (Bond et al., 2008), job performance (Bond & Bunce, 2003), and propensity to be innovative (Bond & Bunce, 2000; Bond, Lloyd, & Guenole, 2012). Traditionally, these are variables that organizations attempt to predict through the use of personality and cognitive ability tests, which candidates frequently take to get jobs and even be promoted. One limitation of those tests is that personality traits and cognitive ability are characteristics that cannot be fundamentally changed. For example, a person who scores high on neuroticism can learn how to manage that characteristic (for example, through ACT) but is likely always to be neurotic. In contrast, as we have described in this book, psychological flexibility, while normally stable if not targeted for change (e.g., Bond & Bunce, 2003), can be fairly rapidly enhanced through ACT. Given that flexibility predicts productivity measures and, unlike personality and cognitive ability, it can also be increased, human resource managers have frequently asked us if the Acceptance and Action Questionnaire-II (AAQ-II), which measures flexibility, can be used in selection and development processes. To date, our response has always been, "We do not have the data to suggest such a use for the AAQ-II." We believe, though, that future research should look at the potential for a measure of psychological flexibility, perhaps tailored to the work environment (Bond et al., 2012), to be used for selecting and developing personnel. If it did serve as a useful predictor and did not demonstrate adverse impact on any groups, then organizations could suggest ACT training for those people who scored below a particular cutoff point on the measure. This would have the advantage of giving candidates a second chance—after undergoing ACT training—in a selection and development process: a second chance that they do not often get when trait measures are given great prominence in selecting and developing people.

Other Innovative Workplace Applications of ACT

In addition to the work being conducted by our own research teams, discussed above, other researchers and practitioners have made use of the ACT model to enhance employees' psychological well-being, performance, social skills, and personal development. In the sections below, we outline the work of Daniel J. Moran, Rachel Collis, Rob Archer, Linda Bilich, and Joseph Ciarrochi, who have developed highly innovative workplace applications of the ACT model.

ACT for Safety

Daniel J. Moran, founder of Pickslyde Consulting in the United States (http.pickslyde.com), has developed ACT-based training for safety-critical industries. His training has particularly been employed to accelerate safety behaviors for workers in manufacturing, construction, and the oil and gas industry. The concepts of values directedness, acceptance, and mindfulness have been adapted and incorporated into the blue-collar industries with a good deal of success, especially when integrated with evidence-based safety programs such as behavior-based safety or McSween's Values-Based Safety Process. Creating accessible metaphors and linking mindfulness to the interests that resonate with front-line employees can boost the effectiveness of ACT-based training. In turn, the improved psychological flexibility from ACT interventions can increase adherence to standard operating procedures and reduce workers' private obstacles toward acting safely (avoiding the discomfort of wearing a hard hat, not feeling like taking the time to complete a safety checklist prior to starting a task).

Moran created ACT for Safety trainings, which have been utilized in collaboration with Quality Safety Edge, a leading behavior-based safety company. A critical aim of all Moran's ACT training events should be to ensure the ideas are presented in a down-to-earth and understandable manner. The more relevant the analogies are to workers' experiences, the more likely they are to influence action. For example, during a training event involving a demolition crew in the Deep South of the United States, it was fitting to discuss the Monkey Trap metaphor in order to relate the idea of acceptance. The audience was filled with avid hunters for whom the following metaphor was more likely to resonate than the more traditional ACT metaphors:

> In a part of the world where people still hunt monkeys for food, they have devised a really interesting way of trapping their game. The hunters cut a small hole in a gourd and hollow it out before tying it to a tree with a vine. Once it is secure, they bait the gourd with banana chips and then go hide in the trees nearby. When the unsuspecting monkey sniffs the scent of bananas while foraging for food, he eventually finds the source of the scent and slips his hand into the gourd to grab the banana chips. When he does so, the trappers jump from the trees and run toward the monkey. Panicked, the monkey tries to pull his hand

> from the gourd, but because he has a handful of banana chips in his clenched fist, he cannot pull his hand out. If he would "just let it go" and "accept the loss" of these banana chips, he could then behave more flexibly and slide his hand back out of the hole. But his unwillingness to lose those banana chips leads to inflexible behavior, which restricts his options and ultimately leads to him being dinner for the hunters. Sometimes it is better to relinquish control and commit your actions toward finding safer and more valuable banana chips elsewhere than to rigidly pursue a single-minded agenda.

The CEO of this particular demolition crew enjoys telling an anecdote that demonstrates his crew's application of the Monkey Trap metaphor. He explains that soon after the ACT for Safety workshop, a late shipment held up progress on a job. The foremen and straw bosses were viciously arguing about whether they should go home early because of this obstacle. Finally, someone chimed in: "There's plenty of work to do without the shipment, so just drop the banana chip! We'll just let that go, and get more productive on the other jobs we *can* do!"

When the ACT interventions are explained in a manner that resonates with the frontline employees and supervisors, they can transform the workers' approach to safety and productivity. ACT for Safety is not a therapeutic endeavor but rather attempts to improve behavioral flexibility for a nonclinical population. This safety approach teaches mindfulness with less focus on traditional "meditation" and greater emphasis on "situational awareness." In addition, the values clarification exercises are crystallized into the much more succinct, but still intensely personal, "What I Care About" survey. When workers clarify what they care about, it helps them become more mindful of the purpose of their work. When oil rig workers or turbine mechanics gain the perspective that they are not simply laboring for a paycheck but for what that paycheck allows them to do (provide for their children, maintain their independence), they can see greater meaning in their work and link these motivations to their committed actions. In addition, knowing the purpose of work and safety actions can reduce risky behaviors, such as cutting corners during a complex task or resisting wearing personal protective equipment. When the aim of ACT is to increase psychological flexibility by undermining unhelpful language processes, it makes sense to reinterpret the basic principles in a manner that is most beneficial for the people you are trying to help. ACT for Safety aims to increase psychological flexibility and quality of life, and it also attempts to reduce injury and death, so there is solid justification for modifying the model.

ACT for Team and Executive Development

Rachel Collis of RJC Consulting (Australia) has been using ACT in her work in organizational settings since 2008. Rachel also writes a blog (with Rob Archer—see below) on using ACT in the workplace (www.workingwithact.com).

Rachel delivers ACT in one-to-one executive coaching sessions and also communicates ACT principles in keynote speeches and corporate workshops in relation to subjects such as managing change, handling difficult conversations, stress management, and well-being. She also uses ACT in team facilitation.

A typical ACT-consistent team facilitation process Rachel might follow involves the following steps:

1. Choosing values

   Start by asking the group, "What qualities are you willing to sign up to today that would help you to achieve the outcomes you want? What qualities do you need from me? Are there any behaviors that we need to watch out for that might derail our discussion? Either in the group or by me?"

   This gives permission for the facilitator to gently bring the group's attention to workable and unworkable behaviors as they occur. It also gives the group permission to raise concerns about unworkable behavior by the facilitator.

2. Getting present

   This might involve encouraging people to slow down and take a moment to "get present" if the discussion is getting stuck or emotions are starting to hijack behavior. We might take five slow, deep breaths or shift awareness to each of the five senses in turn.

   Good facilitators need to really be present to participants' subtle nonverbal cues and then choose how to respond—listening both to the words that are spoken and also *how* those words are spoken, noticing both the people who are speaking and also the people who are silent. Are the quiet ones engaged or subtly signaling something important?

The facilitator is looking for signs that something new could happen in this conversation, a sense that people are becoming more curious and open. The facilitator then encourages that shift into more psychologically flexible behavior.

3. Defusion

   People often come to a team session with a story about what the team is like, how problems should be solved, and what will happen during the discussion. A statement by the facilitator that helps people to hold these stories a little more lightly can be really important:

   "In previous facilitated team sessions you may have been encouraged to say whatever is on your mind, to get it all on the table. I want to take a different approach. Sometimes our minds say really unhelpful things that are best left unsaid. Sometimes we hold ourselves back from saying what is important because our minds tell us we will look stupid. Instead I would like to encourage you to communicate thoughtfully. To ask yourself what you want to achieve, and then what you need to say and do in order to make that outcome more likely. It is okay to pause. It is okay for us to sit quietly for a moment while you have time to choose your response."

4. Acceptance

   When difficult feelings come up, the facilitator models compassion and acceptance, honoring the feelings and acknowledging that those feelings suggest that this really matters, that it is important.

5. Perspective taking

   Perspective taking helps the team to come up with better ideas that are more likely to both achieve desired outcomes and meet with approval of key stakeholders who aren't present at the meeting.

   Ask "Who else is affected by this issue? What is important to them here?"

Perspective taking can also improve communication and defuse conflict: "Jo, before you give your perspective on this, can you just explain how you think Sarah sees the problem?"

6. Choosing broader values

   Ask "How do others see this team? What would you like your customers and coworkers in other areas to say about you?" and lead from that into "What values are you willing to sign up for as a group?"

   If the organization has a preexisting set of corporate values, it is usually helpful to map the team's values onto the values of the organization.

7. Committed action

   People tend to be cynical about team "away days." Their experience is that the discussion at these sessions rarely leads to meaningful actions back in the workplace. So it is very important to come up with a manageable list of actions.

   "What actions will you take as a result of today's discussion? When will you do these things? Who will be responsible? Who will follow up? How do these actions align with your values?"

8. Willingness

   It usually isn't enough to just make a to-do list. It is also important to acknowledge the private events that might get in the way of taking action. This could involve asking: "What is going to be most difficult about this for you? Where might you get stuck?" and then linking the actions to the values and outcomes they have described. Check their level of commitment by asking "Do you want what you have described enough to be willing to have those times of discomfort as you execute this plan?" If the answer is no (and it is important that "no" is an option here), then we might need to either come up with a different plan or focus more directly on increasing psychological flexibility.

ACT for Career Coaching and Development

Rob Archer is an industrial/organizational psychologist based in London. Rob specializes in the application of ACT for career coaching and development. Over the past few years, he has become increasingly convinced that ACT is essential in nontherapeutic contexts, particularly for people who are feeling "stuck" in some way.

Rob's main focus is on helping people who are stuck in their careers. These people are usually in what most would consider a good job, yet find themselves thinking that there must be more to life. They are convinced there's something better out there, if only they knew what it was. Most are highly capable and could do whatever they set their minds to, yet the risk of starting their careers over again often seems too great. So, they end up stuck.

This can go on for years, with people going round and round in circles, trying to find their ideal direction and ending up back where they started, each time a little more frustrated. Rob calls this being "headstuck," because they are stuck inside their heads, trapped between an unwanted present and an uncertain future.

Rob believes that the reason so many people get headstuck is because the human mind is ill equipped to make complex career decisions. In an online presentation he calls "Career Paralysis," Rob outlines how six of the mind's cognitive biases combine to keep us headstuck:

- *Negative bias*—a cautious mind is great when survival is the goal ... but less so for fulfillment.
- *Paradox of choice*—people get stuck not because they have too few choices, but too many.
- *Short-term thinking beats long term*—so meaningful change gets derailed.
- *Thinking in linear patterns*—our minds tend to think in straight lines even though that often keeps us stuck where we are.
- *Decision making based on comparisons*—so we focus on what others value, not what *we* do.
- *Aiming for happiness*—even though having happiness as an objective is often a trap that can keep us stuck.

Getting headstuck is an almost inevitable product of the way we think, especially after the explosion of choice characterized by the information age. So, to beat career paralysis, we need new ways to think about our thinking.

Most traditional career advice rests on the assumption that if we can build self-awareness and better understand what "type" of person we are, we can be "matched" to our ideal job. But Rob believes this approach is at best inadequate and at worst imprisons us still further by promoting self-as-content perspectives that lead to rigid thought and behavior. What we need is a different way of relating to our thoughts that leads to a more flexible approach to career decision making. This is consistent with new approaches to career decision making, such as Hermina Ibarra's *Working Identity*, which encourages readers to conduct small experiments to underpin career change and not to try to "think" themselves into a new career.

Rob's answer is to combine an in-depth career decision process with ACT skills. This ACT-based career intervention has two parts:

1. The first is an analytical decision-making process, which includes many of the traditional techniques associated with career work, for example, building self-awareness and thinking about one's personality, skills, strengths, and values. Rob also introduces key principles from decision science, such as identifying clear decision criteria, to help people make the best, most logical decision possible.

2. But the natural corollary to making a decision is that clients need help with the psychology of change. Traditional approaches generally deal with this by focusing on strengths, boosting confidence, or eliminating uncertainty by advising people to follow their "true" vocation. Rob's view is that this promotes an unrealistic emotional control agenda. After all, it is not really possible to avoid uncertainty—in fact, choosing a new, valued direction will likely make these kinds of emotions *more* likely, not less.

What's needed is a set of skills that allows people to have difficult emotions and thoughts and still move forward in the service of a chosen direction. This is where psychological flexibility comes in. Rob has developed a particular way to weave ACT throughout the career decision-making process that includes the following strategies:

- Normalize the emotions associated with feeling headstuck. This is critical for clients who feel stuck because invariably they feel isolated and alone, comparing themselves to "more successful" people at work.
- Get clients present to their situation by exploring the feelings, emotions, urges, and sensations associated with being headstuck. Rob often uses mindfulness techniques at this stage, especially as a way of changing the pace of career coaching sessions by contacting emotions beyond those permitted by autopilot responses.
- Explore the client's most important values related to work and future life. Clients are usually confused about values, so having a clear, ACT-consistent definition helps. Rob often gives his clients a copy of *The Confidence Gap* (Russ Harris) or some other reader-friendly ACT book to enhance learning at this stage.
- Explore what values mean in practice by looking at the committed actions associated with these values. What will the client do to "live" this value? What does this value look like in five years when you've made the change? What does it look like in two years when you are in transition? What does it look like now, in this moment?
- The natural corollary to the work on values and committed action is to explore the emotional flip side of these values. For example, many clients value freedom and autonomy, yet the flip side to these are often feelings of insecurity and anxiety. Rob works to bring his clients into contact with the reality that by choosing freedom, they will also choose insecurity.
- Clients often assume that they can get rid of difficult emotions by choosing the "right" career. Rob will explore this idea in more depth by asking clients how long they have had difficult thoughts and feelings, and whether their attempts to get rid of them have worked. Rob encourages clients to consider the limits of analysis—is it possible to choose a direction without risk, for example? This work is similar to the kinds of creative hopelessness

exercises that would usually be done much earlier when ACT is delivered in therapeutic settings.

- At this stage, Rob introduces the concepts of willingness and acceptance. Clients are usually receptive to such concepts and strategies, but for some there is a need to explore these ideas more deeply through defusion exercises. Rob tends to promote defusion naturally by referring to "the mind" or even saying to his client "my own mind is telling me I'm not explaining myself very well right now." Rob also uses metaphors like "demons in your rucksack" (based on "passengers on the bus") to promote defusion and to provide a way of speaking about difficult thoughts and emotions in defused ways.
- A natural extension of defusion is to start discussing the self-as-context. Although Rob rarely uses the term "self-as-context," he encourages clients to hold views of themselves lightly by asking them to consider lots of different perspectives about themselves and their situation, all with the aim of building greater behavioral flexibility. (This is in contrast to most types of career coaching, which often emphasize the idea of certain psychological types being compatible with certain jobs.)
- Observing the thoughts and feelings that arise for clients during this process is essential, and Rob's clients are asked to keep a diary documenting their psychological content between sessions and their willingness to experience difficult thoughts in the service of following their valued direction. After all, even after a decision is made life will continue to raise questions. The choice is not whether to have pain or not, but whether to choose the pain of growth or the pain of stagnation.

In sum, Rob's ACT-based career coaching model is designed to help working individuals to accommodate the mind's biases so that they make the best career decisions possible while confronting the need to take positive action. For Rob's headstuck clients, this means being willing to move their careers in a personally valued direction *with* doubts rather than trying to get rid of them first.

ACT for Enhancing Employees' Social Skills

Finally, we would like to highlight the innovative work of Linda Bilich and Joseph Ciarrochi, who have developed an ACT-inspired experiential training program to increase employees' and managers' effectiveness in interpersonal situations (see Bilich & Ciarrochi, 2009). Their program incorporates and cultivates all six of ACT's core processes and has been applied to improve the interpersonal effectiveness of officers working for the New South Wales Police in Australia. Their highly experiential approach seems particularly effective for helping employees develop ACT-related skills such as mindfulness, defusion, and values-based action; practice using these skills in a simulated social interaction; and consider how to cultivate these skills in coworkers (many of the officers involved in the intervention had leadership responsibilities).

During the program, participants are asked to identify a particularly difficult social situation that they may have struggled with or avoided. They are also asked to identify their behavioral value in that situation. During role-plays, participants are supported by the facilitator as they practice ACT skills such as staying present with the other person and noticing the internal events that show up, while using a value to guide their behavior. As part of this work, participants are asked a key ACT question: "Are you willing to have all of the difficult experiences that arise, particularly when trying to behave consistently with your value?"

Bilich and Ciarrochi's program offers a unique and engaging way of cultivating ACT's core process among working groups and takes full advantage of the experiential nature of ACT to improve work-related social skills training. Given the detrimental impact of aversive interpersonal behaviors in the workplace, this type of ACT-based program has great potential for improving working relationships. Moreover, we believe this approach would be useful for any occupations that involve difficult interactions with members of the public (customer service, teaching, nursing, and so on).

Summary

Most people have been able to access detailed information on ACT for only thirteen years (since the publication of Hayes et al., 1999), yet in that relatively short time, significant progress has been made in testing the impact of this intervention on improving mental health in the workplace. As we have discussed in this chapter, we believe that this focus on mental health and the ACT training program we have described only scratches the surface of how ACT and RFT principles can be applied in the workplace. We have pointed to a few horizons toward which ACT can move with regard to work, and we are beginning to see some initial steps toward them. We see this burgeoning area of ACT-inspired practice and research as holding a great deal of promise for developing mindful and effective employees.

Reproduced by permission of Joseph Ciarrochi, PhD (www.acceptandchange.com/original-metaphors/).

Appendix

Handouts

Handout 1: Define Your Values

This written exercise is designed to help you become much more aware of the purpose and direction in your life. For some areas of your life, your values may be easily accessible. For others, you may have to reflect for a while on what you really care about and the type of person you ideally want to be.

There are no right and wrong answers to this type of exercise. It is simply designed to help you become more aware of the particular personal strengths and qualities you personally want to express in your own behavior.

The exercise is designed to help you define your values for five areas of life: health, relationships, work and career, leisure time, and personal growth. You may find the areas overlap somewhat. That's fine. The key thing is to begin identifying the qualities you most want to pursue—essentially capturing the type of person you ideally want to be. What you want your life *to be about*.

Here are some additional tips for completing this exercise:

- Think of your values as the "behavioral guides" that you get to choose for each area of your life.
- They're about how you choose to be—for example, being supportive, loving, patient, competitive, or hardworking are ways of describing values.
- Values can never be achieved, so they are more general than goals and actions.

You do not have to show your answers to anyone, so please take this opportunity to be honest with yourself and discover what you truly value.

Define Your Values: Your Health Values

Think about your values in relation to your health and physical well-being. What are your intentions with regard to diet, exercise, smoking, alcohol, and general self-care and well-being? Do you wish to pursue a healthier lifestyle? If so, what form might that take in your life? If this area of life is important to you, see if you can capture your values regarding the promotion and maintenance of good health.

VALUE STATEMENT:

VALUE REMINDER WORDS:

Define Your Values: Your Relationship Values

In this section, write down a description of the person you choose to be in your various relationships. This section can be divided into relationships with your spouse or partner, children, family members, and friends. In an ideal world, how do you *choose* to relate to the people in your life? How would you treat others if you were the "ideal you" in your various relationships? Describe the personal qualities that you most want to express in any personal and social relationships that are important to you.

VALUE STATEMENT:

VALUE REMINDER WORDS:

Define Your Values: Your Work and Career Values

In your current job, describe the type of employee or manager you most want to be. What personal qualities or strengths do you show at work when you are at your best? What are your values around how to interact with your colleagues? If you are a manager, what type of manager do you choose to be? What are your innermost work values—persistence, hard work, continued development, being supportive to others, career progression, customer service, cooperation, creativity?

VALUE STATEMENT:

VALUE REMINDER WORDS:

Define Your Values: Your Leisure Time Values

Describe the type of leisure time you would most like to have, including hobbies, sports, and leisure activities. What do you or would you most like to pursue for fun and fulfillment in your leisure time? Do you tend to choose having fun, relaxing, or engaging in creative activities and hobbies? What is important to you in this area of your life? Capture the values you would most like to guide your actions during your leisure time.

VALUE STATEMENT:

VALUE REMINDER WORDS:

Define Your Values: Your Personal Growth Values

Describe the types of personal development activities you would be interested in pursuing. This could include training programs you would like to attend; any groups you would like to join; learning new skills or languages; developing greater knowledge about topics that interest you; and spiritual pursuits such as meditation, religion, or yoga. This area could also include contributing to community, political, or environmental causes. If continued personal development is important to you, try to capture the way you would like to be in this area of your life.

VALUE STATEMENT:

VALUE REMINDER WORDS:

Handout 2: Values, Goals, and Actions Worksheet

VALUE → **GOALS** → **ACTIONS**

LIFE AREA: health/relationships/work/ leisure/ personal growth
VALUE REMINDER WORDS

Short-term goals: Next four weeks
1.
2.
3.
4.

Medium-term goals: Next six months to one year
1.
2.
3.
4.

Long-term goals: Next three years or more
1.
2.
3.
4.

VALUE-BASED ACTIONS FOR THE NEXT WEEK

1.
2.
3.

INTERNAL BARRIERS. Record any “unhelpful” thoughts, feelings, urges, or moods that might interfere with value-based goals and actions in this area of your life.

Handout 2a: Values, Goals, and Actions Worksheet (Work Example)

VALUE → **GOALS** → **ACTIONS**

LIFE AREA: health/ relationships/ work/ leisure/ personal growth *WORK*
VALUE REMINDER WORDS ***Dedicated, trusted support, focused on developing members of my team, coach and mentor***

Short-term goals: Next 4 weeks
1. *Have first team huddle before end of the month*
2. *Speak to Julie about cascading coaching and mentoring skills to other team leaders*
3.
4.

Medium-term goals: next 6 months to one year
1. *Meet with each team member to discuss training request for rest of year (by end of Nov)*
2. *Complete coaching/ mentoring certificate by May of next year*
3.
4.

Long-term goals: next three years or more
1.
2.
3.
4.

VALUE-BASED ACTIONS FOR THE NEXT WEEK

1. *Check that Cathy is doing OK when she's back at work on Wednesday*
2. *Speak to Bob about securing training budget for the team (Wed/ Thurs)*
3. *Tell the team about idea of having regular morning team 'huddles' (tomorrow first thing)*

INTERNAL BARRIERS. Record any "unhelpful" thoughts, feelings, urges, moods that might interfere with value-based goals and actions in this area of your life.

Worried about Bob's reaction. Maybe he thinks I'm asking for too much. Team might not be keen on huddles idea.

Handout 2b: Values, Goals, and Actions Worksheet (Relationship Example)

VALUE → **GOALS** → **ACTIONS**

VALUE

LIFE AREA: health/relationships/work/leisure/personal growth

RELATIONSHIP with Julie

VALUE REMINDER WORDS

Loving, appreciative, enabling, supportive

GOALS

Short-term goals: Next four weeks
1. *Have May weekend away booked*
2. *Take Julie to theater last weekend of the month*
3. *Look into evening classes Julie and I could take together*
4.

Medium-term goals: Next six months to one year
1. *Arrange surprise birthday party with Julie's family*
2. *Start evening classes with Julie in art or music*
3.
4.

Long-term goals: Next three years or more
1. *Move to larger house by 2014 with spare room for Julie's painting*
2.
3.
4.

ACTIONS

VALUE-BASED ACTIONS FOR THE NEXT WEEK

1. *Take home flowers tonight. Tell Julie properly how much I've appreciated her support with my parents (tonight)*
2. *Cook Julie dinner (Wed. or Thurs. evening, check tonight)*
3. *Look online for deals for weekend away when we both have days off in May (tomorrow during first break at work)*

INTERNAL BARRIERS. Record any "unhelpful" thoughts, feelings, urges, moods that might interfere with value-based goals and actions in this area of your life.

Always feel soppy and awkward telling Julie how much I care. Might be too tired to cook dinner and will be tempted to get takeout. Embarrassed about starting new class and meeting new people.

Handout 3: Home Practice (To be completed between Sessions 1 and 2)

To get the most out of this training, you are strongly encouraged to practice transferring mindfulness and values-based action skills into your daily life. To help you do this, it is recommended that you complete the following two assignments before we meet again for session 2.

HOME PRACTICE 1
ENGAGE MINDFULLY IN THREE VALUE-BASED ACTIONS OVER THE NEXT WEEK.

During the session you identified three valued actions to perform over the next week. Use your reminder strategies (e.g., wristband or sticker on your phone) to help you remember to perform these actions. A key part of this exercise is to pay attention to what happens. If you do perform your chosen actions, notice what it is like to do so. *Catch a glimpse* of any thoughts and feelings that show up before, during, and after you have performed each action. *Notice* how others respond. *Notice* any consequences of your actions.

If you don't perform one or more of your actions try to notice any external or internal barriers that got in the way.

Record your experiences on the following page of this handout, so that you can discuss your general experiences in pairs in session 2.

HOME PRACTICE 2
PRACTICE MINDFULNESS OF BREATHING EXERCISE AT LEAST THREE TIMES OVER THE NEXT WEEK.

This takes about 10 minutes to complete on each occasion. Remember that these mindfulness meditations offer the richest practice for developing greater present moment awareness.

Record your experiences in the mindfulness diary on the final page of this handout.

HOME PRACTICE 1:
Record of Mindful Engagement in Values-Based Action

Area of your life: health/ relationships/ work/ leisure time/ personal growth
Personal value/ values worked on this week:

List the values-based actions you performed mindfully this week	What did you notice before, during, and after performing these actions?

List any values-based actions you intended to perform but didn't	External barriers (e.g., time/ opportunity)	Internal barriers (e.g., unhelpful thoughts or feelings that popped up and got in the way)

HOME PRACTICE 2: Mindfulness practice diary

Day	Exercise	Duration	Observations and comments
Day 1			
Day 2			
Day 3			
Day 4			
Day 5			
Day 6			
Day 7			

Handout 4: Untangling from Thought Barriers to Values-Based Action

Use this handout to capture any "unhelpful" thoughts that interfere with your effectiveness or your ability to pursue personally valued actions or goals.

Handout 5: Values, Goals, and Actions Map

LIFE AREA	health/relationships/work/leisure/personal growth
VALUE REMINDER WORDS	

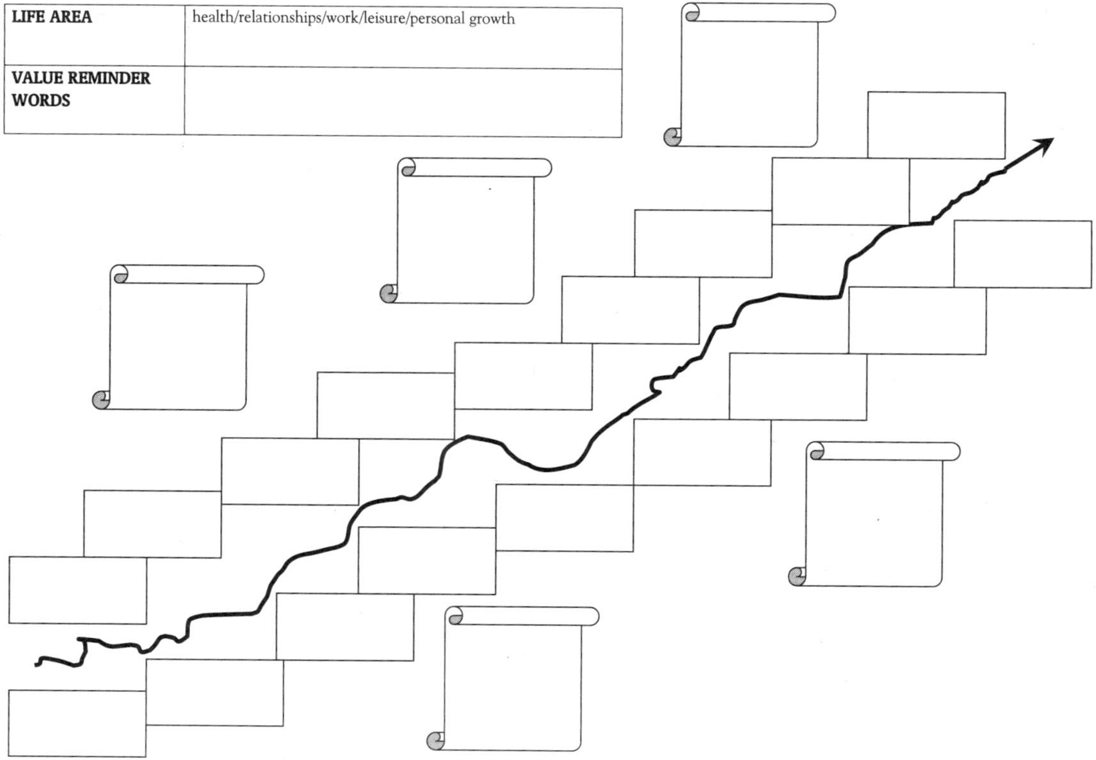

Handout 6: Home Practice (To be completed between Sessions 2 and 3)

To get the most out of this training, you are strongly encouraged to practice transferring mindfulness and values-based action skills into your daily life. To help you do this, it is recommended that you complete the following assignments before we meet again for the final session.

HOME PRACTICE 1
ENGAGE MINDFULLY IN THREE VALUE-BASED ACTIONS OVER THE NEXT WEEK.

Instructions are exactly the same as last week. Use your reminder strategies (e.g., wristband or sticker on your phone) to remember to perform your valued actions, and pay attention to what happens before, during, and after. Use the exercise to become aware of any thoughts and feelings that pull you off course.

HOME PRACTICE 2
WORK TOWARDS FOUR VALUES-BASED GOALS BEFORE SESSION 3

Set yourself the challenge to achieve four *values-based goals* over the next four weeks (before we meet again for session 3). For now focus on the short-term goals you recorded during session 2, or work on the exercises at home to generate additional values-based goals. Stay present and notice what happens as you pursue goals that are guided by one or more of your values.

HOME PRACTICE 3
MINDFULNESS PRACTICE

Get into the habit of practicing mindfulness of the breath or mindfulness of the body and breath three times per week before we meet again.

Practice the cartoon voices technique whenever you notice yourself being overly influenced by unhelpful thoughts.

Practice the physicalizing exercise twice in your own time, and particularly when you notice yourself becoming wrapped up in a difficult feeling or mood.

Start building brief mindfulness into your daily routine – become psychologically present for tasks that you used to perform on automatic pilot – for example, getting ready for work in the morning; eating and drinking; travelling to work; and so on. Practicing a little mindfulness every day is the secret!

Record your experiences in the mindfulness diary on the final page of this handout.

HOME PRACTICE 3: Mindfulness practice diary

Day	Exercise	Duration	Observations and comments
Day 1			
Day 2			
Day 3			
Day 4			
Day 5			
Day 6			
Day 7			

Handout 7: Assessing Value Consistency

This exercise encourages you to assess how *values-consistent* you have been over the past couple of weeks. Use this handout to identify the values you are most interested in pursuing, and then consider the actions that have been consistent and inconsistent with those values over the past two weeks. Have you been bringing your values to life?

Your HEALTH values

Record your key value reminder words for this area of your life:

____

Now reflect on your actions OVER THE PAST TWO WEEKS. To what extent were your day-to-day actions consistent with your health values? For example, did your eating, drinking, and exercise behaviors move you in a healthy direction? To what extent did you purposefully engage in exercise? Did you overdo it on any unhealthy behaviors? How well did you sleep? Think about all your actions over the past couple of weeks related to your health.

Actions that were more consistent with my main health value		Actions that were less consistent with my main health value

On a scale of 1 to 10, how important is this health value to you right now?

(1 = not at all important; 10 = very important) ________________

On a scale of 1 to 10, how value-consistent have your health-related actions been over the past two weeks?

(1 = not at all consistent; 10 = highly consistent) ________________

Handout 7 cont.

Your Relationship Values

Record your key value reminder words for this area of your life:

____

PARTNER	
CHILDREN	
FAMILY	
FRIENDS	

Now reflect on your actions OVER THE PAST TWO WEEKS. To what extent were your day-to-day actions consistent with your most important relationship values? For example, did you relate to others (e.g., partner, family, friends) in ways that are consistent with your values? Did your actions support the development of relationships that you care about? Did you do things to nurture relationships that are important to you? Were some of your social interactions "hijacked" by your thoughts or feelings in the moment? Think about all your actions over the past couple of weeks related to your values around relationships.

Actions that were more consistent with my main relationship value		Actions that were less consistent with my main relationship value

On a scale of 1 to 10, how important are each of your relationship values to you right now?

(1 = not at all important; 10 = very important) ________________

On a scale of 1 to 10, how value-consistent have your relationship behaviors been over the past two weeks?

(1 = not at all consistent; 10 = highly consistent) ________________

Handout 7 cont.

Your Work and Career Values

Record your key value reminder words for this area of your life:

____

Now reflect on your actions OVER THE PAST TWO WEEKS. To what extent were your day-to-day actions consistent with your work/career values? For example, did you engage in behaviors that reflect how you choose to be in your work? Were your interactions with work colleagues values-consistent? Did you take any valued steps toward personal development in relation to work? Think about all your actions over the past couple of weeks related to your main value around work/career.

Actions that were more consistent with my main work/career value		Actions that were less consistent with my main work/career value

On a scale of 1 to 10, how important is this work/career value to you right now?

(1 = not at all important; 10 = very important) ______________

On a scale of 1 to 10, how value-consistent have your work/career behaviors been over the past two weeks?

(1 = not at all consistent; 10 = highly consistent) ______________

Handout 7 cont.

Your Leisure Time Values

Record your key value reminder words for this area of your life:

____

Now reflect on your actions OVER THE PAST TWO WEEKS. To what extent were your day-to-day actions consistent with your recreation and leisure time values? For example, did you engage in behaviors that reflect how you choose to be in your leisure time? Did you pursue activities/hobbies that reflect how you want to be in your leisure time? Were some actions less consistent with your main leisure time value? Think about all your actions over the past couple of weeks related to your values around recreation and leisure time.

Actions that were more consistent with my main leisure time value		Actions that were less consistent with my main leisure time value

On a scale of 1 to 10, how important is this leisure time value to you right now?

(1 = not at all important; 10 = very important) ________________

On a scale of 1 to 10, how value-consistent have your leisure time and recreation behaviors been over the past two weeks?

(1 = not at all consistent; 10 = highly consistent) ________________

Handout 7 cont.

Your Personal Growth Values

Record your key value reminder words for this area of your life:

___

Now reflect on your actions OVER THE PAST TWO WEEKS. To what extent were your day-to-day actions consistent with your values around personal development, learning, and growth? If learning new things is important to you, did you pursue that value over the past two weeks? Did you seek out new knowledge or other growth experiences in a way that is value-consistent? Were some actions less consistent with your personal growth value? Think about all your actions over the past couple of weeks related to your values around personal development and growth.

Actions that were more consistent with my main personal growth value		Actions that were less consistent with my main personal growth value

On a scale of 1 to 10, how important is this personal growth value to you right now?

(1 = not at all important; 10 = very important) ________________

On a scale of 1 to 10, how value-consistent have your personal growth behaviors been over the past two weeks?

(1 = not at all consistent; 10 = highly consistent) ________________

Handout 8: Home Practice (To keep things going now that the program has finished!)

You will hopefully have already made some good progress in developing a combination of mindfulness and values-based action skills. Please do not stop here! These are skills - if you keep using them they become stronger, more automatic, and more integrated into your daily life.

HOME PRACTICE 1
ENGAGE MINDFULLY IN THREE VALUE-BASED ACTIONS OVER THE NEXT WEEK.

Instructions are exactly the same as before. Use your reminder strategies (e.g., wristband or sticker on your phone) to remember to perform your valued actions, and pay attention to what happens before, during, and after. Use the exercise to become aware of any thoughts and feelings that pull you off course.

HOME PRACTICE 2
WORK THROUGH THE WHOLE VALUES-BASED ACTION PROCESS ON YOUR OWN TIME

Take away some of the blank handouts and continue defining your values in each area of your life. If your values are not well defined and familiar to you, they will not operate as a prominent guide to action. As you define your values, get into the habit of identifying a series of more concrete goals and actions that will help to bring your values to life. And maybe start becoming a little bolder! Gradually increase patterns of action that are guided by values. Keep on the lookout for new opportunities to bring your values to life. Practice engaging in personally valued actions even when unhelpful or difficult thoughts and feelings are showing up. Welcome your passengers along for the ride!

HOME PRACTICE 3
MINDFULNESS PRACTICE

Continue practicing mindfulness of the breath or mindfulness of the body and breath three times per week. Many people find it helps to continue with regular mindfulness meditation practice throughout their lives.

Continue using brief daily mindfulness exercises – get into the habit of using the three steps to present moment awareness at regular intervals during the day.

Practice the cartoon voices technique whenever you notice yourself being overly influenced by unhelpful thoughts.

Practice the physicalizing exercise when you notice yourself becoming wrapped up in a difficult feeling or mood.

REMEMBER THAT MINDFULNESS IS LIKE
A PSYCHOLOGICAL MUSCLE—IT DEVELOPS
WITH REGULAR PRACTICE!

References

Archer, R. (2012, July). *How ACT is being used in organisations to help improve performance and wellbeing: Time management course.* Workshop delivered at ACBS World Conference X, Washington, DC.

Baer, R. A. (2003). Mindfulness training as a clinical intervention: A conceptual and empirical review. *Clinical Psychology: Science and Practice, 10,* 125–143.

Baer, R. A. (Ed.). (2010). *Assessing mindfulness and acceptance processes in clients: Illuminating the theory and practice of change.* Oakland, CA: New Harbinger.

Barkham, M., & Shapiro, D. A. (1990). Brief psychotherapeutic interventions for job-related distress: A pilot study of prescriptive and exploratory therapy. *Counselling Psychology Quarterly, 3,* 133–147.

Bass, B. M., & Avolio, B. J. (1999). *Training full range leadership: A resource guide for training with the ML.* Redwood City, CA: Mind Garden.

Batten, S. V. (2011). *Essentials of acceptance and commitment therapy.* London: Sage.

Bieling, P. J., McCabe, R. E., & Antony, M. M. (2006). *Cognitive-behavioral therapy in groups.* New York: Guilford Press.

Biglan, A., Hayes, S. C., & Pistorello, J. (2008). Acceptance and commitment: Implications for prevention science. *Prevention Science, 9,* 139–152.

Bilich, L. L., & Ciarrochi, J. (2009). Promoting social intelligence using the experiential role-play method. In J. T. Blackledge, J. Ciarrochi, & F. P. Deane (Eds.), *Acceptance and commitment therapy: Contemporary theory, research and practice.* Bowen Hills, Queensland: Australian Academic Press.

Biron, M., & van Veldhoven, M. J. P. M. (2012). Emotional labor in service work: Psychological flexibility and emotion regulation. *Human Relations.* doi: 10.1177/0018726712447832.

Black, C. (2008). *Working for a healthier tomorrow.* Report commissioned by the Secretaries of State for Health and Work and Pensions. Norwich, England: Stationery Office.

Bohlmeijer, E. T., & Hulsbergen, M. (2008). *Voluit leven: Mindfulness of de kunst kan het aanvaarden, nu als praktisch hulpboek* [Living to the full: Mindfulness or the art of acceptance now as a practical help book]. Amsterdam: Boom.

Bond, F. W. (2004). ACT for stress. In S. C. Hayes & K. D. Strosahl (Eds.), *A practical guide to acceptance and commitment therapy.* New York: Springer.

Bond, F. W. (2012). Enhancing the effectiveness of transformational leadership with acceptance and commitment therapy (ACT). Manuscript in preparation.

Bond, F. W., & Bunce, D. (2000). Mediators of change in emotion-focused and problem-focused worksite stress management interventions. *Journal of Occupational Health Psychology, 5,* 156–163.

Bond, F. W., & Bunce, D. (2003). The role of acceptance and job control in mental health, job satisfaction, and work performance. *Journal of Applied Psychology, 88,* 1057–1067.

Bond, F. W., & Flaxman, P. E. (2006). The ability of psychological flexibility and job control to predict learning, job performance, and mental health. *Journal of Organizational Behavior Management, 26,* 113–130.

Bond, F. W., Flaxman, P. E., & Bunce, D. (2008). The influence of psychological flexibility on work redesign: Mediated moderation of a work reorganization intervention. *Journal of Applied Psychology, 93,* 645–654.

Bond, F. W., & Hayes, S. C. (2002). ACT at work. In F. W. Bond & W. Dryden (Eds.), *Handbook of brief cognitive behaviour therapy*. Chichester, England: Wiley.

Bond, F. W., Hayes, S. C., Baer, R. A., Carpenter, K. C., Guenole, N., Orcutt, H. K., et al. (2011). Preliminary psychometric properties of the Acceptance and Action Questionnaire–II: A revised measure of psychological flexibility and acceptance. *Behavior Therapy, 42,* 676–688.

Bond, F. W., Hayes, S. C., & Barnes-Holmes, D. (2006). Psychological flexibility, ACT, and organizational behavior. *Journal of Organizational Behavior Management, 26,* 25–54.

Bond, F. W., Lloyd, J., & Guenole, N. (2012). Preliminary psychometric properties of the work-related acceptance and action questionnaire. Manuscript submitted for publication.

Boorman, S. (2009). *NHS Health and Well-Being Review*. Leeds, England: Department of Health.

Brinkborg, H., Michanek, J., Hesser, H., & Berglund, G. (2011). Acceptance and commitment therapy for the treatment of stress among social workers: A randomized controlled trial. *Behaviour Research and Therapy, 49,* 389–398.

Brown, J. S. L., Cochrane, R., Mack, C. F., Leung, N., & Hancox, T. (1998). Comparison of effectiveness of large scale stress workshops with small stress/anxiety management training groups. *Behavioural and Cognitive Psychotherapy, 26,* 219–235.

Brown, R. A., Lejuez, C. W., Kahler, C. W., & Strong, D. (2002). Distress tolerance and duration of past smoking cessation attempts. *Journal of Abnormal Psychology, 111,* 180–185.

Bunce, D. (1997). What factors are associated with the outcome of individual-focused worksite stress management interventions? *Journal of Occupational and Organizational Psychology, 70,* 1–17.

Centre for Mental Health. (2010). *The economic and societal costs of mental health problems in 2009/10*. London: Author.

Chaskalson, M. (2011). *The mindful workplace: Developing resilient individuals and resonant organizations with MBSR*. Chichester, England: Wiley.

Ciarrochi, J., & Bailey, A. (2008). *A CBT practitioner's guide to ACT: How to bridge the gap between cognitive behavioral therapy and acceptance and commitment therapy*. Oakland, CA: New Harbinger.

Clayton, T. M. (1995). *Changing organizational culture through relational framing.* Master's thesis, University of Nevada, Reno.

Cox, T., Griffiths, A., Barlowe, C., Randall, R., Thomson, L., & Rial-Gonzalez, E. (2000). *Organisational interventions for work stress: A risk management approach.* Health and Safety Executive research report 286/2000. Norwich: Stationery Office.

Crane, R. (2009). *Mindfulness-based cognitive therapy.* Hove, England: Routledge.

Cummings, T. G., & Worley, C. G. (2009). *Organization development and change* (9th ed.). Mason, OH: South-Western/Cengage Learning.

Dahl, J. C., Plumb, J. C., Stewart, I., & Lundgren, T. (2009). *The art and science of valuing in psychotherapy: Helping clients discover, explore, and commit to valued action using acceptance and commitment therapy.* Oakland, CA: New Harbinger.

Dahl, J., Wilson, K. G., & Nilsson, A. (2004). Acceptance and commitment therapy and the treatment of persons at risk for long-term disability resulting from stress and pain symptoms: A preliminary randomized trial. *Behavior Therapy, 35,* 785–801.

de Board, R. (1978). *The psychoanalysis of organisations.* London: Tavistock.

Dimidjian, S., & Linehan, M. M. (2008). Mindfulness practice. In W. T. O'Donohue & J. E. Fisher (Eds.), *Cognitive behavior therapy: Applying empirically supported techniques in your practice.* Hoboken, NJ: Wiley.

Donaldson-Feilder, E., & Bond, F. W. (2004). Psychological acceptance and emotional intelligence in relation to workplace well-being. *British Journal of Guidance and Counselling, 34,* 187–203.

Drossel, C. (2008). Group interventions. In W. T. O'Donohue & J. E. Fisher (Eds.), *Cognitive behavior therapy: Applying empirically supported techniques in your practice.* Hoboken, NJ: Wiley.

Flaxman, P. E., Blackledge, J. T., & Bond, F. W. (2011). *Acceptance and commitment therapy: The CBT distinctive features series.* Hove, England: Routledge.

Flaxman, P. E., & Bond, F. W. (2006). Acceptance and commitment therapy in the workplace. In R. A. Baer (Ed.), *Mindfulness-based treatment approaches.* San Diego, CA: Elsevier.

Flaxman, P. E., & Bond, F. W. (2010a). A randomised worksite comparison of acceptance and commitment therapy and stress inoculation training. *Behaviour Research and Therapy, 48,* 816–820.

Flaxman, P. E., & Bond, F. W. (2010b). Worksite stress management training: Moderated effects and clinical significance. *Journal of Occupational Health Psychology, 15,* 347–358.

Flaxman, P. E., & Bond, F. W. (2010c). Acceptance and commitment training: Promoting psychological flexibility in the workplace. In R. A. Baer (Ed.), *Assessing mindfulness and acceptance processes in clients: Illuminating the theory and practice of change.* Oakland, CA: New Harbinger.

Flaxman, P. E., Söderberg, M., Bond, F. W., & Lloyd, J. (2011, July). *Acceptance and commitment training at work.* Paper presented at ACBS World Conference IX, Parma Italy.

Fledderus, M., Bohlmeijer, E. T., Pieterse, M. E., & Schreurs, K. M. G. (2012). Acceptance and commitment therapy as guided self-help for psychological distress and positive mental health: A randomized controlled trial. *Psychological Medicine, 42,* 485–495.

Fledderus, M., Bohlmeijer, E. T., Smit, F., & Westerhof, G. J. (2010). Mental health promotion as a new goal in public mental health care: A randomized controlled trial of an intervention enhancing psychological flexibility. *American Journal of Public Health, 100,* 2372–2378.

Fletcher, L., & Hayes, S. C. (2005). Relational frame theory, acceptance and commitment therapy, and a functional analytic definition of mindfulness. *Journal of Rational-Emotive and Cognitive-Behavioral Therapy, 23,* 315–336.

Forsyth, J. P., & Eifert, G. H. (2008). *The mindfulness & acceptance workbook for anxiety: A guide to breaking free from anxiety, phobias, and worry using acceptance and commitment therapy.* Oakland, CA: New Harbinger.

Giga, S. I., Cooper, C. L., & Faragher, B. (2003). The development of a framework for a comprehensive approach to stress management interventions at work. *International Journal of Stress Management, 10,* 280–296.

Goetzel, R. Z., Anderson, D. R., Whitmer, R. W., Ozminkowski, R. J., Dunn, R. L., Wasserman, J., & Health Enhancement Research Organization (HERO) Research Committee. (1998). The relationship between modifiable health risks and health care expenditures: An analysis of the multi-employer HERO health risk and cost database. *Journal of Occupational and Environmental Medicine, 40,* 843–854.

Grandey, A. A. (2003). When "The show must go on": Surface acting and deep acting as determinants of emotional exhaustion and peer-rated service delivery. *Academy of Management Journal, 46,* 86–96.

Hardy, G. E., Shapiro, D. A., Haynes, C. E., & Rick, J. E. (1999). Validation of the General Health Questionnire-12 using a sample of employees from the healthcare services. *Psychological Assessment, 11,* 159-165.

Harris, R. (2007). *The happiness trap.* London: Constable & Robinson.

Harris, R. (2009). *ACT made simple: An easy-to-read primer on acceptance and commitment therapy.* Oakland, CA: New Harbinger.

Hayes, S. C. (1984). Making sense of spirituality. *Behaviorism, 12,* 99–110.

Hayes, S. C. (2004). Acceptance and commitment therapy and the new behavior therapies: Mindfulness, acceptance, and relationship. In S. C. Hayes, V. M. Follette, & M. M. Linehan (Eds.), *Mindfulness and acceptance: Expanding the cognitive-behavioral tradition.* New York: Guilford Press.

Hayes, S. C. (2010, June). Values, verbal relations and compassion: Can we do a better job of facing global challenges. Association of Contextual Behavioral Sciences World Conference 8, Reno, Nevada.

Hayes, S. C., Barnes-Holmes, D., & Roche, B. (Eds.). (2001). *Relational frame theory: A post-Skinnerian account of human language and cognition.* New York: Kluwer Academic.

Hayes, S. C., Bissett, R., Roget, N., Padilla, M., Kohlenberg, B. S., Fisher, G., et al. (2004). The impact of acceptance and commitment training and multicultural training on the stigmatizing attitudes and professional burnout of substance abuse counselors. *Behavior Therapy, 35,* 821–835.

Hayes, S. C., Bond, F. W., Barnes-Holmes, D., & Austin, J. (Eds.). (2006). *Acceptance and mindfulness at work: Applying acceptance and commitment therapy and relational frame theory to organisational behaviour management.* New York: Haworth Press.

Hayes, S. C., Bunting, K., Herbst, S., Bond, F. W., & Barnes-Holmes, D. (2006). Expanding the scope of organizational behavior management. *Journal of Organizational Behavior Management, 26,* 1–23.

Hayes, S. C., Luoma, J. B., Bond, F. W., Masuda, A., & Lillis, J. (2006). Acceptance and commitment theory: Model, processes and outcomes. *Behaviour Research and Therapy, 44,* 1–25.

Hayes, S. C., & Smith, S. (2005). *Get out of your mind and into your life: The new acceptance and commitment therapy.* Oakland, CA: New Harbinger.

Hayes, S. C., Strosahl, K. D., Bunting, K., Twohig, M., & Wilson, K. (2004). What is acceptance and commitment therapy? In S. C. Hayes & K. D. Strosahl (Eds.), *A practical guide to acceptance and commitment therapy.* New York: Springer.

Hayes, S. C., Strosahl, K., & Wilson, K. G. (1999). *Acceptance and commitment therapy: An experiential approach to behavior change.* New York: Guilford Press.

Hayes, S. C., Strosahl, K., & Wilson, K. G. (2012). *Acceptance and commitment therapy: The process and practice of mindful change.* New York: Guilford Press.

Hayes, S. C., Strosahl, K. D., Wilson, K. G., Bissett, R. T., Pistorello, J., Toarmino, D., et al. (2004). Measuring experiential avoidance: A preliminary test of a working model. *Psychological Record, 54,* 553–578.

Hayes, S. C., Villatte, M., Levin, M., & Hildebrandt, M. (2011). Open, aware and active: Contextual approaches as an emerging trend in the behavioral and cognitive therapies. *Annual Review of Clinical Psychology, 7,* 141–168.

Hayes, S. C., Wilson, K. G., Gifford, E. V., Follette, V. M., & Strosahl, K. (1996). Experiential avoidance and behavioral disorders: A functional dimensional approach to diagnosis and treatment. *Journal of Consulting and Clinical Psychology, 64,* 1152–1168.

Hilton, M. (2005). *Assessing the financial return on investment of good management strategies and the WORC project.* University of Queensland. Retrieved from http://www.qcmhr.uq.edu.au/worc/Documents/Hilton_Paper(2005).pdf.

Hilton, M. F., Whiteford, H. A., Sheridan, J. S., Cleary, C. M., Chant, D. C., Wang, P. S., & Kessler, R. C. (2008). The prevalence of psychological distress in employees and associated occupational risk factors. *Journal of Occupational & Environmental Medicine, 50,* 746–757.

Hobfoll, S. E. (2002). Social and psychological resources and adaptation. *Review of General Psychology, 6,* 307–324.

Holman, D. J., Axtell, C. M., Sprigg, C. A., Totterdell, P., & Wall, T. D. (2010). The mediating role of job characteristics in job redesign interventions: A serendipitous quasi-experiment. *Journal of Organizational Behavior, 31,* 84–105.

Jex, S. M., Bliese, P. D., Buzzell, S., & Primeau, J. (2001). The impact of self-efficacy on stressor-strain relations: Coping style as an explanatory mechanism. *Journal of Applied Psychology, 86,* 401–409.

Johns, G. (2010). Presenteeism in the workplace: A review and research agenda. *Journal of Organizational Behavior, 31,* 519–542.

Judge, T. A., & Piccolo, R. (2004). Transformational and transactional leadership: A meta-analytic test of their relative validity. *Journal of Applied Psychology, 89,* 755–768.

Kabat-Zinn, J. (1990). *Full catastrophe living: The program of the stress reduction clinic at the University of Massachusetts Medical Center.* New York: Dell.

Kanter, J. W., Busch, M., & Rusch, L. C. (2009). *Behavioral activation.* Hove, England: Routledge.

Kashdan, T. B., Barrios, V., Forsyth, J. P., & Steger, M. F. (2006). Experiential avoidance as a generalized psychological vulnerability: Comparisons with coping and emotion regulation strategies. *Behaviour Research and Therapy, 44,* 1301–1320.

Kessler, R. C., & Frank, R. G. (1997). The impact of psychiatric disorders on work loss days. *Psychological Medicine, 27,* 861–873.

Kessler, R. C., Merikangas, K. R., & Wang, P. S. (2008). The prevalence and correlates of workplace depression in the National Comorbidity Survey Replication. *Journal of Occupational & Environmental Medicine, 50,* 381–390.

Klatt, M. D., Buckworth, J., & Malarkey, W. B. (2009). Effects of low-dose mindfulness-based stress reduction (MBSR-ld) on working adults. *Health Education and Behavior, 36,* 601–614.

Lappalainen, R., Lehtonen, T., Skarp, E., Taubert, E., Ojanen, M., & Hayes, S. C. (2007). The impact of CBT and ACT models using psychology trainee therapists: A preliminary controlled effectiveness trial. *Behavior Modification, 31,* 488–511.

Lejeune, C. (2007). *The worry trap: How to free yourself from worry & anxiety using acceptance and commitment therapy.* Oakland, CA: New Harbinger.

Lloyd, J., Bond, F. W., & Flaxman, P. E. (in press). Identifying psychological mechanisms underpinning a cognitive behavioural therapy intervention for emotional burnout. *Work & Stress.*

Locke, E. A., & Latham, G. P. (1990). *A theory of goal setting and task performance.* Englewood Cliffs, NJ: Prentice Hall.

Locke, E. A., & Latham, G. P. (2002). Building a practically useful theory of goal setting and task motivation: A 35-year odyssey. *American Psychologist, 57,* 705–717.

Longmore, R. J., & Worrell, M. (2007). Do we need to challenge thoughts in cognitive behavior therapy? *Clinical Psychology Review, 27,* 173–187.

Lundgren, T., Dahl, J., Strosahl, K., Robinson, P., Luoma, J., & Melin, L. (2012). A Bull's-Eye Values Survey: A psychometric evaluation. *Cognitive and Behavioral Practice, 19,* 518–526.

Luoma, J. B., Hayes, S. C., & Walser, R. D. (2007). *Learning ACT: An acceptance & commitment therapy skills-training manual for therapists.* Oakland, CA: New Harbinger & Reno, NV: Context Press.

McCracken, L. M. (1998). Learning to live with the pain: Acceptance of pain predicts adjustment in persons with chronic pain. *Pain, 74,* 21–27.

McCracken, L. M., & Yang, S-Y. (2008). A contextual cognitive-behavioral analysis of rehabilitation workers' health and well-being: Influences of acceptance, mindfulness, and values-based action. *Rehabilitation Psychology, 53,* 479–485.

McKay, M., Forsyth, J. P., & Eifert, G. H. (2010). *Your life on purpose: How to find what matters and create the life you want.* Oakland, CA: New Harbinger.

Meichenbaum, D. (1985). *Stress inoculation training.* New York: Pergamon.

Meier, L. L., Semmer, N. K., Elfering, A., & Jacobshagen, N. (2008). The double meaning of control: Three-way interactions between internal resources, job control, and stressors at work. *Journal of Occupational Health Psychology, 13,* 244–258.

Milczarek, M., Schneider, E., & Rial Gonzalez, E. (2009). *Stress at work—facts and figures.* Luxembourg: European Agency for Safety and Health at Work.

Miller, W. R. (1983). Motivational interviewing with problem drinkers. *Behavioral Psychotherapy, 11,* 147–172.

Miller, W. R., & Rollnick, S. (2002). *Motivational interviewing: Preparing people for change* (2nd ed.). New York: Guilford Press.

Mitmansgruber, H., Beck, T. N., & Schüssler, G. (2008). "Mindful helpers": Experiential avoidance, meta-emotions, and emotion regulation in paramedics. *Journal of Research in Personality, 42*, 1358–1363.

Moran, D. J. (2011). ACT for Leadership: Using acceptance and commitment training to develop crisis-resilient change managers. *International Journal of Behavioral Consultation and Therapy, 7*, 68–77.

Murphy, L. R. (1996). Stress management in work settings: A critical review. *American Journal of Health Promotion, 11*, 112–135.

National Institute for Occupational Safety and Health. (2002). *General social survey.* Retrieved from http://www.cdc.gov/niosh/programs/workorg/risks.html

National Institute for Occupational Safety and Health. (2004). *Worker health chartbook* (Publication no. 2004-146). Cincinnati, OH: Author.

Oliver, J., Morris, E., Johns, L., & Byrne, M. (2011). *ACT for life: Group intervention for psychosis manual.* London: South London and Maudsley NHS Foundation Trust.

Oliver, M. I., Pearson, N., Coe, N., & Gunnell, D. (2005). Help-seeking behavior in men and women with common mental health problems: Cross-sectional study. *British Journal of Psychiatry, 186*, 297–301.

Parent-Thirion, A., Macias, E. F., Hurley, J., & Vermeylen, G. (2007). *Fourth European working conditions survey.* Dublin: European Foundation for the Improvement of Living and Working Conditions.

Richardson, K. M., & Rothstein, H. R. (2008). Effects of occupational stress management intervention programs: A meta-analysis. *Journal of Occupational Health Psychology, 13*, 69–93.

Sainsbury Centre for Mental Health. (2007). *Mental health at work: Developing the business case* (Policy Paper 8). London: Author.

Schaubroeck, J., Jones, J. R., & Xie, J. L. (2001). Individual differences in utilizing control to cope with job demands: Effects on susceptibility to infectious disease. *Journal of Applied Psychology, 86*, 265–278.

Schmidt, N. B., Richey, J. A., Cromer, K. R., & Buckner, J. D. (2007). Discomfort intolerance: Evaluation of a potential risk factor for anxiety pathology. *Behavior Therapy, 38*, 247–255.

Segal, Z., Williams, J. M. G., & Teasdale, J. D. (2002). *Mindfulness-based cognitive therapy for depression.* New York: Guilford Press.

Seymour, L. (2010). *Common mental health problems at work: What we know about successful interventions (a progress review).* London: Sainsbury Centre for Mental Health.

Seymour, L., & Grove, B. (2005). *Workplace interventions for people with common mental health problems: Evidence review and recommendations.* London: British Occupational Health Research Foundation.

Shaw Trust. (2006). *Mental health: The last workplace taboo.* London: Author.

Sobocki, P., Jönsson, B., Angst, J., & Rehnberg, C. (2006). Cost of depression in Europe. *Journal of Mental Health Policy and Economics, 9*, 87–98.

Stahl, B., & Goldstein, E. (2010). *A mindfulness-based stress reduction workbook.* Oakland, CA: New Harbinger.

Stewart, I., Barnes-Holmes, D., Barnes-Holmes, Y., Bond, F., & Hayes, S. C. (2006). Relational frame theory and industrial/organizational psychology. *Journal of Organizational Behavior Management, 26*, 55–90.

Stride, C., Wall, T. D., & Catley, N. (2007). *Measures of job satisfaction, organisational commitment, mental health and job-related well-being: A benchmarking manual*. Chichester: Wiley.

Strosahl, K. D., & Robinson, P. (2008). *The mindfulness and acceptance workbook for depression: Using acceptance and commitment therapy to move through depression and create a life worth living*. Oakland, CA: New Harbinger.

Thomas, C. M., & Morris, S. (2003). Cost of depression among adults in England in 2000. *British Journal of Psychiatry, 183*, 514–519.

Törneke, N. (2010). *Learning RFT: An introduction to relational frame theory and its clinical application*. Oakland, CA: New Harbinger.

van der Klink, J. J. L., Blonk, R. W. B., Schene, A. H., & van Dijk, F. J. H. (2001). The benefits of interventions for work-related stress. *American Journal of Public Health, 91*, 270–276.

Varra, A. A., Hayes, S. C., Roget, N., & Fisher, G. (2008). A randomized control trial examining the effect of acceptance and commitment training on clinician willingness to use evidence-based pharmacotherapy. *Journal of Consulting and Clinical Psychology, 76*, 449–458.

Vilardaga, R., Luoma, J. B., Hayes, S. C., Pistorello, J., Levin, M. E., Hildebrandt, M. J., et al. (2011). Burnout among the addiction counseling workforce: The differential roles of mindfulness and values-based processes and work-site factors. *Journal of Substance Abuse Treatment, 40*, 323–335.

Walser, R. D., & Pistorello, J. (2004). ACT in group format. In S. C. Hayes & K. D. Strosahl (Eds.), *A practical guide to acceptance and commitment therapy*. New York: Springer.

Wenzlaff, R. M., & Wegner, D. M. (2000). Thought suppression. In S. T. Fiske (Ed.), *Annual review of psychology* (Vol. 51, pp. 59–91). Palo Alto, CA: Annual Reviews.

White, J. (2000). *Treating anxiety and stress: A group psycho-educational approach using brief CBT*. Chichester, England: Wiley.

Williams, K. A., Kolar, M. M., Reger, B. E., & Pearson, J. C. (2001). Evaluation of a wellness-based mindfulness stress reduction intervention: A controlled trial. *American Journal of Health Promotion, 15*, 422–432.

Wilson, K. G., & Blackledge, J. T. (1999). Recent developments in the behavioral analysis of language: Making sense of clinical phenomena. In M. J. Dougher (Ed.), *Clinical behavior analysis*. Reno, NV: Context Press.

Wilson, K. G., & DuFrene, T. (2010). *Things might go terribly, horribly wrong*. Oakland, CA: New Harbinger.

Wilson, K. G., Sandoz, E. K., Kitchens, J., & Roberts, M. E. (2010). The Valued Living Questionnaire: Defining and measuring valued action within a behavioral framework. *The Psychological Record, 60*, 249–272.

Zapf, D. (2002). Emotion work and psychological well-being: A review of the literature and some conceptual considerations. *Human Resource Management Review, 12*, 237–268.

Zettle, R. D. (2007). *ACT for depression: A clinician's guide to using acceptance and commitment therapy in treating depression*. Oakland, CA: New Harbinger.

Paul E. Flaxman, PhD, is senior lecturer in psychology at City University London. He specializes in adapting acceptance and commitment therapy (ACT) to help improve employees' mental health and performance. Evaluations of Paul's ACT interventions have been published in numerous scientific papers and books, and he has been invited to present his research at conferences around the globe. Paul recently directed two major projects focused on delivering ACT and other mindfulness-based interventions to public sector workers across the United Kingdom.

Frank W. Bond, PhD, is professor of psychology and director of the Institute of Management Studies at Goldsmiths, University of London. His research and consulting work focus on the psychological and organizational processes that underpin peak performance and well-being in the workplace.

Fredrik Livheim, MS, is a licensed clinical psychologist at FORUM, a research center for psychosocial health at the Karolinska Institute in Stockholm, Sweden. He has trained more than 400 professionals in how to use ACT in group format to improve employees' mental health. His research focuses on the use of ACT in group format in the workplace.

Foreword writer **Steven C. Hayes, PhD**, is a founder of acceptance and commitment therapy and a professor of psychology at the University of Nevada. An author of thirty-four books and more than 470 scientific articles, he has shown in his research how language and thought lead to human suffering. Hayes has been president of several scientific societies and has received several national awards, including the Lifetime Achievement Award from the Association for Behavioral and Cognitive Therapy.

Index

A

B

C

D

E

F

G

H

I

JKL

M

N

O

P

R

S

T

U

V

W

XYZ